How to restore

Norton Commando

YOUR step-by-step guide to restoring a Norton Commando, complete with comprehensive instructions and hundreds of colour photos

Chris Rooke

www.veloce.co.uk

First published in February 2020, reprinted May 2020 and 2025 by Veloce, an imprint of David and Charles Limited. Tel +44 (0)1305 260068 / e-mail info@veloce.co.uk / web www.veloce.co.uk.
ISBN: 9781787113947
© 2020 Chris Rooke and David and Charles. All rights reserved. With the exception of quoting brief passages for the purpose of review, no part of this publication may be recorded, reproduced or transmitted by any means, including photocopying, without the written permission of David and Charles Limited.
Throughout this book logos, model names and designations, etc, have been used for the purposes of identification, illustration and decoration. Such names are the property of the trademark holder as this is not an official publication. Readers with ideas for automotive books, or books on other transport or related hobby subjects, are invited to write to the editorial director of Veloce at the above email address. British Library Cataloguing in Publication Data – A catalogue record for this book is available from the British Library. Design and DTP by Veloce.

ENTHUSIAST'S RESTORATION MANUAL™

How to restore

Norton Commando

YOUR step-by-step guide to restoring a Norton Commando, complete with comprehensive instructions and hundreds of colour photos

Chris Rooke

Contents

Introduction 6
  A bit about the author 6
  Acknowledgements 7

1. Buying a bike to restore .. 8
  Lessons learnt 14

2. Golden rules for restoring a bike 15
  Ten golden rules for a successful rebuild 15
  Lessons learnt 17
  Rules of the workshop 17

3. Preparing to dismantle .. 18
  Lessons learnt 20

4. Beginning to dismantle .. 21
  Lessons learnt 24

5. Removing the main electrics 25
  Lessons learnt 27

6. Dismantling the rear wheel & brake assembly 28
  Lessons learnt 31
  Rear wheels on earlier models 32

7. Removing the carbs, airbox & remaining wiring. 33
  Lessons learnt 35

8. Draining the oil 36
  Lessons learnt 38

9. Removing the swinging arm & timing cover 39
  Lessons learnt 45

10. Dismantling the timing & primary chaincases 46
  Lessons learnt 52

11. Dismantling the gearbox 53
  Lessons learnt 58

12. Removing the cylinder head 59
  Lessons learnt 65

13. Removing & dismantling the crankcases 66
  Lessons learnt 71

14. Removing the front wheel, forks & yokes 72
  Lessons learnt 75

15. Dismantling the wheels 76
  Lessons learnt 79

16. Chroming, polishing, painting & parts 80
  Lessons learnt 83

17. Polishing engine casings & other alloy parts 84
  Lessons learnt 87

18. Reassembling the crankshaft & crankcases .. 88
  Lessons learnt 94

19. Fitting the crankcases & isolastics 95
  Lessons learnt 101

20. Rebuilding the front forks & front wheel 102
  Lessons learnt 105

21. Refitting the front wheel & front calliper .. 106
  Lessons learnt 109

22. Fitting the timing case 110
  Lessons learnt 113

23. Fitting the cylinder barrels 114
  Lessons learnt 118

24. Refurbishing & refitting the cylinder heads 119
  Lessons learnt 125

25. Rebuilding the gearbox 126
  Lessons learnt 134

26. Primary chaincase reassembly 136
  Lessons learnt 142
  Earlier models 143

CONTENTS

27. **Carburettors**.................. 144
    Lessons learnt....................... 151

28. **Fitting the head steady** 153
    Lessons learnt....................... 155

29. **The starter motor**......... 156
    Lessons learnt....................... 159

30. **Horn & oil feed system** 160
    Lessons learnt....................... 163

31. **Handlebar switches**..... 164
    Lessons learnt....................... 167

32. **Wiring & electrics** 168
    The charging system............. 170
    The ignition system............... 172
    The lighting system (and instruments).................... 174
    Lessons learnt....................... 177

33. **Fitting the support plates** 178
    Lessons learnt....................... 179

34. **Refitting the rear wheel & mudguard** 180
    Lessons learnt....................... 185

35. **Refurbishing the brakes** 186
    Lessons learnt....................... 192
    Earlier models with drum brakes............................. 192

36. **Painting the tank & side panels** 193
    Lessons learnt....................... 198

37. **Fitting the tank & side panels** 199
    Lessons learnt....................... 200

38. **Commissioning, teething & riding**.......... 201
    Commissioning 201
    Teething problems 204
    Riding 207
    Lessons learnt....................... 207

39. **Summing up** 208

40. **Recommended publications & equipment**. 212
    Publications 212
    General workshop tools........ 213
    More recommended tools..... 214
    Sockets................................. 214
    Special tools 214
    Power tools........................... 215
    Spare nuts, bolts, washers and thingummies 215
    Consumables........................ 216
    Keeping things clean 216
    Freezer bags 216
    Other essential tools............. 216
    Bike lift 216
    Lessons learnt....................... 217

41. **Recommended suppliers** 218
    Recommended parts and service suppliers............. 218
    Owners' clubs....................... 219
    Facebook groups................. 219

Index 224

This book is dedicated to the memory of Frank Cuomo, a wonderful man who was taken from us far too soon. He will be sadly missed by all who knew him.

Introduction

So what's this book all about? Basically, it's a user-friendly workshop manual, covering the complete strip down and total restoration of a 1975 850 Norton Commando MkIII Roadster. The idea is that this manual complements other workshop manuals in a friendly and readable style; it doesn't replace, for example, the factory *Norton Workshop Manual*, but is a companion, and helps makes sense of some of the info in there, explaining jobs more fully, with the aid of many colour photos. Although the manual deals specifically with an 850 MkIII Commando, I hope that there is enough in common with the other Commando models, together with specific information about them, to make the manual relevant to all Commandos.

It is important to note that while I am an experienced mechanic and I have restored many classic cars and bikes over the years, I am a novice when it comes to working on Norton Commandos. I therefore make mistakes – and learn from them – and I freely share them here to help you avoid them (and feel better about your own mistakes!), while guiding you through how to overcome them. In this way, I hope to cover some of the things that other manuals miss out or gloss over; this is a manual written by an amateur home restorer, for amateur home restorers.

Please be aware that this manual is aimed more at the relative novice who is contemplating working on their bike, maybe for the first time, and has limited knowledge of rebuilding a Commando.

However, I would hope that even those with more experience working on Commandos will still find the manual helpful.

Above all, this manual is written in a friendly, conversational style, which many owners have found extremely readable and accessible, resulting in a manual that is very useful and informative.

The manual features:
• Over 750 full colour photos covering every part of the restoration in detail
• Content written in a friendly, informal way that's accessible to all
• No jargon and no impenetrable gobbledygook
• The knowledge of a home restorer without access to garage quality machinery
• Full documentation of all my mistakes so that you can avoid them – and laugh about them!
• A friend in book-form for your workshop, to help you through the bad times
• Lots of advice about upgrades and options for you to consider
• Relevant info on all models of Commando, although based on the rebuild of an 850 MkIII
• Detailed coverage of all areas of dismantling, refurbishment and rebuilding
• Coverage of everything: electrics, engine, gearbox, wheels, paintwork, forks, brakes, etc.

A BIT ABOUT THE AUTHOR

I was born and brought up in Oxford, where I first started to learn about all things mechanical. My dad was very mechanical and I inherited that talent from him, and grew up dismantling clocks and anything else I could get my hands on – although the putting back together part was often lacking! I also developed a love of engines and motorcycles (I don't know where in the family that came from!) and at the age of 12 I bought my first moped: a Raleigh Runabout that I used to ride around the garden and on which Dad would somehow take me for rides around

INTRODUCTION

the local countryside. Later, I had two scooters: a Vespa 125 and a Lambretta SX200. My first legal bike was a Casal moped at the age of 16. The Casal was a cheap 'Sports moped' akin to the Yamaha FS1-E (which many of my friends had) but much cheaper – in every way. After that, when I turned 17 I bought my first real motorbike, a BSA Starfire 250 (for £60) that had the first engine I ever rebuilt (after the oil pump seized) and actually went again afterwards! I then had a brief affair with a Suzuki 350 Rebel before buying the love of my life, a 1954 Matchless 350 G3LS heavyweight single that I turned into a chopper/cruiser and converted to 500cc. That bike was my only transport for many years until it was stolen. Those were my really memorable biker years, including breaking down in France and me and the bike being brought home in the back of an estate car, and being the last vehicle over the Woodhead Pass before it was closed due to heavy snow! Ah, those were the days. During my ownership of the Matchless (Idiot Wind), my friend Alan bought a 750 Norton Commando Combat that was 'interesting' – more info on that in the next chapter.

I then rebuilt a Triumph T100 for a friend and bought myself a Triumph Bonneville T140V, which my then girlfriend (now my wife) and I rode on a camping holiday to Spain – nearly the end of a great relationship! I sold the bike shortly after and was then bikeless for many years.

My focus then shifted to my career as a teacher, and with my knowledge of mechanics, etc, I obviously became a teacher of … Drama! (That's another story.) That, together with buying houses, getting married, etc, meant that my passion for classic bikes was put on the back burner (sound familiar?).

However, later on I bought an E-Type Jaguar and spent nine years restoring it. It was during this restoration that I managed to combine my love of mechanics with my love of literature and wrote my first manual. After that, I was forced to sell the E-Type when I took early retirement from teaching (30 years was enough). I've since been lucky enough to buy several classic bikes, restore them and write restoration manuals for them – there's a manual on rebuilding Kawasaki Z1s and a manual and buyer's guide on Triumph Tridents to go with the E-Type manual. And now, here's the Norton Commando manual.

As previously mentioned, this manual is designed to be read in conjunction with other manuals such as the *Haynes Manual*, but especially the official *Norton Workshop Manual*, and I would highly recommend that you buy a copy of that as soon as you can.

I would like to think that this manual helps to demystify some of the more impenetrable elements of the *Norton Workshop Manual*, but there is still some information in there that goes alongside what you'll find in here, and the two go hand-in-hand. The *Haynes Manual* is also a good backup; if you're about to plunge into a full restoration it's probably worth buying that too.

With regards to the *Norton Workshop Manual*, I would recommend you buy a hard copy: don't just download a virtual copy from the internet (which you can do for free). I don't know why, but it's really hard to read a manual on the computer as opposed to in book format. I initially just downloaded the workshop manual because it was free, but when I later bought a hard copy I wished I had done so earlier, as I'd missed so much.

If you're contemplating a full or part restoration of your Commando, then I hope you'll find this manual useful. It's designed not only to be informative, but also as a comforting friend in the workshop when things go wrong – and they will! This book will help you overcome all the problems and allow you to build the bike of your dreams, as I did.

Good luck, and keep the faith.

Chris Rooke
Sheffield

ACKNOWLEDGEMENTS

I would also like to take this opportunity to thank all those who have offered advice and support in the creation of this manual: the Norton Owners' Club, the various parts suppliers and members of various Facebook groups, and special thanks to Ashley, Phil and Simon at Andover Norton, who were particularly knowledgeable and helpful, and provided some of the photos of earlier models for this manual.

As someone new to Commandos I have strived very hard to ensure that the information contained herein is correct, and I have had the manual checked over by marque experts in an attempt to ensure there are no errors. However, just to be doubly sure, there is a Facebook page set up specifically to detail any corrections, amendments or new information, etc, about what's in the manual: 'Norton Commando Restoration Manual Updates.'

Chapter 1
Buying a bike to restore

Well, back in the '70s, I rode a Norton Commando 750 Combat Roadster and so I thought it was time I bought another one and restored it – that sounds so simple!

When I say I rode one, I did; it belonged to my very good friend and flat-mate, Alan Boby, when we were both students at Portsmouth Polytechnic in the late '70s. At the time, I owned a Matchless 350 G3LS custom cruiser (What can I say? It was the '70s and I was only 18), and Alan had the Commando, which I regularly rode, both as rider and as pillion – and it was an absolute nightmare!

When Alan bought it, it was only four years old, but they had clearly been four long, hard years and the bike was a little tired (pretty knackered, in fact). If we'd owned it today, then we would have stripped it down and rebuilt it from scratch, as that's what it needed, but back then we were students with only a pair of mole grips between us, no garage or outside space, and even less money. Maintenance consisted of working at the kerbside, doing whatever was absolutely essential to get the bike on the road and nothing more (even then maintenance was a full-time occupation!). See photo 1.1 of me on my Matchless, and photo 1.2 of Alan's legendary (infamous) Combat Roadster, back in the day.

In the year or so that Alan had his Commando, this is what went wrong:

• The clutch slipped really badly, especially under hard acceleration, and led to several embarrassing occasions of being 'burnt-off' at the lights by much less powerful machines – when you're 18 that's really annoying!
• Not only did the clutch slip, but it also dragged, and engaging first was always a nightmare, as was trying to hold it on the clutch when stationary.
• One evening, we were riding the Commando to Oxford when all the electrics, including the lights, failed.

1.1 Me on my Matchless in France.

1.2 Alan's 'legendary' Norton Commando 750 Combat Roadster.

BUYING A BIKE TO RESTORE

We discovered that the wire from the alternator had sheared off inside the chaincase (thank you, Lucas). Being young and foolish, instead of turning back, we pulled the illumination bulb out of the speedo and stuffed that in the back of the headlamp (as we knew it would only take a small current) and rode the bike about 60 miles in almost total darkness with a headlamp that was more of a glow than a light. At least by some miracle we weren't killed.

- A while later, with the electrics still not great (they never were), we borrowed the battery out of the Yamaha XS650 owned by the guy next door and went off for a run. He was in the army and was away on duty so we figured it would be okay. It turned out he wasn't away on duty, and it definitely wasn't okay! (Apparently he had spent half an hour trying to start the bike before discovering that some b*****ds had stolen his battery! Did we know anything about it? We just smiled weakly, owned-up, and prayed.)
- Another time, when I was riding pillion, the throttle cable snapped. The only way we could get the throttle to work was by me, as pillion, pulling the broken cable while Alan did the rest. I was happy enough with this arrangement, but Alan wasn't!
- I once got to ride the bike all the way back to Oxford by myself! Unfortunately, Alan admitted that the bike had a 'slight misfire.' In reality, this meant that the bike had a massive misfire and cut out every two seconds, making for the worst, most annoying ride on a motorcycle I have ever endured. I think I was suffering from whiplash by the time I arrived, and I was ready to throw the bike in the river! The fault turned out to be a loose connection on one of the ignition coils.
- The final ignominy, and the last straw for Alan, was when he was riding along one day and the bike suddenly lost power and stopped. The problem was easily identified: the cylinder barrels had fractured around their base, causing the barrels and the cylinder head to simply lift clean off the crankcases! I would have said 'unbelievable,' but then, with that bike, it wasn't. Note that this was almost certainly caused by the engine being tuned beyond its limits (the Combat engines in particular were well known for this), and later on, when Norton brought out the 850 Commando, they sensibly strengthened the bottom of the barrels and added four through bolts that ran from the top of the cylinders right down the length of the barrels, clamping them firmly in place and reducing the stress on the bottom section – maybe Alan's wasn't the only bike to suffer this fate?![1]

In case you think that this was a one-off, just read the Wikipedia entry for the Norton Commando. (PS – This isn't a list of faults, it's the actual main entry for the Commando on Wikipedia!):

"The Norton Commando was introduced in 1967 at the Earls Court Show. The first production machines completed in April 1968 had frame failure problems, which were resolved with the introduction of an improved frame in January 1969.

"There were numerous other design problems that were gradually addressed over the years, although some persisted to the end. The early clutches could not handle the engine torque, and two small internal pins would shear off, leading to severe slippage (later resolved).

"The sidestand tended to break off, particularly if the owner insisted on starting the machine on the sidestand, leaving a hole in the frame beneath the engine, while the centre-stand was too short to provide good support for the motorcycle, dragged on the pavement, and tended to break in half (both later improved).

"The engine rubber mounting system, which isolated the rider from vibration very well, left the engine to its own devices, and it shook like a commercial paint can shaker at idle.

"The rocker arm oil supply pipe was steel, and would fracture from vibration (later improved). The head steady would also fatigue and fracture from vibration (later improved). The Amal carbs had float needle leakage from vibration, which led to flooding and fires, exacerbated by having the ignition points located under the right-hand carb (relocated to the right side of the engine after the first year). And the carburettors wore out prematurely from vibration (persistent problem).

"The main bearings were of two types at first, ball and roller. In 1972 both bearings became roller-type, and the crankcase was stiffened. These main roller bearings, in the now stiffer case, would gall at high revs, leading to main bearing failure (resolved after the Combat model debacle, using the German-made 'Superblend' bearing). The threaded aluminium knobs holding the seat would strip, leaving the seat loose (never resolved). The chain guard mount would fracture (later improved).

"The exhaust pipe manifold nuts were problematic to the end, loosening from vibration, no matter how tightly they were fastened, leading to a ruined cylinder head and constant rattling of the header pipes. The brakelight switches were unreliable, leading, at times, to no brakelight indicator (front was improved with disc brake). The steering head bearings were ball-type, and took a permanent set under the bearing pre-load, leading to weaving at speed (later switched to roller bearings). There was a rear chain oiler which covered the rear wheel in oil, and had to be pinched off by the owner.

"The speedometer drive mechanism operated from the rear wheel, with a long cable to the speedometer. This drive mechanism wore out very quickly, as did any replacement, leading to no speedometer reading (never resolved). The early tachometer drive jutted from the right side of the engine, and was vulnerable to being struck and snapped off (relocated to front of engine). The primary chain tensioning bolt tended to loosen at inconvenient times. The rear chain adjusting bolts pushed, rather than pulled, the rear axle, and would bend, making them difficult to turn. Nor were there index

---

[1] As for Alan, he saw the light! He got the bike repaired (!) and then sold it for the princely sum of £720 to fund the purchase of a Suzuki GSX 1100, which he still owns to this day. Funnily enough though, he recently retired and bought himself another 750 Commando – there's just something about them!

HOW TO RESTORE NORTON COMMANDO

marks to allow equal axle positioning on the right and left side of the swing arm. The ignition switch mount would break from vibration (later relocated)."

Now, that isn't the best Wikipedia entry for a motorcycle I've ever read! But, the thing is, it's an honest one.

The Commando was created at very short notice, as a stop-gap model, whilst the next wonderful Norton engine was developed (similar story to that of the Triumph Trident T150 / BSA Rocket 3). Hence, the bike used the old 750 Norton Atlas engine (which in turn was a design dating back to the 1940s), but tuned and slanted forward to look better (and arguably improve air cooling) and mounted in rubber bushes to try and stop the inevitable severe vibration that prevented contemporary twin cylinder bikes from being much more than 650cc. (The Atlas was a 750 but was heavily de-tuned to avoid vibration). Note that Triumph/BSA tackled the vibration problem in a different way, by developing a Triple – another supposedly 'stop-gap' model. (The new Hinckley Triumph Bonnevilles and 961 Commandos, etc, are much, much bigger and don't vibrate – but their engineers are just very, very clever!)

The rubber mountings gained the exotic title of 'isolastic' and these were marketed not as a desperate attempt to stop vibration but as a wonderful new mounting system that improved road holding and comfort. Combined with the inspired name of 'Commando' the publicity department was on top of its game. The thing was, that although it was a very rushed model (about five months from inception to launch, I think), the bike looked right, with its sportily forward-canted engine and jazzy alloy foot peg supports etc. And not only that, it went brilliantly too! It was an immediate hit with both the motorcycling press and the general public alike, and production continued for eight years until 1975 (needless to say that, as with the Triumph Trident, the much vaunted replacement model never appeared). Also note that some limited Commando production continued after 1975 for a couple of years. Victory was snatched from the jaws of defeat.

The main problem was always going to be the engine (and to a lesser extent the gearbox), as the design was already out-of-date and the engine already at the limit of its available power. But the public wanted more, and various attempts to tune the engine were made by Norton, including producing the 'Combat' model (as owned by Alan), which was very much over-tuned and was a disaster on all fronts. I think that it cost Norton over £1,000,000 in warranty claims and probably more in loss of reputation.

Norton finally sat down and re-designed the engine properly in 1973, in order to make it more reliable and try and regain some kudos. The result was the 850 Commando with many improvements, including strengthened lower barrels (!) with through bolts from the top of the cylinders going down into the crankcases. (Alan's experience certainly showed the need for these!) Other good news was that the bike was now an 850! The bad news was that it was now a little slower than the 750 and had lost its sporting edge. It was starting to become more of a fast tourer than a street racer. Also the bike retained its four-speed gearbox, which by the mid '70s wasn't acceptable. The problem was that the AMC gearbox couldn't really be altered to take five-speeds, unlike the Triumph which gained five speeds in the early '70s. However, the Commando didn't really need five speeds due to its immense torque, which meant it could pull in any gear – though it wasn't a great selling point.

Finally, in 1975, the Commando underwent its last metamorphosis into the MkIII, with electric start, left-hand gear change and proper switchgear! (The latter two features dictated by new American legislation). Once again this mirrored the Triumph Trident, which was now re-launched as the T160 with all the above improvements (although their Lucas starter tended to work a lot better!). Both sets of engineers had managed to provide their bikes with left-hand gear changes by running a large shaft, called a cross-shaft, across the engine and through the primary chaincase. (I tend to call them bodge shafts, but I'm just old and cynical; they actually work very well in both cases – much to most people's surprise – especially mine!) Unlike the Commando, the Trident's bodge, erm, I mean cross-shaft, even actually runs *through* the crankcases, missing all vital organs by a hair's breadth!

This was an exciting new dawn for both Triumph and Norton, but then, of course, this new light was quickly extinguished when what was by then Norton Villiers Triumph (NVT) collapsed at the end of 1975 and the Commando and Trident, whose lives had been inextricably linked, were no more (although Commandos continued to be made in small numbers after this up to the autumn of 1977).

So, here we are, with me considering buying a Commando to restore (although given all the above I'm not sure why!).

Basically, there were three models of Commando:

- The original Fastback 750
- The later Roadster and Interstate 750s
- The later Roadster and Interstate 850s

See photos 1.3 and 1.4 of a Fastback and an Interstate Commando.

(There was actually a bewildering array of Commando models, including the funky custom Hi-Rider, the Interpol police bike and the John Player Special racer – for full details on all the models I would recommend you read the *Norton Commando Essential Buyer's Guide* by Peter Henshaw.)

Now, personally, I don't like the look of the original Fastbacks: they're very singularly styled and (again, like the original 'breadbin'-tanked Trident T150) you either love them or you don't. The latter, in my case.

So maybe a 750? Then there's really just the choice between the small tanked Roadster and the large tanked Interstate. The Roadster tank is small and cute but not very practical, whereas the Interstate tank is large and rather bulbous (to my eyes) but very practical. So which one to go for? For me, that's an easy decision as I've always gone for form over function (looks rather than practicality), so it'd be the

BUYING A BIKE TO RESTORE

1.3 Commando Fastback.

1.4 Commando Interstate.

Roadster for me every time. Some of those 750s from the early '70s were gorgeous and 'pure' as some enthusiasts might say before the 'middle-aged spread' of the 850.

However, for some reason I've always loved the idea of electric start on a bike (I guess it's because these came out when I was 17 and they just seemed so cool) so I didn't discount an 850 MkIII. Plus, my earlier experience with Alan's 750 Combat didn't really endear me to the 750.

So I started looking for a bike to restore, which would ideally be either a 750 or 850 MkIII Roadster. I perused the listings on eBay looking for a suitable candidate – preferably a complete bike, but in need of total restoration. There were quite a few bikes advertised but they were mainly either bikes in seemingly good to excellent condition or complete wrecks imported from the States with half the parts missing, for which they were asking silly money.

NB: My main advice if buying from the likes of eBay is that ANY bike looks good in a general, middle-distance photo: if you put a concours bike next to a real heap and took a photo, they wouldn't look much different. Always ask for close-ups, as it's only then that the true condition of the bike can begin to be seen; general, middle-distance photos tell you very little about the condition of the bike. Of course, seeing the bike 'in the flesh' is the only way to appraise it properly.

I also put out a few feelers, and almost immediately a friend from one of the motorcycle Facebook groups I belong to – who runs a small business specialising in importing bikes from the States (Z1Classics) – got back to me saying that he had a bike that I might be interested in. It was an 850 MkIII Roadster recently re-imported from the USA. The only problem was that it was in fair running condition, not a restoration basket case.

There's good news and bad news when planning to restore in fair condition. The bad news is mainly the cost – you'll be paying a premium for a bike that's running and roadworthy with parts that are in fair condition (but not good), but you'll still need to pay to restore them, just as you would with a basket case, yet the bike cost twice as much to buy as a non-runner.

The good news is that you have a pretty good idea that all the parts are there, and hopefully in pretty much the right order (you never know what previous owners have done). Also, if you're restoring a particular model of bike for the first time then it's always advisable to buy a bike that's pretty much fully assembled, so you've a fair idea where everything goes. If you buy a bike in boxes then you won't even know what half the parts are, let alone where they all go! Not only this, but, from my experience, a bike that is in fair condition, especially an old Brit, is actually in need of a full restoration anyway and is more tired than it might at first appear. This was the case for just about every bike I've ever restored; and it turned out to be the case for the Commando, too!

Anyway, not only did Frank at Z1Classics have the bike for sale, but it was local and I knew him to be a good, reliable and trustworthy seller, which is so important. So the deal was done and for the princely (but fair) sum of £7000 I was now the proud owner of a Norton Commando 850 MkIII Roadster with electric start. Many thanks to Frank for making the purchase an enjoyable experience (unlike many experiences I've had in the past! Note: you can tell an awful lot about a bike from the owner – another disadvantage of eBay).

Having brought the bike home in a hired van, my first impression of

HOW TO RESTORE NORTON COMMANDO

my new Commando was that it was indeed in too good condition! I wanted a bike to restore, and here was a machine that was running and looked okay. However, as I inspected the bike more closely, and began to dismantle it, it became clear that the bike really needed a proper rebuild anyway (as is often the case with bikes in 'fair' condition).

From a distance, the bike looked good, but the first thing I noticed was that the tank and side panels had been poorly resprayed using black aerosol and the finish wasn't great (although it's not easy to see this in the photos); there was a broken fin on the cylinder head; the front mudguard was damaged; the front fork yokes had been hand-painted silver in situ and had had some fairly poor quality stainless brake hoses fitted; the battery was missing; and the bike also had a bad oil leak and had wet-sumped[2] so badly that ALL the oil in the tank had drained into the sump, despite this being an 850 MkIII model which was fitted with anti-drain valves.

Apart from that the bike was just a bit tatty and tired throughout, with spots of rust and damage here and there and various loose parts. However, it had an almost brand new 'pea-shooter' upswept exhaust system fitted, which looked good, and brand new tyres (although they were actually already a few years old, and the bike had clearly just not been used since they'd been fitted – they still had the manufacturer's labels stuck to their treads!) I could tell that this bike might well run okay, but in its present condition it would never be a joy to ride and would be a lot like Alan's 750, on which we just spent our time chasing faults round the bike without really curing them. Riding a classic bike is a wonderful feeling if the bike's going well; if it's not, it's just depressing and annoying. See photos 1.5-1.13.

1.5 Bike as bought, timing side.

1.6 Bike as bought, drive side.

So, my plan was to get the bike started (as I was going to rebuild the engine anyway, I wasn't too worried about the wet-sumping issue) and take it for a run to find out what was working and what required attention,

---

[2]Wet-sumping is where a bike that has a separate oil tank that holds all the oil (and is therefore a dry-sump engine) drains all the oil out of the oil tank and fills the engine full of oil. As the engine wasn't designed to run like this it can cause oil starvation if the bike is started after wet-sumping as although when the bike has wet-sumped, the crankcases are full of oil, ironically the crankshaft and big end bearings can suffer from oil starvation as there's no oil in the tank to go into the oil pump and be pumped into the crankshaft etc until the oil in the engine has been re-circulated back into the tank. There is also the possibility of encouraging oil leaks to develop if the bike is started like this. As a result, it's recommended that if your bike has wet-sumped you should drain the oil from the engine and put it back in the oil tank before starting the engine. Note: bikes that have engines without oil tanks are designed to store all the oil in the engine (a wet-sump engine) and so they can't actually wet-sump as the oil's already in there, eg Kawasaki Z1s.

BUYING A BIKE TO RESTORE

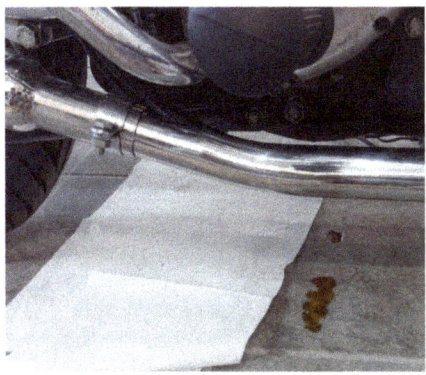
1.7 The engine was leaking quite badly.

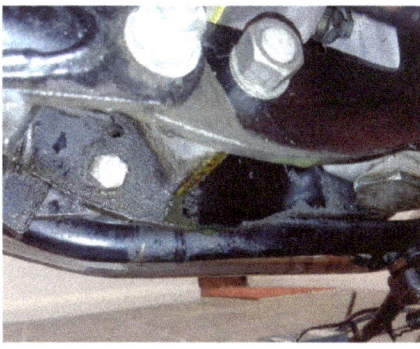
1.8 The underside of the engine suggests leaks have been there for some time.

1.9 Broken fin on the cylinder head – someone who shouldn't have been has been working on the bike.

1.10 The near side downpipe is slightly discoloured, suggesting the engine has been running a little hot on this side.

1.11 Everything there – just a bit tired and tatty.

1.12 Leaking tappet inspection covers.

1.13 Seat won't close properly.

as this would be a big help in the restoration. For instance, was the gearbox working properly, with smooth, easy, positive changes, or did it jump out of gear or have a false neutral somewhere? Information like this helps when you restore a bike as you know what to look out for and what parts might need replacing, and the only way to find this out is by riding the bike.

I duly bought a new, high-powered Motobatt AGM (Absorbed Glass Mat) battery, added some fresh fuel, tickled the carbs, applied the choke (always required in my cold basement workshop) and pressed the starter button to see what might happen. Blow me down if the damn thing didn't start! However, there was a cloud of smoke out of one of the

HOW TO RESTORE NORTON COMMANDO

exhausts to rival a London smog, and the engine was very lumpy – and the whole thing shook and rattled like a bag of spanners.

In the end, I decided not to take it for a test ride as the whole bike was clearly not right, and it was just a bit too dangerous for my liking. So I'd have to check every part carefully after I'd dismantled it for excess wear, and err on the side of caution, replacing parts that might not necessarily require it, just for peace of mind – and to not have to do it all again!

LESSONS LEARNT
- Buying the right bike to restore is one of the most important parts of the whole restoration process.
- Do as much research as possible about your chosen model before entering the market.
- Know what you want from your restoration before you begin: do you want a 100 per cent concours machine or a custom street racer? This will affect what bike you're looking for as a basis for your restoration.
- There are a few bike dealers that specialise in importing bikes for restoration, and they are always a good starting point – but choose your company carefully as some importers tend to sell relatively expensive machines for what they are. Find a company like Z1Classics (on Facebook).
- eBay is always a good starting point, but photos can be very deceptive, especially when taken from a distance.
- A bike in fairly good condition will cost just as much to restore as one in tatty condition as the parts might be okay, but will still need to be restored. It therefore makes more financial sense to buy a bike in poor condition rather than a similar one in okay condition as you'll end up doing the same amount of work on both. For example the paintwork on a decent bike may be in pretty good condition when compared to that chipped and dented one over there, but you'll still need to have the tank repainted if you want the bike to look top dollar.
- If you're restoring a model for the first time, avoid basket cases as you'll have no idea where all the parts go.
- If you want to have the finished bike fairly standard, then go for a bike that looks original and relatively untouched, rather than a bike that's been customised over the years with such items as uprated brakes, forks, suspension, etc. You'll pay over the odds for such a bike and then spend a whole lot again putting it back to standard. An original bike that may be very tired and a bit rusty is a far better option.
- Good owners sell good bikes; bad owners sell anything.
- If possible, take the bike for a run before beginning the restoration, as that will tell you what's working and what isn't.

Chapter 2

Golden rules for restoring a bike

TEN GOLDEN RULES FOR A SUCCESSFUL REBUILD

Rule 1

The first rule about dismantling a bike (or anything mechanical) is to take as many photos before and during dismantling as possible – and then take some more. You simply can't take too many photos of how things look and where they go, etc. In this day and age of digital photography there's no excuse for not taking copious amounts of pictures. I think I took something like 500 photos during the dismantling process alone, chronicling the disassembly as thoroughly as possible. These proved invaluable during the reassembly process when I encountered a part that I wasn't sure which way round it went, and there was no mention of it in the manuals. Being able to look back at how it was originally is so helpful. (Does the spacer go behind or in front of the nut?)

Under NO CIRCUMSTANCES should you fool yourself into thinking, "I'll remember how this goes together, there's no need to take any photos." This is simply not true. I often can't even remember how to reassemble parts I only took apart a few days ago let alone those that have lain untouched for several months/years – as parts of a full restoration often do. Not taking pictures is just laziness – you tell yourself there's no need as you'll remember, but in truth it's just that you simply can't be bothered to take pictures (I know, I've been there). Do this and you will regret it in a big way (and my words will come back to haunt you!)

Even such photos of where the wiring loom runs can be invaluable later on – don't forget to take some of these as well as all the mechanical bits.

Rule 2

Rule 2 is to bag all parts up as you dismantle the bike and LABEL THEM as you take them apart. My patent method is to use freezer bags labelled with a marker pen and stored in plastic storage boxes. Most parts can simply be bagged (and sealed) up with the contents clearly written on the outside of the freezer bag. As they are plastic they can be filled with oily or greasy parts without a problem and they won't rot or split. You can also add oil where necessary to ensure that parts don't go rusty in storage. I then have a large plastic storage box to cover each section of the bike: for example, electrical, cylinders and cylinder head, crankcase internals, electrics, front forks, etc, and parts are kept together in them. The only time I don't bag things up is if they are too big or are VERY easily identifiable, eg the swinging arm or rear shock absorbers. Otherwise 'bag and tag' everything, regardless. Not only this but try to separate parts as much as possible, so, for instance, you should have many bags for the various parts of the primary chaincase, rather than having one huge bag for the entire contents! I even have bags with just one nut in them (carefully labelled!); it makes reassembly so much easier when you know exactly what things are.

Rule 3

Rule 3 is to briefly assess the condition of each item before bagging it and storing it. I tend only to examine parts in detail as I begin to reassemble everything and restore/replace as necessary then. However, there are some parts that require longer to recondition than others, so if you have an idea of what is required you can make that a priority. For example, if you discover you need a re-bore as you take the engine apart

HOW TO RESTORE NORTON COMMANDO

you can get pistons etc, and the re-bore itself organised earlier than later, so you aren't waiting several days/weeks for a part that can hold up the entire job.

One particular example of this was with my chroming. I already knew I needed to re-chrome several parts and wanted to chrome others and I rang my local chrome platers for a chat about how they wanted them prepared before taking them in (all paint removed, not shot blasted – too rough a surface – and old chrome left as is), during which they told me how long the waiting time was … five months! Yes, five whole months as they were so busy. I therefore knew that my first priority following dismantling was to take all the requisite parts for chroming and get in the queue! In the end they were able to do this in a shorter time than quoted – but I was very lucky, and it was still a long time before they were ready.

Rule 4
Most parts will be oily and/or greasy and pretty horrible. Use WD40 liberally on oily/greasy parts to clean them down to a basic acceptable level for storage. Full cleaning/refurbishment can be carried out as necessary at a later date. If absolutely necessary, use white spirit to clean such parts, but WD40 is a lot more user friendly and does a great job. Conversely, if parts are too dry or rusty then also spray them with WD40 to protect them from further deterioration. If you then put them in freezer bags they will be protected from moisture etc and so prevent further rusting.

Rule 5
Decide what you want out of your rebuild and plan accordingly. For example, I knew that I wanted to complete a high quality nut and bolt rebuild to create what I think of as a stunning bike, which was largely original but with modern upgrades where appropriate, so not 100 per cent original. This meant I would have all engine parts blast cleaned, much additional chrome work, upgraded parts where applicable/available/affordable, new bearings throughout, a powder-coated frame, stainless steel wheel rims and spokes with polished hubs and new tyres, stainless fasteners throughout, etc. This meant that I had to make sure I had the following in place: a chrome plating company, an engineering firm, wheel rebuilders, instrument restorers, parts suppliers, a knowledge of where to buy good quality custom/upgraded parts etc. As well as planning ahead, begin scouring the internet for companies that sell upgrades and other parts for your bike so you know what options are out there. Companies I used are listed at the back of this manual.

Rule 6
Make sure you have the time and money in place for such an undertaking. Rebuilds always take far longer than anticipated and as time goes by more and more other jobs begin to mount up that demand your time (and money!) so make sure you are able to stay focussed and get the job completed even when it takes two or three times longer than you'd planned.

Ensure your life is fundamentally stable enough to support a rebuild. As well as time, money, space, tools, etc, problems can arise from unrelated things such as having children, moving house/job/city, holidays, home improvements, illness, getting divorced, etc. Life gets in the way.

Always remember the golden rule that rebuilds have an inverse time to completion ratio. This means that the nearer you get to finishing the restoration, the slower the rate of progress. So the first few days are spent happily pulling the bike apart thinking that this is easy and you'll have it finished in no time. Then things start to slow down as you have to find new parts and get old ones repaired, and then the spare room needs redecorating, and your partner insists you go on holiday, and your job suddenly changes, and before you know it your rate of progress has slowed right down to a crawl and gets steadily slower as the rebuild continues. Therefore, according to the law of inverse time to completion 20 per cent of the rebuild is completed in one week, 30 per cent in one month, 40 per cent in three months, 50 per cent in six months, 70 per cent in a year, 80 per cent in 18 months and so on. Beware: this is a mathematical certainty and can't be avoided! You have been warned. (Note: by definition this also means that no restoration is ever 100 per cent complete!)

Rule 7
Know your limitations. Make sure you have the necessary expertise, temperament and patience to complete such a project, and where you haven't, find suitable specialists to complete the work for you. I'm lucky in that I've always had some mechanical/practical ability (inherited from my father), and having learnt the hard way as a teenager pulling bikes apart and not being able to put them back together I now know I'm old enough and wise enough to get things finished. However, there are still things that I know I'm no good at (like paintwork) and if necessary I give these jobs to others. Know your own strengths and weaknesses and use professionals/friends and contacts as necessary. This also goes for such work as chroming, re-boring and maybe valve guide fitting.

Rule 8
Ensure you have enough tools, equipment and space to complete a restoration. I've built up a large array of tools over the years and am in the fortunate position of being able to buy anything I haven't already got, especially in terms of special tools required. This is a big bonus. There is a list of the special tools and general tools I used during the rebuild at the end of the book.

I have a basement-cum-garage and that gives me sufficient room – room to work, room to assemble the bike, room to store all the parts of the bike, room for my tools. Remember that a bike in bits takes up at least three times the room of a complete bike. I have a good workshop with a decent bench that is solid, plus a recent acquisition of a bike lift, which is fantastic. If you can afford one then definitely go for it – by far the best tool I've bought in years. How I ever managed to crawl around on the floor rebuilding bikes before I'll never know. My knees are still recovering

GOLDEN RULES FOR RESTORING A BIKE

to this day. With a bike lift you can either sit or stand and work on the bike at the perfect height – it makes the whole job so much easier and enjoyable. The second best tool I ever bought is a cordless socket wrench, used for undoing locked/very tight nuts and bolts throughout the bike, and especially inside the engine: with this amazing tool you don't have to lock the engine to stop the nut from just turning. With this tool it shocks the nut into releasing without the need to lock the engine. It can also be used on other nuts and bolts on the bike that are very tight or rusted solid. Again, this is in the tools section at the end of the book.

Rule 9

Make sure you really love your bike and want to rebuild it – it simply won't get finished otherwise. Want to go down the pub every night or follow other interests? Forget it. If you don't really want it, it won't happen. When things go wrong with the rebuild (and they will) you need to have the desire and commitment to face the problem, take it apart, and start again.

Rule 10

When working on the bike and it's not going right – the nut that's hard to reach simply won't go on or a part won't fit – STOP WORK! Go for a breather and a cuppa (or even better leave it overnight) and come back to it refreshed and relaxed. I guarantee that the nut will suddenly screw on, or those parts that don't fit will suddenly go together. If you don't have that break but continue working then you will cross-thread the nut and break the parts you're trying to fit together. (Same applies if you need the loo!) By the same token don't set yourself goals for a work session. For instance, don't say, "I'll just fit the rear brake pedal" or whatever, as the pedal will jam for some unexpected reason and you'll end up rushing to try and get it to fit as time runs out. Instead, just say to yourself, "I'll spend two hours on the bike," so that, whether you only get one nut fitted or the whole engine rebuilt in that time, it's okay. In line with this, you'll also discover that the simple jobs always turn out to be the hardest: refitting the pistons, no problem; putting the little screw back on the bracket that holds the side panel, complete nightmare!

LESSONS LEARNT

• Ignore these rules at your peril. You can complete a rebuild without following some or any of the above – it's just that it's a lot harder.
• Never forget the fundamental 'law of inverse time to completion' and go with the flow.
• You *will* make mistakes – but accept them, learn from them, move on; your understanding of mechanics and the bike itself will increase.
• If you've read the rules and are unable to adhere to them, then either pay someone else to rebuild the bike for you or buy a bike that's already been restored – there's always work to be done on any classic bike, no matter how well (or not!) it's been restored, and much joy can be derived from tinkering with a bike rather than fully restoring it.
• Keep the faith.

RULES OF THE WORKSHOP

• Proportion of time spent working on bike in the workshop: 10 per cent. Time spent looking for that flipping tool you had in your hand just a few seconds ago: 90 per cent.
• Any nut, screw or washer that is dropped onto the garage floor immediately transports to a third dimension, and will only return after many hours of fruitless searching … and only then after a replacement has been ordered.
• Proportion of time spent sleeping in bed: 10 per cent. Proportion of time spent wide awake in bed trying to work out why the crankcases won't fit together: 90 per cent.
• Ability to listen to someone for longer than five minutes without your mind wandering off to the rebuild: nil.
• Time waiting for parts to be delivered and waiting in, not wanting to miss the parcel: infinite.
• Ability to enjoy holidays when you know they're taking up valuable rebuild time and money: low.
• Having to explain why all the other essential and urgent jobs that need doing round the house should be put on hold until after the rebuild: relentless.
• Worrying that when the parts' suppliers ring and leave a message with someone else, they might accidentally say how much they cost.
• Going out to a posh do with oil under your fingernails and cuts on your hands: normal.
• And of course you're greatest fear: Worrying that when you die your partner will sell your bikes for what you told them you paid for them!

And finally, never forget this mathematical equation. It has been scientifically proven that the formula for the number of bikes you need is $X + 1$ (where X equals the number of bikes you already own!)

Chapter 3
Preparing to dismantle

Before starting work my first task was to decide what kind of restoration I wanted. Did I want a 100 per cent original bike with only original parts built to concours standard? Or a modern street bike/café racer with all the modern custom upgrades I could think of? Or a semi-original restoration with the odd upgrade and aftermarket part? In my case it was the latter. Remember, it's your bike, so restore it as you see fit, but just try to decide what you want at the beginning so you know where you're headed, and so you don't have to make major changes half way through the rebuild.

If you've a good idea of what bike you want to have at the end of the restoration then you can plan accordingly and begin assembling the necessary parts at the earliest opportunity, especially if you require parts or services that are hard to obtain or which have a long lead time.

In my case, I wanted to build a bike that was largely original but with a few tweaks and changes to make it look good and be a bit special. This is what I planned at the start in terms of changes/upgrades:
• Polish the hubs and fit stainless steel spokes to the wheels – and possibly change to stainless steel rims rather than re-chrome the original steel ones (which is what I ended up doing. I could have changed to alloy rims, rather than stainless steel, but in the end I decided to keep with the more original look of the standard rims).
• Have the tank and side panels repainted in the original red, not that I wanted the bike original, but by coincidence that was my favourite colour choice anyway.
• Fit stainless steel parts where appropriate/possible – engine casing fasteners, most nuts/bolts/fasteners throughout the bike where obtainable, including all engine casings and wheel spindles etc.
• Replace the rear shocks with new upgraded ones, depending on what's available.
• Polish engine outer casings to a high finish, and vapour-blast all engine and gearbox casings. I like a bit of bling!
• Upgrade the front disc brake – either fit a better master cylinder, or upgrade the whole thing with new a new calliper and disc – or possibly twin discs. (In the end I fitted an upgraded calliper and disc from Norvil, and an upgraded master cylinder from Andover Norton).
• Fit LED bulbs where possible. Some owners say that LED headlamp bulbs don't provide a decent beam at night, but I had no intention of using the bike at night, so that wasn't an issue. However, I do like to ride with my headlamp on at all times (it's a personal thing – you either do or you don't) and LED bulbs take far less current than the original filament bulbs and therefore put far less strain on the charging system. LED bulbs are also slightly brighter and so can possibly be seen more easily in the daylight.
• I was also interested in looking at upgrading the electrical/charging system. However, as I dismantled the bike I was stunned by the uniqueness and ingenuity of the charging system on my 850 MkIII. It was fitted with not one, but two Zener diodes (regulators), each one attached to the alloy foot peg mountings to aid heat dissipation (Zener diodes take excess power from the charging system by releasing heat). Not only that, but a large capacitor was fitted which retains some charge so the bike can be started with a flat battery. In the end I went on to fit a Boyer Power

PREPARING TO DISMANTLE

Box that replaced all of the above and more, and is apparently much more efficient.

Other than that everything was to be cleaned, restored, replaced, re-chromed or polished as necessary to make the bike look good and run as sweetly as possible.
• I was also keen to fit upgrades where appropriate. At this point I wasn't sure what was available, but these are on my list: electronic ignition, an upgraded head steady, a good oil seal for the tacho drive, a good anti-drain valve (the MkIII already has one fitted – but as my engine had clearly wet-sumped, it wasn't working!), an upgraded starter motor, a new air filter to replace the massive MkIII airbox, and any other engine modifications as recommended by other owners (Facebook is good for this) and the various parts suppliers.

You should also waste no time in finding the following services:
• A list of very reputable suppliers of spare parts. You will almost certainly be buying a whole host of parts for your bike during the restoration and finding reliable and efficient parts suppliers who only sell either original parts (NOS: new old stock) or quality replacement parts and who deliver quickly will be important.
• Try to build a list of enthusiasts and contacts who can help you and give advice and help when you need it (and you will need it!). The best place to start is by joining one of the owners' clubs (see back of book for details) and looking on the web and Facebook for pages and forums where you can ask for advice (again see the back of the book for details). Good parts suppliers are also a great source of knowledge and expertise.
• A good metal finishers (chroming and polishing) to chrome parts as necessary and buff any alloy parts you want shiny unless you're polishing them yourself, as I did in some cases – they do it better than I can!
• A decent machine shop to carry out any necessary work on the engine, eg a re-bore or head skim as well as being able to properly mend broken fins etc on the cylinder block where necessary (a decent company will make an almost invisible repair).
• A really good painters for the tank and panels – ensure they are VERY familiar with painting tanks to ensure they're ethanol resistant and won't peel or bubble round the vulnerable tank filler cap area, and make sure you end up with a paint job that will really set the bike off, rather than detract from it.
• Unless building the wheels yourself, a recommended wheel builders who can either refurbish your existing wheels to original or carry out such additional work as polishing the hubs, fitting stainless steel spokes and/or rims and fitting new tyres (to save you the hassle of trying to find a good motorcycle tyre fitters later on).
• Somewhere to take your parts for blast cleaning. Be aware that some parts are softer than others and can be badly damaged by blast cleaning if the wrong process is used. For example the carburettors are made of much softer aluminium alloy than the crankcases and can only be cleaned with a gentle method such as vapour/aqua-blasting (carb manifolds on Commandos are even softer).
• Somewhere to powder-coat your frame and other parts as required (or spray it; as is your want).
• A large wad of cash to spend on your bike without question or thought – the restoration is clearly a top priority and takes precedence over all other household expenditure such as holidays (clearly unnecessary) and the purchase of such fripperies as soft furnishings and other household items – although generous (or at least regular) gifts to your other half should be maintained at all times to ensure that the restoration continues smoothly and without interruption!

Finally, don't forget the two golden rules to dismantling:
• Take copious photos of EVERY aspect of the dismantling procedure before taking it apart so you have full reference material when trying to put it back together. For instance, does the washer go in front or behind the bracket? Which way round does the battery box go? How does the rear light assembly fit together? These may seem like simple things but when you come to reassemble everything a few months later it's suddenly not quite so straightforward.
• As you dismantle parts put them in plastic freezer bags and label them with a permanent marker. Keep the parts as separate as possible by using multiple bags rather than one large one with a large amount of parts in it.

I know I've mentioned these before, but I make no apologies for repeating them because they are so essential. If you only take two things from this book, take these.

My plan was as follows:
• Completely dismantle the bike, briefly inspecting each part as it came off so I could see if there were any parts that were badly damaged or missing that may be hard to source so I could begin my search for them straight away or make a note of any parts that required specialist attention.
• Take the appropriate parts (mainly engine cases, frame and other cycle parts) to the specialist vapour/aqua-blast cleaners for cleaning.
• Assess cycle parts with regards to suitability/cost for re-chroming. If they're in very poor condition it might be better to replace them with aftermarket parts. Similarly, due to the high cost of chroming it may be cheaper to buy replacements than pay for re-chroming. (But some aftermarket parts are not as good quality as the originals, so refurbishing original items is usually preferential to buying remanufactured ones).
• Take the appropriate parts to the chrome platers for chroming or polishing ASAP.
• Send tank and panels off for re-painting.
• Send the wheels off to a specialist wheel builders (stainless spokes and stainless rims).
• Send the frame away for powder-coating.
• Having assessed the various parts of the engine/gearbox assembly decide what work is required (re-bore etc) and what parts need replacing and have the necessary work completed and replacement parts ordered accordingly. (I intend to use only recommended specialists for

HOW TO RESTORE NORTON COMMANDO

machining work, as I used to use my local machine shop but I've decided their work just isn't really top quality. If you're going to have work done, have it done properly. I'm also going to only use specialist parts suppliers to source parts, as there are just too many cheap and poorly made replacement parts available on the internet from suppliers of unknown provenance. Always worth looking on the internet, but beware cheap parts that are poor quality.)
• Begin engine reassembly whilst waiting for other parts to arrive.
• Retrieve frame.
• Whilst waiting for all the parts to be cleaned/chromed/repainted, recondition and reassemble the crankshaft, con-rods and crankcases.
• Refit the front forks and front wheel to the frame ready to accept the rebuilt crankcases, and then slowly reassemble the engine in the frame.
• Re-wire bike using new or reconditioned parts where appropriate, and upgrade the charging system.
• Buy replacement cycle parts where necessary, such as mudguards.
• Assemble cycle parts.
• 'Spanner up' by going round the bike, checking that all nuts and bolts, etc, are fully tightened.
• Fill bike with requisite fluids and start engine. Check all is well.
• Give bike a full road test, check all torque settings and sort out teething problems as necessary.
• Sit back and enjoy the completed restoration. (Bearing in mind Rule 6 of the top ten golden rules!)

• Simple!
Finally, make sure you have the correct tools to hand. In the back of this book you will find a whole chapter dedicated to the tools you may require to rebuild a Commando, and I suggest you have a look at this before you start, but apart from general garage tools there are a few essentials/desirables that I'll mention now:
• A bike lift. If you can afford one and have the space for one, then go for it. Best tool I ever bought – not as expensive as they used to be.
• Buy a cordless impact driver (like they use in garages to remove wheel nuts, etc – although theirs tend to be air driven). This tool allows you to undo many nuts on the bike that are either done up very tightly, or rusted, or that normally require locking the engine in some way to prevent the nut just turning instead of unscrewing. The 'shock and awe' of the impact driver overcomes all these problems, and nuts that in the past drove me mad and sometimes took days to remove (literally), come off in a matter of seconds. Not cheap but so, so wonderful.
• Alongside the normal AF, a good set of Whitworth spanners and sockets. Almost needless to say there are a complete mix of threads and sizes on the bike that have no rhyme nor reason. Most nuts and bolts tend to be Whitworth so a good set of spanners and sockets is essential. On MkIII Commandos there is also the odd metric nut here and there, just for good measure.
• Special tools for dismantling the engine. I usually have to find some way of improvising a tool to remove a certain part, as the original workshop tool is NLA (no longer available), but, in the case of the Commando, all the special tools are still available (re-manufactured) and they're not that expensive. So it's definitely worth investing in either a full set before starting work, or buy them individually as you go along, as they make the whole job so much easier and stress free – plus, there's much less chance of causing damage to vulnerable parts (Yes, I've done that too many times to admit to, and when it happens it hurts and you have several days of self-recrimination to go through before paying out ten times the value of the special tools to get things mended). Special tools available from the main suppliers are listed in the back of this book.
• A car trolley jack to help support the engine whilst dismantling it – see chapters on dismantling the bike.

LESSONS LEARNT
• Make a plan for the restoration but be prepared to change it as work progresses.
• Find parts suppliers and service providers ASAP.
• Join clubs and/or Facebook groups to source advice and support when necessary.
• Make sure everything's ready before starting to dismantle.
• Check you have the correct tools and equipment.
• Find a good supplier of flowers and chocolates.

Chapter 4
Beginning to dismantle

So, finally time to get the bike on the ramp and begin the dismantling. My method is basically as follows:
• Put the bike on the lift, put it on its main stand, and strap it down carefully (later on I was very glad I had!).
• Leave the lift on its lowest setting and first and foremost remove the battery. After that, I kind of work my way from the top down – seat, tank, handlebars, instruments, rear mudguard, the electrics under the seat and tank.
• After this I raise the lift to its half way up position and begin removing the back wheel and other cycle parts (battery tray, airbox etc)
• I keep going until all that's left is the front wheel and forks and the engine and gearbox in the frame.
• Raising the lift to its full height, I then begin to dismantle the engine and gearbox in the frame, with the frame acting as a glorified engine stand allowing dismantling to take place relatively easily and safely.
• When the gearbox is out and the cylinder head, barrels, timing case and primary chaincase have been removed, the crankcases can be lifted out of the frame (what remains of the engine now being light enough to lift and carry).
• The very last job is to remove the front wheel and forks.
• The bike is now fully dismantled.

Well, that was the plan anyway – now back to reality! With the battery safely removed, together with both side panels, I removed the seat, which should have been very simple but undoing the hinge (as only fitted to MkIII models, I believe) actually had me confused for a while. In the end I removed the four cross head screws that held the seat to the hinge (see photo 4.1) before removing the two bolts that hold the remainder of the hinge to the frame later on, as access was easier, but I could have just removed the two hinge mounting bolts on the frame.

After this I turned to the fuel tank. The tank should have been attached to the frame via four studs on the tank (two at the front, sitting on a number of rubber washers going into brackets on the frame, and two rubber 'cotton reel' ones at the rear, bolting into a strap under the frame). However, in my case the tank was simply sitting on the front brackets with no bolts done up

4.1 The seat hinge screws (MkIII).

HOW TO RESTORE NORTON COMMANDO

at all, and the rear mounting strap was missing completely! The only things holding the tank on were the two fuel pipes, and when these were removed, the tank simply lifted away. See photos 4.2 and 4.3. At least it made for easy removal!

I gave the tank a quick check over and it immediately became clear that it had been given a poor quality respray in black. Photo 4.4 shows that it is covered in small pin holes, which are a sign that the surface wasn't properly prepared and was probably greasy. Not only that, but it would appear that the bike was originally red as that is the colour on the underside of the tank. See photo 4.5. This was a nice coincidence, as I had already decided to respray the bike red, so it was now even more fitting.

I then immediately put the tank and side panels into a large plastic box, for protection. In my experience, the main likelihood of damage to fuel tanks is not when the tank's on the bike, but from accidents in the workshop when in storage. Things can fall on it, or it can be dropped etc. I therefore always store tanks (and panels) in a strong plastic box when off the bike.

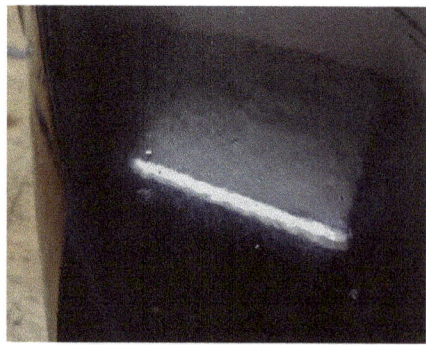

4.4 Poor paintwork on the tank – probably caused by not degreasing the surface properly before spraying.

4.2 Seat and tank removed – very easily in this case!

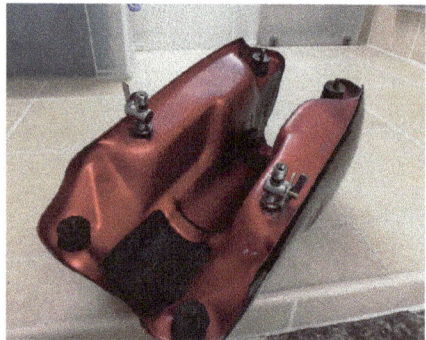

4.5 It would appear the bike was originally painted red.

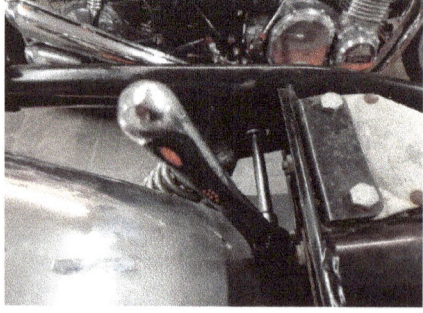

4.3 Front mounting brackets for the tank – at least they were still there, unlike the rear ones!

4.6 Removing the seat hinge from the frame (MkIII).

BEGINNING TO DISMANTLE

After this, I fully removed the seat hinge from above the left-hand rear shock absorber (see photo 4.6), and at the same time I was beginning to appreciate just how big the airbox on an 850 MkIII really is. See photo 4.7. I think that the airbox was introduced to enable the bike to pass much more stringent environmental legislation in the USA. The airbox was there both to help reduce pollution in the exhaust fumes, by re-burning some fumes, and to reduce air intake noise from the carburettors – hence its considerable size. I also removed the grab rail at this point, which is just clamped to the rear frame loop by metal brackets. See photo 4.8. I then turned my attention to the handlebars and instruments. The first thing I did here was drain the hydraulic fluid from the front brake in readiness to remove the lever assembly from the handlebars. See photo 4.9. I always find that brake fluid makes a mess no matter how careful you are, but the good news is that it's hygroscopic – it absorbs water. If it's spilt then you can wipe the area with a damp cloth and the fluid magically disappears.

NB: I now know that I should have removed both callipers from their mounting first (MkIIIs also have a rear disc brake, as well as the front), and used the hydraulics to push out the rearmost piston from the Norton-Lockheed callipers as, due to their unique design, it's really hard to remove the rear piston when the calliper's off the bike. Pushing the rearmost piston with hydraulic pressure makes the job a lot easier.

I then removed the headlamp from the nacelle to expose the wiring within, and took even more photos than usual of how it was before dismantling, to ensure it all went back in the correct order later on! See photo 4.10. I disconnected the wiring to the right-hand handlebar switch from the headlamp (see photo 4.11), and then removed the brake lever and master cylinder from the front of the switch. See photo 4.12 of the assembly removed and photo 4.13 of where it screws onto the front of the handlebar switch. Note that a quick initial inspection revealed that the front brakelight switch was broken. See photo 4.14.

4.7 Beginning to see just how big that MkIII airbox really is!

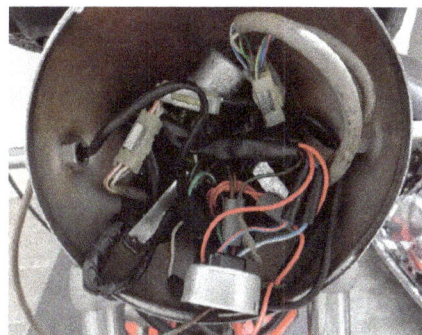

4.10 Take copious photos of the headlight wiring before disconnecting.

4.8 The grab rail is just clamped to the rear frame loop.

4.9 Draining brake fluid and disconnecting the front brake calliper.

4.11 Right-hand handlebar wires removed from headlamp.

HOW TO RESTORE NORTON COMMANDO

4.12 Master cylinder removed from the switchgear.

4.13 Switchgear still in place on the handlebars.

4.14 Initial inspection reveals a broken brake light connection.

4.15 Switch and throttle removed from the handlebars.

4.16 Wires trapped and cut through between the headlamp and headlamp nacelle.

4.17 Clutch lever and left-hand switchgear removed.

With the brake lever removed I was then able to remove the right-hand handlebar switch, together with the throttle grip, which comes away from the throttle cable when the switch itself is removed. See photo 4.15. Note that I also discovered that a PO (previous owner) had trapped the wiring between the headlamp rim and the nacelle and this had been cut through. (See photo 4.16.) You should never trust what has been done to a bike by a PO.

After this, I removed the left-hand handlebar switch by disconnecting its wiring and the clutch cable before removing it from the handlebars. See photo 4.17. I then removed the handlebars from the top yoke and the top 'layer' of the bike was now dismantled, and already it was looking like a basket case. See photo 4.18.

LESSONS LEARNT
- Dismantle from the top down.
- Strap the bike down securely! Later on in the dismantling process, due to my gross negligence, the bike nearly came off the lift, and I was very glad I'd strapped it down properly.
- On disc brake models, ideally use the hydraulic fluid in the brake system to push the rearmost piston out of the callipers before dismantling.
- Always remove the battery first – I learnt that the hard way on a previous rebuild when I shorted out a live wire to earth.
- Never trust anything done or claim to have been done by a PO – unless you know that they're a good mechanic, assume that they're not.
- Brake fluid is hygroscopic so if it's spilled, just put water on it and that'll just wash it away.
- Don't forget to keep taking those photos! I think that by this point I'd already taken about 50.
- Once taken off the bike, store your tank and panels in a strong storage box with a lid to avoid accidental damage.

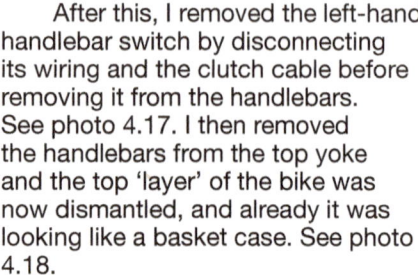

4.18 Handlebars removed from a suddenly emasculated bike.

Chapter 5
Removing the main electrics

I continued to dismantle the bike by removing the instruments and the electrics. I began by removing the speedo and tacho, which proved to be slightly more difficult than I anticipated. The clocks are mounted on top of the forks and held on by the fork top nuts. I therefore unscrewed the fork top nuts, but they were in turn screwed onto the damper rods inside the forks. I therefore had to hold the locknut on the damper rod to enable me to unscrew the fork top nut from the damper rod. See photo 5.1. With the nut removed, the instruments were lifted away. See photo 5.2.

With the speedo and tacho removed it was time to remove the instrument panel (see photo 5.3, MkIII only) but in order to this I first needed to remove the headlamp shell. I therefore removed the front indicators, which hold the headlamp shell to the mounting ears (see photo 5.4), which then allowed me to remove the shell by pulling it free from the wiring loom. See photo 5.5. Note that the small cylindrical indicator relay is also housed in the headlamp shell.

With the headlamp out of the way I was able to remove the instrument panel from the top yoke. See photo 5.6. Before removing the

5.1 Removing the nut from the top of the forks holding the instrument brackets in place.

5.2 Instruments liberated!

5.3 Instrument panel and ignition switch ready for removal.

25

HOW TO RESTORE NORTON COMMANDO

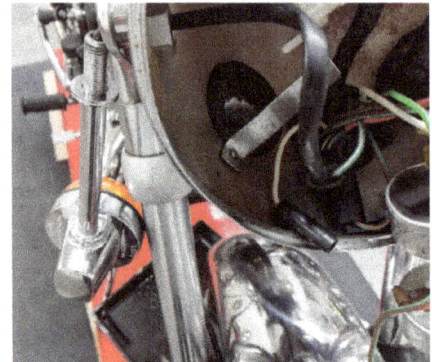

5.4 Removing the indicators from the headlamp.

5.5 With the indicators removed, the headlamp shell comes away.

5.6 Removing the instrument panel from the top yoke.

5.7 Take copious photos of the wiring to the ignition switch and the warning lights.

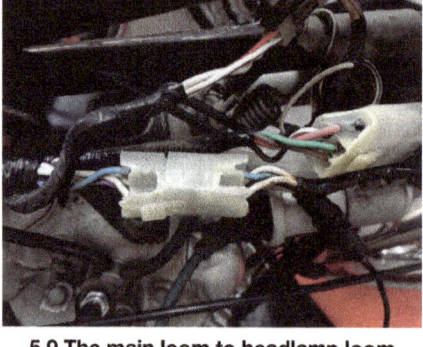

5.9 The main loom to headlamp loom connectors don't look too happy.

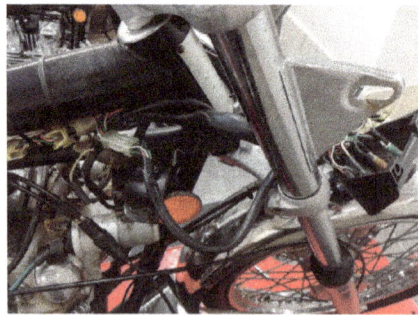

5.8 Preparing to unplug the instrument panel loom from the main loom.

5.10 Removing the ignition coils and condensors.

ignition switch I took care to take copious photos of the wiring. See photo 5.7. With the ignition switch wires disconnected I prepared to unplug the remaining wires from the main wiring loom via the multi-pin connector, leaving the warning lights still in situ. See photo 5.8. At this point I also unplugged the main wiring loom connectors, which didn't look too happy. See photo 5.9. Maybe a new loom would be on the menu.

After this, I removed the bracket that holds the twin ignition coils, together with the condensers and ballast resistor mounted between them (not visible in the photos – see Chapter 32 for more info). However, these are usually only required for contact breaker ignition and so would be removed with the fitting of electronic ignition (although some electronic ignition systems still recommend that the ballast resistor still be used, so always check). See photos 5.10 and 5.11. The condensers ensure that the points don't burn out and the ballast resistor ensures that enough current still goes to the coils when the electric starter is engaged, which takes most of the available current.

With the electrics from the front section of the bike removed, I turned to the wiring and electrics under the seat. To begin with, I removed the starter solenoid (see photo 5.12) and then the rectifier and the large blue, spring-mounted capacitor. If you look at photo 5.13 you can see the starter solenoid hanging free in front of the rectifier with the capacitor behind it. The rectifier changes the AC current from the alternator into DC and the

REMOVING THE MAIN ELECTRICS

5.11 Ignition coils on the bench.

5.12 Removing the starter motor solenoid.

capacitor stores a little charge so the bike can still be started with a flat battery. The starter has a solenoid so that the full electric current required to run the starter motor doesn't go through the switch gear; if it did it would very quickly burn out the switchgear. The starter button sends a small current to the solenoid, that in turn engages and connects the full current from the battery to the starter motor via heavy-duty power leads.

Finally, I removed the two Zener diodes, one from each of the alloy support plates on each side of the bike (although I think that earlier models had only one Zener diode). See photo 5.14. Zener diodes are a fairly basic form of regulator that allows excess current from the alternator to be turned into heat and dissipated through heat sinks – in this case the support plates. (On many British machines of the era, the Zener diode was mounted under the headlamp on a finned alloy heat sink, which was designed and placed to allow for maximum air cooling.) Apparently, two smaller Zener diodes are more efficient than one large one. I decided to look into changing and upgrading the charging system as the rebuild progressed (and I did indeed later upgrade the charging system with a Boyer *Power Box*, replacing the capacitor, rectifier and Zener diodes).

LESSONS LEARNT
- The fork top nuts are also attached to the damper rods inside the forks.
- You need to remove the headlamp shell to gain access to the instrument panel mounting screws (MkIII).
- You only need condensers with points, and the same generally goes for ballast resistors, where fitted.
- The indicator relay is inside the headlamp.
- These bikes were fitted with a capacitor to enable starting with a flat battery.
- Two Zener diodes were fitted to MkIIIs rather than the usual one, and they were cleverly and unobtrusively mounted to the alloy support brackets.

5.13 Starter solenoid hanging down in front of the rectifier and large blue capacitor.

5.14 One of the two Zener diodes on the support plates.

Chapter 6
Dismantling the rear wheel & brake assembly

Time to remove the rear wheel and silencers. First of all, I removed both shock absorbers to allow as much movement of the swinging arm as possible, which always helps when removing a rear wheel. See photo 6.1. I then removed the exhaust system. My bike had clearly had a new exhaust system fitted very recently, which on my model should have been one with annular discharge silencers and a balance pipe between the downpipes. However, the exhaust system on my bike had been replaced with one with 'pea shooter' silencers and without the balance pipe. The balance pipe was fitted as a means of helping the bike meet stricter emissions legislation, and the annular discharge silencers were quieter. Contrary to popular belief, apparently the annular discharge silencers didn't actually reduce performance, and neither did the balance pipe affect performance. However, in my eyes (and that of many other owners) the pea shooter silencers simply look the part, as does the removal of the balance pipe. So I was very happy with the system as fitted, apart from discolouration to the downpipe on the left side, which I decided to have re-chromed.

The main difference between the earlier models and the MkIII as far as the exhaust system is concerned is the way the downpipes attach to the cylinder head. After many, many years of the original exhaust clamps repeatedly coming loose, often even leading to the downpipes actually falling out of the head, Norton finally got to grips with things for the MkIII and used a proper screw-in exhaust clamp that doesn't come loose (allegedly). Hurrah!

The method I used to unscrew the clamps on my bike was to utilise

6.1 Removing the shock absorbers.

DISMANTLING THE REAR WHEEL & BRAKE ASSEMBLY

a 'C' spanner in the form of a rear shock absorber adjuster, which worked admirably. See photo 6.2. With the downpipes freed, I unbolted the (new) silencers from the (new) rubber mounted silencer brackets, and then removed the brackets themselves. See photo 6.3.

After this, I removed the right-hand (main) section of the rear wheel spindle. See photo 6.4. On a MkIII the rear wheel mounting is different to previous models owing to the fitting of a rear disc brake, and this means the hub, bearing, shock absorber (inside the rear hub) and speedometer drive are all slightly different as well – for a start the speedo drive is on the left on a MkIII. In the case of all Commandos, the right-hand wheel spindle goes through the wheel hub and screws into a second short wheel spindle on the left-hand side of the bike that holds the rear sprocket on. The rear wheel can therefore be removed without the need to remove the rear sprocket and rear chain – apparently!

With the spindle removed I half removed the rear calliper to get it out of the way. However, I should have removed it completely from the bottom bolt on the shock absorber to get it right out of the way (apparently some models of the rear disc braked MkIII had a hook on the rear loop to hold the calliper out of the way, but it was missing on mine) but I didn't do this and the calliper remained partly in the way for the rest of the operation, whilst I began to try and ease the rear wheel out. My mum's favourite saying: "Lazy people take the most trouble" comes to mind.

However, the wheel jammed against the rear mudguard. I tried various different ways to get it out, but to no avail. I checked the workshop manual (always a good idea – preferably before starting work!) and it said: "You may have to lean the bike over to get the wheel out past the mudguard." Hmm. As the bike was up on the lift and there was no-one else available to help 'lean the bike over' I wasn't impressed – how do you do this on your own when you've had a puncture in the middle of nowhere? In the end, I simply decided to remove the rear mudguard first, which I duly did by removing the three mounting bolts from the front inside of the mudguard and then the bracket over the rear frame loop. See photo 6.5. With the mudguard removed the wheel came out easily – but so much for the 'quick release' idea! (See below for some info on the earlier models.)

After this, I undid the split link on the rear drive chain and removed the nut on the short wheel spindle on the left, enabling me to remove the rear sprocket and speedo drive. See photo 6.6. An initial inspection revealed the poor condition of the rear sprocket, as expected. If you look at photo 6.7 you can see that the teeth are all slightly hooked and have burrs on one side. This was an ex-sprocket! Preliminary inspection of the speedo drive showed no obvious problems. See photo 6.8.

With the rear wheel and mudguard now off the bike I discovered … the horn! I had been told that the horn on a Commando was one of the first things to be fitted on the assembly line – and now I could see why! If you look at photo 6.9 you can see the horn mounted in the middle of the frame behind the engine plates and just above the swinging arm. If that ever went wrong then it really would be a job to get to it!

Leaving the horn in place for a while I turned my attention to the rear brake system. At this point I made (another!) basic error. I didn't read the manual properly as 'I knew what I was doing' and removed the front and rear callipers without first using the hydraulic pressure to push the rearmost of the two pistons out. The design of the iconic Norton-Lockheed

6.2 Unscrewing the MkIII downpipe clamps with the aid of a shock absorber adjuster.

6.3 Removing the rubber-mounted silencer hangers.

6.4 Preparing to remove the rear wheel.

6.5 The rear wheel comes out easily without the mudguard in the way. The rear calliper should have been removed completely.

HOW TO RESTORE NORTON COMMANDO

6.6 Rear sprocket and rear chain being removed.

6.7 Initial inspection of the rear sprocket shows the expected excessive wear. Note the hooked teeth with burrs on the ends.

6.8 Speedo drive assembly from the left-hand side of a MkIII.

6.9 So, people weren't joking when they said that the horn on a Commando was inaccessible.

callipers is such that removing the rearmost piston with the calliper off the bike is a total pain. I had to take mine down to the engineers later and get them to remove mine. Anyway, in blissful ignorance I continued working …

I drained the rear master cylinder through the calliper and removed the calliper together with its mounting plate and began to remove the combined master cylinder and rear brake pedal assembly. See photo 6.10. With this off, I then split the brake assembly into its three main assemblies for storage: the master cylinder, the right-hand footpeg bracket and the brake lever. See photos 6.11, 6.12 and 6.13. Finally, I removed the hydraulic brakelight switch, having photographed the wiring (not so I would know which way round the two wires went – on a switch it doesn't usually matter – but so I would know that these were the two wires for the brakelight switch during reassembly – wiring looms can be a disorientating mess on reassembly, with no clues as to what wires go where!). See photo 6.14.

By this time the iconic alloy support plates on each side of the bike were nearly off, so I undid the last couple of bolts and removed them from the bike. See photo 6.15. I then began to remove the oil tank. See photo 6.16. I first undid the two rubber mountings from either side of the top of the oil tank, then realised that there was an extra mounting bolt at the bottom of the tank, securing it to the battery tray, which was particularly hard to get to. I therefore removed the horn, giving me sufficient access to get to the mounting. See photo 6.17. It was still hard to access even then.

With the oil tank partially removed from the frame I drained the remnants of oil that were still in

6.10 Beginning to remove the rear master cylinder and brake pedal assembly.

DISMANTLING THE REAR WHEEL & BRAKE ASSEMBLY

6.11 Rear brake and master cylinder assembly on the bench.

6.12 Separating the brake pedal and master cylinder assemblies.

6.13 Separating the brake pedal from the footpeg mounting.

6.14 Removing the hydraulic brake light switch – having photographed the connections first.

there (most of it was in the sump as the bike had wet-sumped – mainly due to the fact that the anti-drain valve had seized open in the timing cover, as I was later to discover). I left draining the oil to this point as it was easier to drain the oil past the frame and swinging arm with the tank partially out of the frame. See photo 6.18. With the oil drained from the tank, I then removed the oil feed pipe, together with its attached filter (see photo 6.19) and I was then able to withdraw the oil tank from the frame. See photo 6.20

Removing the oil tank then provided me with much better access to the central frame area and the remaining wiring and airbox.

LESSONS LEARNT
• The original annular discharge silencers as fitted to the MkIIIs were often blamed for reducing the power input on Tridents and Commandos, but they were in fact very efficient – the jury's out as to how power was reduced from earlier models, if indeed, it ever was.
• MkIII Commandos actually have exhaust clamps that stay tight in the cylinder head!
• The rear wheel assembly is understandably different on a MkIII as they were fitted with a disc brake rather than a drum brake. They are

6.15 Removing the iconic support plates.

6.16 Support plates off, ready to remove the oil tank.

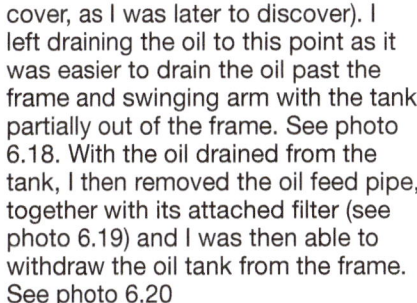
6.17 Removing the horn to give greater access to the oil tank mountings.

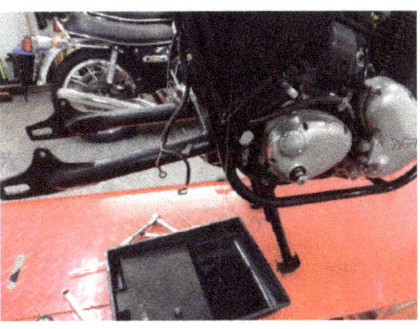
6.18 Draining the remnants of the oil tank.

6.19 Removing the oil feed pipe.

HOW TO RESTORE NORTON COMMANDO

6.20 Oil tank removed giving better access to the remaining wiring.

6.22 The left side of an early hub showing where the three bolts from the sprocket locate.

6.23 The right-hand side of an early hub, with the alloy cover removed, showing where the three bolts from the sprocket come through the hub.

6.21 Rubber bungs in the hubs of early bikes are removed to give access to the three bolts holding the sprockets on.

6.24 Three different types of rear sprocket. On the right is the early 'bolt-on' type. At the top is the later 'pronged' type, which had small rubber shock absorbers and an extra bearing. On the left is the MkIII version with extra bearing and the prongs now replaced with five vanes.

all designed to be 'quick release' enabling the wheel to be removed without the sprocket – allegedly!
• To check a chain for wear whilst on the bike, pull it away from the sprocket – the further away you can pull it, the more worn the chain.
• Rumours that the horn on a Commando is very hard to access are true!
• The rear master cylinder and brake assembly on a MkIII are easily accessible.
• Use hydraulic pressure to force out the rearmost piston on a Norton-Lockheed brake calliper *before* draining the fluid and removing the calliper from the bike.
• There's an extra hidden, and completely inaccessible, bottom mounting bolt on a Commando oil tank – as per usual for British bikes of the era!
• Commandos tend to wet-sump – even on MkIIIs when the anti-drain valve has seized open!

REAR WHEELS ON EARLIER MODELS

I think that all Commandos had rear wheels with two spindles – a long one through the hub and a short one through the sprocket – so that the rear wheel could be removed without disturbing the rear sprocket – hopefully! However, they differed in style.

Very early Commandos had rear sprockets that were bolted to the rear hub with three bolts – and no shock absorber! To remove the wheel you remove the three rubber bungs from the right-hand side of the wheel which gives access to the three bolts, and by undoing these, the wheel can be removed. See photo 6.21. Note that these early wheels only had two bearings in total: two in the hub and none in the sprocket itself – as the sprocket is bolted to the hub it doesn't require a separate bearing. See photos 6.22 and 6.23 of an early hub, showing where the three bolts locate.

Later wheels had a similar but slightly more sophisticated arrangement. They had three long prongs to replace the three bolts, and these prongs had rubber pads either side to create a shock absorber. These wheels should be able to be removed by simply pulling the wheel away from the sprocket after the speedo drive had been removed. Note that these sprockets also had bearings inside them.

Then came the MkIII which used five vanes to replace the three prongs of the earlier models, which engage with rubber pads in the hub and enable drive through a shock absorber with a greater contact area. They also had an extra bearing in the sprocket. See photo 6.24 showing all three different types of rear sprocket.

Chapter 7
Removing the carbs, airbox & remaining wiring

The next jobs were to remove the carburettors, airbox and remaining wiring. With the oil tank out of the way I was able to remove the rectifier followed by the capacitor (see photos 7.1 & 7.1A) before turning my attention to removing the carburettors from the cylinder head. This was one of those seemingly simple jobs that turned out to be far more difficult than it first appeared. The carbs are mounted on long, curved inlet manifolds that are very close together (not splayed). The manifolds are so close together that there is no way to get a spanner onto the nuts on the carburettor flanges between the manifolds, so that was out. The only other option was to remove the manifolds from the cylinder head. These were attached by Allen screws, with enough room to apparently get to them quite easily, however, I quickly discovered that this wasn't so.

Although the heads were accessible there wasn't room between them and the back of the carbs to get the 'L' shaped Allen key into the heads on the middle two screws. After some research I discovered that some manuals recommend that you cut down the short side of an Allen key so it can get in. However, after much fiddling and using an Allen key with a ball end on the long side, I was able to just get enough purchase on the Allen screws to loosen them – fortunately they weren't too tight. (Later on, when it came to reassembling the carbs, I did cut down an Allen key, so I might as well have done it at this point anyway.)

Having also pulled off the two

7.1 Removing the rectifier.

7.1A Removing the capacitor.

7.2 Removing the carburettors – eventually.

7.3 Both carbs removed, and then tied out of the way.

HOW TO RESTORE NORTON COMMANDO

carb balancing pipes that run into the airbox, the carbs were free. See photo 7.2 of the first carb removed and photo 7.3 of both removed. Not only had it been difficult to remove the carbs but I now realised that I was unable to remove them from the bike as the throttle and choke cables ran through and round the top engine mounting in such a way that they could not be removed without dismantling the head steady first. Not being sure at this point of how to dismantle the head steady, I simply temporarily tied the carbs out of the way at the front of the engine.

With the carbs finally out of the way I could finally remove the airbox – or so I thought! Removing the carbs had actually made no difference to freeing it from the frame and it could only be moved about ½in in any direction. Eventually I decided that the easiest course of action was to bend the front airbox mounting bracket flat, sufficient that it passed under the frame and allowed the airbox to slide forward. I eventually succeeded in bending the mounting bracket flat, despite it being 10 times thicker than necessary for its job – of course. See photo 7.4.

However, whilst I was at least now able to move the airbox forwards slightly, I was still unable to completely remove it, but at least I was able to finally reach the last section of wiring. In this case that comprised the instrument warning light control unit, or assimilator (this controls the ignition warning light) which sits under the airbox. See photo 7.5. I was also able to remove the battery tray, and this allowed the main wiring loom to be removed at last! See photo 7.6. However, even with all this out of the way, the airbox was still too big and awkward to be pulled out from the centre of the frame. Bugger.

7.6 Main wiring loom finally off!

7.4 Bending the top airbox mount flat to try and remove it from the frame.

7.7 Trying to squeeze out the airbox.

7.5 Disconnecting the warning light control panel (assimilator) and battery tray.

7.8 It didn't want to come out at all.

REMOVING THE CARBS, AIRBOX & REMAINING WIRING

It was a bit like trying to complete some weird puzzle on *The Krypton Factor* or whatever. I tried turning it in all directions, trying to find an angle or side that would allow the airbox to come out between the frame and the cylinder barrels, but it didn't want to know. But this was one problem that wasn't going to defeat me, and in the end I managed to find an angle that allowed the box to almost be removed (see photos 7.7 and 7.8), and then used pure brute force and ignorance to get it out. It worked! Hurrah! The airbox was finally out! (See photo 7.9.) After that I moved it to the bench where it sat looking back at me like a disgruntled frog from some weird Disney cartoon. See photo 7.10. That airbox is BIG! In retrospect I should have waited until I'd removed the cylinder head and barrels before trying to remove the airbox – and people say that the horn is hard to remove!

With the airbox completely out I was able to remove the various brackets to the rear of the frame used to hold various electrical items etc. See photo 7.11. I was also finally able to remove the carburettors from the engine by disentangling the cables from the head steady. This involved removing the throttle slides to be able to remove one of the choke cables and pull it through the head steady. See photo 7.12. Note that I intended to replace the carbs with new Amal Premier ones as the originals tend to wear so badly. More on this later.

LESSONS LEARNT
• Removing the carburettors is not as easy as it seems. The best solution is to cut down an Allen key, but you can get round it.
• The airbox on a MkIII is big – very, very BIG!
• I think that the airbox can only be properly removed after the cylinder head and cylinder barrels have been removed – nightmare!
• What on earth is an 'indicator warning light control box' or assimilator, when it's at home? A little bit over-complicated I feel?
• Original Amal carburettors tend to wear out very quickly, and experience has taught me that it's often better to replace them with new ones (or replace them with a Mikuni carb or similar) rather than try to recondition the originals. More (much more!) on this later.

7.9 It's finally out! A combination of ingenuity and brute force.

7.11 Removing the last mounting plates from the rear of the frame.

7.10 The airbox looking like a rather startled frog!

7.12 Carbs finally removed from the bike.

Chapter 8
Draining the oil

With most of the ancillaries removed it was time to begin dismantling the engine. Having already drained the oil from the oil tank, my first job was to drain the oil from the engine, and then remove the various oil pipes etc. See photo 8.1. To begin with I removed the rocker feed pipes from either side of the cylinder head (see photo 8.2) and then turned my attention to the bottom of the sump. Under there I found the sump drain plug and the large nut securing the sump oil filter. See photo 8.3.

The remaining two bolts and the flat bladed screw are engine bolts, holding the crankcases together. Just above all these on the timing side were also the timing plug and

8.1 The engine ready to be stripped down.

8.2 Preparing to remove the rocker oil feed pipes.

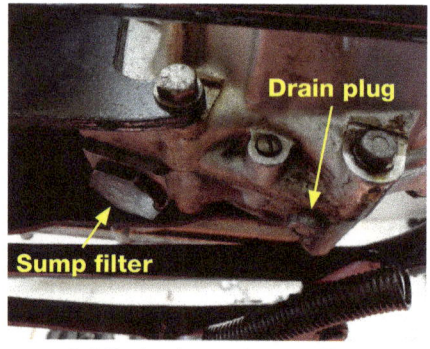

8.3 Drain plug and sump filter.

DRAINING THE OIL

a plugged oilway. See photo 8.4. The timing plug is there so it can be removed and replaced with a little plunger that engages with the crankshaft holding it at exactly 38 degrees BTDC (before top dead centre) so the engine can have the ignition timing set accurately (you can use it to accurately set the little plate in the timing cover, and hence set the timing exactly). The plug is just there to blank off the drilling for one of the oil pump oilways. I placed my drain tank underneath the sump and removed the sump plug – a large quantity of oil drained out, as I was expecting, due to the engine having wet-sumped. See photo 8.5.

After this, I looked at the oil filter behind the gearbox. See photo 8.6. One of the real plus points on all but the earliest Commandos is having a proper, cartridge oil filter, which is far superior to most motorcycle oil filters of the time. Not only that, but the engines still boast a sump oil filter, just for good measure: Now that's proper filtration! However, all I needed to do now was remove the filter – easy. Not! First of all, I removed the large jubilee clip acting as a locking ring, as seen in photo 8.6 and then tried to unscrew the filter – it wouldn't budge. After several fruitless attempts at removing it by hand, and after nearly giving myself a hernia, I had to think again.

Luckily, I remembered that I did have an old oil filter removal tool kicking about from when I used to service my own cars (many, many years ago – they go straight to the garage these days) and managed to unearth it. To be honest it was never a great tool, but after several failed attempts I finally managed to get a good grip on the filter and eventually unscrewed it. See photo 8.7. Note that I'm wearing latex gloves. Draining the oil etc is such a messy business that wearing disposable gloves is almost essential (I suffered from major dry skin problems on my hands years ago due to using high-powered garage hand cleaners, and to this day I still don't have proper fingerprints as a result – latex gloves are highly recommended when dealing with very oily/dirty parts).

When the filter finally came free, more oil than I was expecting drained out of it – beware. See photo 8.8. With the filter removed the oil filter body and oil pipes were ready to be removed. See photo 8.9. The oil filter body and the remaining oil pipes were then removed and the usual resulting oily mess was ready to be bagged and tagged. See photo 8.10

The final reservoir of engine oil to be drained was in the Primary Chaincase. On Commandos the Primary Chaincase oil is separate to the oil in the rest of the engine and needs to be drained separately as a result. Strangely, on most models (all models before the MkIII) there is no drain plug and the only way to drain

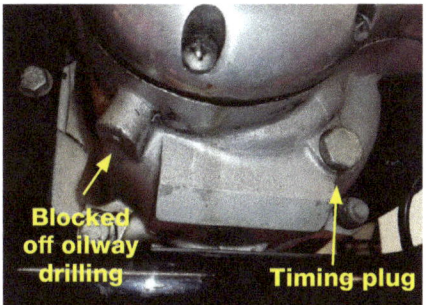
8.4 Timing plug and blanked-off oilway.

8.5 Draining the oil from the sump.

8.6 The engine oil filter.

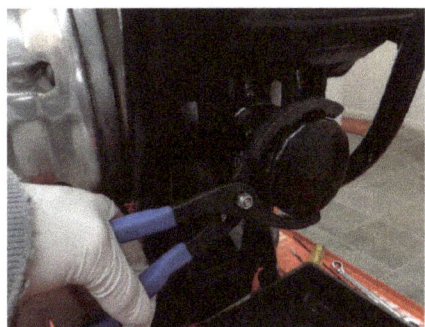
8.7 Removing the oil filter.

8.8 Oil filter draining – quite a bit of oil.

HOW TO RESTORE NORTON COMMANDO

8.9 Oil filter mounting ready for removal.

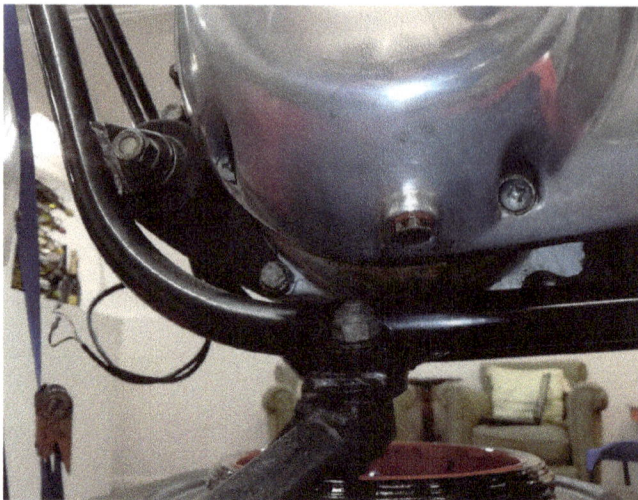

8.11 Oil drain plug on the primary chaincase – peculiar to MkIIIs.

8.10 Oil filter housing and pipes removed.

8.12 Draining the oil from the primary chaincase.

the oil in the primary chaincase is by removing the cover – not the best system. So on the MkIIIs, as well as having a primary chaincase with screws around the edge to keep it oil tight, Norton also added a drain plug – wow! See photo 8.11. Removing this plug allowed me to drain the last of the engine oil in readiness for stripping the engine. See photo 8.12.

LESSONS LEARNT
- It's always good to know what all the nuts and bolts and plugs etc are in the bottom of the crankcases.
- Commandos were fitted with not one, but two oil filters – and one of them is a proper full-flow cartridge type. Excellent!
- Why do people ALWAYS overtighten cartridge oil filters so they're impossible to remove!?
- Latex gloves are great for oily jobs if you want to save your skin – literally!
- The oil in the primary chaincase on Commandos is separate to the rest of the engine oil

Norton didn't fit a drain plug in the primary chaincase before the MkIII because …?

Chapter 9
Removing the swinging arm & timing cover

With the engine drained of oil it was finally time to start stripping the engine. See photo 9.1. First of all I decided to remove the swinging arm to get it out of the way. On a MkIII the swinging arm bearing shaft is held in position by two cotter pins in the body of the arm. See photo 9.2. (I think earlier models used a single lock screw.) I undid the two nuts and this allowed me to then drive the cotter pins upwards and remove them. See photo 9.3. The top of the cotter pins should have little 'Top-hat' rubber seals on top of them to keep the oil in and the water out, but they were missing on my bike.

After this I removed the two alloy end caps from each side of the swinging arm, which are a compression fit on a MkIII, but they were just loosely pressed in, in my case, and were quite easy to prise out. See photo 9.4. If they're difficult to remove, then one way is to insert a self-tapping screw into the middle of the cap and pull it off with mole grips. I just used small screwdriver on mine and they came off very easily, together with their two felt oil seals. See photo 9.5. (I believe that on earlier models the end caps are simply screwed on, and can be

9.1 Engine ready for dismantling.

removed by removing the screw). Rather cleverly, Norton threaded the inside of the swinging arm shaft to enable it to be withdrawn. In the manual it says that the front engine mounting bolt on the isolastics fits this thread, and so it turned out to be.

I spent some time looking for a suitable bolt amongst all my stash of such things, but found nothing. I therefore removed the front engine bolt (see photo 9.6) and screwed that into the swinging arm shaft. See photo 9.7. This enabled me to remove the swinging arm quite easily by turning the bolt with a spanner whilst pulling it

HOW TO RESTORE NORTON COMMANDO

outwards at the same time. See photo 9.8. The shaft was then duly removed. See photo 9.9. At the same time, the swinging arm came free, complete with its bushes and their rubber oil seals still in situ. See photo 9.10. Little did I know at the time, but removing the front isolastic mounting bolt (and then not replacing it) was to have dire consequences when I removed the head steady later on.

I was pleasantly surprised to discover that both the swinging arm shaft and the bushes were coated with a good film of oil and looked to be in very good condition. All Commando swinging arms should be lubricated with 140w oil, not grease, and Norton provided a lubrication nipple to allow oil to be pumped in as required. So far, so good. However, the main problem with this was that owners (and some garages!) saw the nipple and assumed it was a grease nipple, and pumped the swinging arm full of grease instead of oil. This led to the premature wear of the shaft and bushes as they were starved of lubrication due to the grease being thicker and not reaching where it was needed – inside the bushes.

So, Norton had a re-think for the MkIII and came up with a novel solution to stop people pumping grease in – they removed the lubrication nipple altogether! Can you see the potential problem with this? Whilst it undoubtedly stopped owners from pumping grease into the swinging arm, it also prevented them from pumping much needed oil in as well! So, that's why I was pleasantly surprised to find oil in there, and I'm still trying to work out how to put oil back in there when the swinging arm is rebuilt, without the benefit of

9.2 Two cotter pins holding the swinging arm shaft in place.

9.3 Removing the cotter pins.

9.4 Alloy end plates weren't properly fitted on my bike, and came out easily. Otherwise, use a self tapping screw or similar to pull them out.

9.5 The end plate removed, together with the two felt seals.

9.6 The swinging arm bearing shaft is now revealed, with an internal thread to aid removal.

9.7 Removing the front engine bolt.

9.8 Front engine bolt screwed into the bearing shaft, which is then removed by turning and pulling.

REMOVING THE SWINGING ARM & TIMING COVER

9.9 Bearing shaft removed.

9.10 Swinging arm removed, with bushes still fitted.

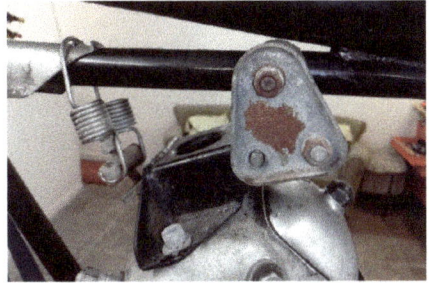

9.11 Removing the top head steady.

a lubrication nipple – but there must be a way! (I was later to learn that the swinging arm bushes are generously lubricated during assembly and have oil-soaked felt pads inserted and this seems to be enough to keep the swinging arm lubricated.)

Anyway, removing the swinging arm signalled the end of the dismantling of various cycle parts and I could finally turn my attention to the engine. It was at this point in the dismantling that I made a very basic, and near fatal error that could have been very serious for both myself and the bike. I decided that the first thing to be done was to remove the head steady between the cylinder head and the frame. Again, on a MkIII these were improved from earlier models by the addition of a damping spring to further reduce vibration and engine movement at idle, and the modification apparently works well (earlier models can be upgraded, and there is even a simple upgrade to further improve the MkIII models – more on this in the rebuilding section). I therefore innocently began to dismantle the top engine steady, oblivious to the chaos I was about to unleash. I began by removing the nuts holding the triangular side plates that are the main structural part of the head steady. See photo 9.11

All seemed to go well until I actually removed the side plates from their mounting studs. At this point the whole bike suddenly and uncontrollably lurched forward and came very close to falling off the bike lift. If it had done so it could have caused major injury to both itself and me (don't forget that the bike was about 4ft up in the air at this point). Thankfully though, the bike stabilised and remained upright on the lift. I was in shock. What on earth had gone wrong?

I quickly realised my basic schoolboy error, caused in this case, as with most accidents, by complacency, ignorance and arrogance. It suddenly dawned on me that the main stand on most Commandos (apart from the early models) is not actually attached to the frame, as with every other bike of the era that I'm familiar with, but to the engine plates! I had previously removed the front engine bolt in order to use it to remove the swinging arm, and now I had just also removed the main part of the top engine steady. This meant that the engine was now free to rotate in the engine frames around the last remaining bolt – the rear isolastics mounting. On a normal bike this wouldn't be an issue as the engine would just sit there. But on my MkIII Commando, the whole weight of the bike was on the main stand, which in turn was attached to the engine frames, and with the engine now free to rotate, it did – it suddenly fell forward and downwards at high speed. This led to the top of the main stand rotating backwards by about 15 degrees, causing the whole bike to suddenly lurch forward by several inches. Very scary.

I was saved by two things: firstly I had strapped the bike down pretty well and whilst this allowed the bike to lurch forward, it prevented it from falling off the lift. Secondly, there is (very fortuitously) a crossmember on the frame, underneath the engine, and that prevented the engine from rotating any further round, and so, in turn, prevented the main stand from rotating any further backwards. Note also that the springs on the head steady, as fitted to MkIIIs, had tried to hold on bravely in the face of extreme adversity, and I was very grateful for this sacrifice. See photo 9.12 of how far the engine rotated downwards and photo 9.13 of how its movement was halted by the frame crossmember under the engine. Also see photo 9.14 showing the remains of the cylinder head steady which clung on gallantly.

So, I was lucky to have survived what could have been a very nasty accident. What had gone wrong? In hindsight I realised that I just been arrogant and slap-dash. This was the umpteenth bike I'd rebuilt and so I never even thought of checking where the centre stand was mounted before stripping it down - I mean, they're all bolted to the frame, right? I was a bit blasé and gung-ho and this lack of proper checking and care had almost been the death of me and the bike.

All I can say in my defence is that at least I had carefully strapped the bike to the lift and that this helped to save the day, preventing the bike from toppling over, but it was still a stupid schoolboy error that could have led to serious injury to both myself and the bike – or bikes, plural, if it had fallen the other way and landed on one of my other bikes! It doesn't bear thinking about, but I do know someone that this happened to! Beware! Lesson well and truly learnt.

Note that the engine frames and engine wouldn't have moved at this point if the rear wheel, swinging arm and rear shocks were still in place. They serve to hold the engine frames in place and not rotate around the top isolastic mounting, so if you just want to remove the engine with the rest of the bike still together, you don't need to worry about the engine suddenly rotating forwards, as in my case.

Anyway, with the disaster narrowly averted I now had to work out how to dismantle the engine and remove it, without further moving the main stand. I decided to continue

HOW TO RESTORE NORTON COMMANDO

9.12 Near-disaster! The engine hinges forward and nearly topples the bike off the lift.

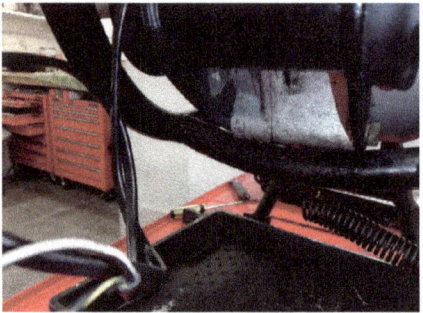

9.13 Saved by the frame cross member ...

9.14 ... and the top engine mount, which bravely clung on!

dismantling the engine in its new position as far as I could (at least it was stable now that it had come to rest) before finding a new way of supporting the engine and frame that didn't involve the centre stand.

At this point, rather than removing the head and barrels, I decided to remove the timing cover, for reasons best known to myself (I was itching to get inside the engine and see what was in there, and couldn't wait!). I therefore used my impact driver (with the correct size bit fitted!) to loosen the timing case screws. As with nuts etc that are tight, I usually find that a short, sharp shock is way better at loosening these items than concerted pressure. See photo 9.15. I then checked, double checked, and finally triple checked that I had actually managed to remove all the timing cover screws.

I can't tell you how many times cases have been damaged by owners trying to prise them off without realising that they have accidentally left a screw in position. It's a weird fact of mechanics that you sometimes get blind to casing screws and it is much, much easier than you might think to miss one, and either spend fruitless hours trying to remove a case that won't budge, or worse still, cracking the case as you try to force it off.

9.15 Using an impact driver to remove the screws securing the timing case.

However, as expected, with the screws removed, the timing cover showed no signs of wanting to come off. I therefore resorted to my tried and trusted method of removal – heat and a block of wood. If the casing has been sealed with a non-hardening gasket cement such as Wellseal, then heating the cover will soften the gasket cement and the cover should come off much more easily. However, if hardening gasket cement was used (which is often the case with older bikes) then heating the case won't have much effect. The only way to find out which gasket cement was used is to try heating the case and see what happens.

In this case, having heated the casing, it showed no signs of wanting to budge, and so my next problem was to find a way of pulling or pushing it off. As with many such casings it was flush with the inner casing all the way round, and there was nothing to get a purchase on to tap it off from behind. Hmm. I then remembered that there was the pressure release valve to the rear of the casing, and I could possibly use that to help me remove the casing. I found that the wooden shaft of one of my hammers was small enough to get between it and the oil feed pipes, and I used it to lever the casing forward and break the seal. See photo 9.16.

However, levering the casing off using the above method is not really recommended! You run the risk of cracking or damaging the oil feed pies, or even the casing. Note that I used a wooden shaft as a lever – never use anything hard such as metal as you WILL damage the casing in some way or other. Also note that before I did any levering I checked for the fourth time that I had removed all

REMOVING THE SWINGING ARM & TIMING COVER

9.16 Starting to remove the timing cover with heat and a wooden hammer shaft, but wait ...

9.17 ... in my haste I'd forgotten to first remove the points!

the casing cover screws! One other major thing to note is that you should NEVER EVER use a screwdriver to try and prise apart casings. You WILL damage the mating edges of the cases and have to live with the guilt forevermore (I know, I've been there).

Anyway, in this case, levering against the oil pressure relief valve with a wooden hammer shaft worked, and the timing cover came away. Result! But wait, something was wrong, as although the cover was loose, it wouldn't come away fully. Hmm, something wasn't right. I very soon realised my mistake. I was generally being a numpty at this point (everyone has phases like this), and having already failed to notice that the centre stand was fitted to the engine plates, I now also suddenly realised that I was trying to remove the timing cover without having first removed the points and advance/retard unit!

Feeling very foolish (as I deserved to) I quickly removed the points cover from the timing case to reveal the ignition points that sit behind it. See photo 9.17. Note that I intended to replace the original points system with electronic ignition as it is simply far superior, and a 'no-brainer' as part of a restoration as far as I'm concerned, unless you are a complete originality freak (as the ignition is behind a cover no-one will know what ignition system you have without removing the cover first). The only real question being what make of electronic ignition to fit. More on this later.

Anyway, I belatedly removed the points from their backplate by removing the small pillar bolts that hold them in place, and left them hanging by the wire that goes from them, through the casing, and up to the ignition coils. Removing the points revealed the advance and retard unit sitting behind them. The advance and retard unit is a mechanical unit that uses centrifugal force to advance the ignition timing as engine speed increases and then retards it again as engine speed decreases. Most electronic ignition systems do away with the need for the advance/retard unit as the spark is advanced electronically rather than mechanically, but don't lose or damage it, just in case!

The advance and retard unit is held onto the end of the camshaft taper by friction as it's an interference fit. The end of the camshaft has a female taper in the end and the advance and retard unit has a corresponding male taper to fit inside it. When the advance and retard unit is tightened onto the camshaft with its central bolt, it binds onto the shaft and stays put. To remove the advance and retard unit you need to break the interference fit between it and the camshaft. In order to do this, remove the central bolt that slides through the advance/retard unit and screws into the end of the camshaft (see photo 9.18), and then replace it with a bolt of a slightly larger diameter that screws into the threaded section of the advance and retard unit. Insert the bolt until it tightens up against the end of the camshaft, at which point the unit may come away, but if it doesn't, gently tap the bolt sideways, and the mechanism should then simply fall off the end of the camshaft. See photo 9.19 of the advance and retard unit on the bench with its mounting bolt in place and the larger bolt, which screws into the mechanism in order to remove it, next to it.

The timing case was now virtually ready to be fully removed (see photo 9.20), but I still had the

HOW TO RESTORE NORTON COMMANDO

9.18 Removing the advance and retard mechanism by first removing the central bolt.

9.19 Advance and retard mechanism removed, with larger diameter withdrawal bolt to the right.

9.20 Timing case now ready for removal!

pump to the bottom left, and the timing chain running from the crankshaft to the camshaft on the right – but nothing to the top left of the case!

I quickly realised that when the engine was originally developed there would have been something driven in the top left that is no longer required – a dynamo or magneto? Needless to say (and very luckily) Norton never got round to changing the case and so it remains partially empty – but still retains its iconic shape from the outside. Other marques, such as AJS/Matchless, changed the shape of their timing cases when they removed magnetos and dynamos and as a result the timing cases were badly butchered and looked terrible. So although there was nothing in the top left of the case on the Commando, at least the case still looked good!

(What a shame that Norton wasn't able to fit its new-fangled starter motor to the timing case instead of the primary chaincase! In terms of looks it would have been the perfect position, but apparently they tried to fit it there, originally, but were thwarted by not being able to fit a 'backfire device' to prevent damage in the event that the engine backfired whilst the starter was engaged. Apparently several timing cases were destroyed in the attempt! A shame, as it was crying out to be fitted there).

I then suspended work on the timing case as I needed to lock the engine in order to remove the pinions from the crankshaft and camshaft sprocket, and to do this I needed to dismantle the primary chaincase. I therefore turned my attention to properly securing the engine and frame before dismantling the primary chaincase. To begin with, I removed the sidestand, which is mounted on a bolt together with a sleeve. See photo 9.22. Removing the sidestand also removed the last obstacle underneath the engine and I put my cunning plan into operation to support the engine and frame, so as to enable me to fully dismantle the bike. I used a car trolley jack and a stout piece of wood that was wide enough to go right across the frame. I then started to jack the engine plates up (which at this point were lower than the frame following the unfortunate removal of the front engine bolt) and then kept going even after the wood came up under the frame. I raised the frame just enough to enable the main stand to be flipped back up out of the way, ready for removal. I then added some extra straps to hold the bike

wiring from the points going through the cases. Pulling the long wires back through the cases is a bit of a pain, so in this case I simply cut the wires off as I thought I wasn't going to be re-using the points. (I was later to discover that I did still need the wires in order to wire-up the electronic ignition, and I was lucky that they were still long enough to fit after my having cut them off).

With the points and associated wiring removed, the timing case now lifted away, and the innards of the timing case were revealed. I must say that I was a little taken aback to find that there wasn't that much in there. See photo 9.21. There was the oil

9.21 Timing case removed to reveal ... well, not much!

REMOVING THE SWINGING ARM & TIMING COVER

9.22 Side stand removed.

9.24 Main stand removed.

9.23 Supporting and lifting the engine under the frame.

steady and the bike was now secure and the engine and frame supported in such a way as to allow complete dismantling of the engine and engine plates to take place. See photo 9.23

My final job before continuing with the dismantling of the engine was to remove the now redundant main stand from its mountings on the engine plates. See photo 9.24.

LESSONS LEARNT

- The swinging arm on Commandos should be oiled with 140w oil, not greased.
- The inside of the swinging arm shaft is threaded to allow for easy removal by screwing the front engine mounting bolt into it.
- On most Commandos (apart from early models) the main stand is bolted to the engine plates, not the frame!
- Do not dismantle the top head steady with the front isolastic bolt removed, and with the bike on its centre stand! (Unless the rear wheel is still in situ.)
- Head steadies on MkIIIs have added tensioning springs.
- Check, double check and then check again that you have removed all the screws from a casing before trying to remove it.
- Never ever try to remove a casing by levering it off with a screwdriver – you WILL damage the cases.
- If the casing won't come off (90 per cent of the time) try heating it round the edge to melt the gasket cement.
- Use a block of wood on any exposed edges to try and knock a casing off.
- Don't try and knock the casing sideways as they are usually held in place with dowels.
- If a casing won't come off, go away and clear your mind for a few hours, then return with a fresh approach – if you keep on at it you'll end up doing something stupid.
- There's not much machinery inside a Commando timing case – but at least it still looks the part.
- If you have the bike on a lift then make sure it is securely strapped down – I'm very, very glad that I did.

Chapter 10
Dismantling the timing & primary chaincases

With the engine and frame secured it was time to begin dismantling the primary chaincase. This would also allow me to complete the dismantling of the timing case by enabling me to lock the engine and remove the crankshaft and camshaft pinion nuts.

Having already drained the oil from the primary chaincase (MkIIIs have drain plugs – luxury!) the first job was to remove the gearlever (see photo 10.1) by loosening its clamping bolt. However, I later learnt that this was unnecessary and could actually help to remove the casing if left in situ. After this, I removed all the mounting screws around the edge of the case (this being a MkIII). If it had been an earlier model I would just have undone the central retaining bolt (and caught the oil in a drip tray). I then used my blowtorch to gently heat the edge of the casing in order to melt the sealant and, after a few careful taps with my hide mallet, the casing came away quite easily. See photo 10.2.

It's useful to note that if the cover is reluctant to come away you can remove the inspection cap, and then you can use the hole to pull the cover

10.1 Gear lever off, ready to remove the primary chaincase.

10.2 Chaincase removed revealing the primary chain, starter motor, and clutch assembly.

DISMANTLING THE TIMING & PRIMARY CHAINCASES

10.3 Starter motor removed by simply undoing the remaining two mounting screws.

off. Also, you can leave the gearlever on, as the spigot it's mounted on comes off with the cover, and use the gearlever as something to pull on. These are usually only necessary on MkIII models though, as earlier models have the notorious 'rubber ring' seal which doesn't stick the cases together like gasket sealant. Notorious, as it has a tendency to leak oil. More on this in the rebuilding section.

With the cover removed, the internals of the casing were revealed, and all looked in pretty okay order. To the left is the rotor and stator, which provide charge to the battery, to the right is the clutch assembly, and between them is the primary chain, and somewhere behind that is the starter motor drive gear and hydraulic primary chain tensioner – both of which are peculiar to the MkIII.

I decided to have a go at removing the starter motor from the rear of the case and was very surprised to discover that it was held on solely by the two remaining screws in the casing. Great stuff! See photo 10.3. Note that the motor is actually held on by three screws, but one of them also holds the outer primary chaincase, so had already been removed. As I had already removed all the wiring, the starter motor simply lifted out and was put aside for refurbishment and upgrading later on.

Next up was the clutch. The clutch plates are held together with a very strong circular spring plate on the outside of the unit, and the spring plate itself is held in position by a large circular circlip round its edge. There is a very simple but really essential special tool for relieving the pressure on the spring plate in order to remove the circlip and hence remove the spring plate. As the tool is easily available from the usual Norton stockists (as listed in the rear of the manual) and is pretty cheap, then it makes perfect sense to use it. As well as being very difficult, it would also be very dangerous to attempt removal without it, so I would definitely recommend buying one. See photo 10.4 of the tool in use. Simply tighten it up to relieve the pressure on the circlip. After this, prise the circlip out (see photo 10.5) and the spring plate will then simply come away. See photo 10.6 of the spring plate with the tool removed, showing just how dished it is, and that gives an idea of just how much tension it exerts when in situ and nearly flat. I then removed the clutch plates using my favourite method of pulling them out with a small magnet. See photo 10.7.

With the clutch plates removed, I undid the rotor nut using my wonderful cordless impact driver. See photo 10.8. The advantage of this is that I didn't have to worry about having to lock the engine in order to remove the nut and it just came off so easily. Several years ago, a few years BCID (Before the Cordless Impact Driver) removing such a nut could be a complete pain in the backside – with this great tool it's a doddle. Without an impact driver you need to lock the engine first, usually with a piece of wood jammed in the primary chain, or with a rod inserted through the small ends of the con-rods, if the cylinder barrels are already removed.

After this, I removed the stator (which fits around the rotor) by undoing the three nuts that hold it in position. See photo 10.9. This enabled me to then pull the stator and rotor off the crankshaft. See photo 10.10. Behind the rotor, on the crankshaft was a large washer and thin spacer together with the Woodruff key for the rotor. I prised out the Woodruff key and then slid the large washer and thin spacer off the crankshaft. See photo 10.11. I was unsure why the thin spacer was there (as there's no mention of it in the parts catalog) but I assumed it was there to ensure that the end of the rotor lined up with the outside edge of the stator. This is to be checked on reassembly.

With the rotor and stator out of the way I had access to the backplate

10.4 The clutch spring removal tool in place.

10.6 Clutch spring and circlip removed.

10.5 With the removal tool tightened, the large circlip is removed.

10.7 Removing the clutch plates with a magnet.

HOW TO RESTORE NORTON COMMANDO

10.8 Undoing the rotor nut with a cordless impact driver.

10.11 Washers from behind the rotor and Woodruff key.

10.9 Removing the stator.

10.12 Removing the backplate from behind the rotor.

10.10 The stator and rotor removed.

10.13 With the backplate removed, the starter motor gearshaft can be withdrawn.

that held the starter motor drive gear, and duly removed it by undoing the three nuts that were locked with tab washers, before pulling the plate away. See photo 10.12. This is a feature particular to the MkIII models.

With the backplate removed I was able to pull out the starter motor gear shaft (see photo 10.13), the starter motor drive gear on the crankshaft (see photo 10.14), and the sprag bearing and the washer

behind it (see photo 10.15). The sprag bearing is a very clever piece of kit in that it will only turn one way. This means that when the starter motor is engaged, the bearing locks and allows the starter motor to turn the

DISMANTLING THE TIMING & PRIMARY CHAINCASES

10.14 The starter motor geardrive is also pulled away.

10.16 The gearlever cross shaft can also be pulled through.

10.15 Followed by its sprag bearing and mounting plate.

10.17 The mounting plate for the hydraulic chain tensioner being removed.

engine over (anti-clockwise). When the engine has started, the sprag gear spins freely (clockwise) allowing the engine to turn, but the starter motor to remain stationary. Clever. More detail on this in later sections.

I was also able to pull the gear cross shaft (MkIII) out through the back of the chaincase, together with the coupling that joins the cross shaft to the gear shaft, behind the engine. The coupling can be seen sitting on top of the casing in photo 10.16. After this I removed the black cover plate for the hydraulic chain tensioner. See photo 10.17. It was only after I removed it and wiped it down that I realised it wasn't black but steel grey. See photo 10.18. It soon became clear that the whole chaincase was covered in a thin black film of old oil residue. It's important to understand that this oil residue was covering every part of the chaincase, covering the clutch plates, inside the chain rollers, etc. Definitely time to give everything a very thorough, deep clean.

With the (steel grey) plate removed, it revealed the hydraulic tensioner behind it (once again particular to the MkIII), which looked to be a very nicely engineered piece of kit (but apparently it doesn't work too well, so I need to look into it a bit more prior to reassembly). See photo 10.19. Next, I employed another special tool, the clutch locking tool, in order to lock the clutch and undo the clutch hub nut. The clutch hub nut spins very freely, so I needed to lock the hub, as even my cordless impact driver wouldn't undo it otherwise. See photo 10.20 of the clutch hub locked and the central hub nut being

10.18 The mounting plate is not black, but grey!

removed. I then left the clutch locking tool in place, which also serves to lock the engine, in order to undo two very tight nuts in the timing case.

Turning to the timing case, I prepared to use my cordless impact driver to remove the two tight nuts – the oil pump drive on the timing

HOW TO RESTORE NORTON COMMANDO

10.19 The hydraulic tensioner assembly revealed.

10.22 Removing the two bolts holding the oil pump in place.

10.25 The timing chain and tensioner assembly.

10.20 Locking the engine with the special tool to firstly remove the clutch hub nut.

10.23 The timing chain, oil pump drive and camshaft sprocket nut removed.

10.26 The valve timing showing ten chain roller pins between timing marks, with the crankshaft pinion timing mark at the bottom.

10.21 Preparing to remove the oil pump drive and camshaft pinion with the cordless impact driver.

10.24 The timing case empty, apart from the crankshaft pinion and chain tensioner.

side crankshaft and the nut holding the camshaft sprocket in place. See photo 10.21. But before removing the above, I undid the two bolts holding the oil pump in place and removed it to get it out of the way. See photo 10.22. I was then able to remove the oil pump drive and camshaft sprocket nut and pull the timing chain and its two sprockets off their shafts. See photo 10.23. The timing case was now empty apart from the crankshaft pinion (which drives the timing chain). See photo 10.24. I then removed the chain tensioner, see photo 10.25.

I checked the valve timing marks to satisfy myself that all was as it should be. The timing chain was set correctly at ten chain roller pins between timing marks on the sprockets. See photo 10.26. Also note the second timing mark on the first sprocket, which lines up with the timing mark on the crankshaft pinion. I then used another special tool to remove the crankshaft pinion. See photo 10.27. This is another special tool that is virtually essential. If you try to remove the crankshaft pinion without this tool (which isn't that cheap) you risk doing serious damage to the crankcases. The tool looks like the baddies' spaceship from James Bond's *You Only Live Twice,* which they use to capture the American space capsule (see photo 10.28) and is the only one to have jaws thin enough to fit behind the crankshaft

pinion. These jaws are designed to fit in the spaces left in the triangular washer behind the pinion and allow you to tighten the central bolt and pull the pinion off. See photo 10.29. The timing side casing was now empty, revealing the rollers of the main bearing inside the crankcases. See photo 10.30.

Switching back to the primary chaincase, I employed another special tool to remove the engine sprocket from the crankshaft. See photo 10.31. With the engine sprocket released I was able to remove the primary chain assembly. See photo 10.32 of the chaincase with the primary chain removed. Note the large starter gear sitting in the rear of the casing. I could now remove this, and, as I did so, I marked it as to which side faced outwards to aid reassembly. Also note the spacers on the gearbox mainshaft which sit behind the clutch. These are used to align the primary chain (which will be checked on reassembly) and need to kept safe. See photo 10.33 of the primary chain, engine sprocket, clutch assembly, clutch hub nut and locking washer, and the three clutch spacers.

DISMANTLING THE TIMING & PRIMARY CHAINCASES

10.27 Removing the crankshaft timing pinion.

10.28 The pinion removed by a special tool resembling the spacecraft from *You Only Live Twice!*

10.29 The crankshaft pinion, three-sided washer, and blanking plate.

10.30 Timing case empty, revealing the main bearing in the crankcases.

10.31 Removing the engine sprocket with yet another special tool!

10.32 Primary chaincase with the primary chain removed. Note the spacers on the gearbox mainshaft.

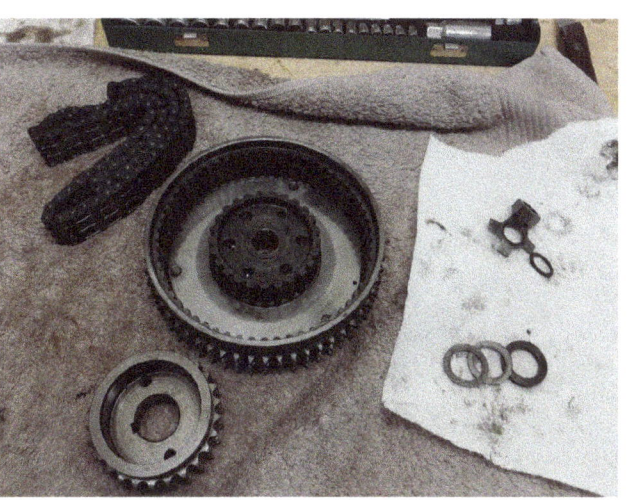

10.33 The primary chain, engine sprocket and clutch assembly removed, together with the spacers behind the clutch.

HOW TO RESTORE NORTON COMMANDO

10.34 Removing the hydraulic primary chain tensioner.

10.36 Inserting a bolt to remove the starter gear.

10.35 Inner chaincase removed.

10.37 The starter gearshaft removed, releasing the starter gear from the casing.

After this, I removed the hydraulic chain tensioner followed by the chaincase mounting nut just next to it (see photo 10.34) which then allowed me to remove the inner chaincase by simply rocking it loose, exposing the crankcases and gearbox behind it. See photo 10.35. My final job was to remove the starter gear from the inner chaincase housing. In order to do this I screwed a bolt into the threaded gear shaft (see photo 10.36) and this allowed me to withdraw the shaft and free the gear from the casing. See photo 10.37. I also marked this gear as to which side faced outwards for ease of refitting.

The disassembly of the primary and timing chaincases was now complete.

LESSONS LEARNT

- You can leave the gearlever on when removing the primary chaincase (on MkIIIs) and use it to help pull the casing away.
- Only MkIIIs had primary chaincase drain plugs – on other models, be ready to catch the oil when removing the casing – if there's any oil left in there!
- Special tools – they're a bit of a godsend. On many bikes of this era, special tools are stipulated for various jobs – but they are no longer available! So you then have to find some way of fabricating a tool or being creative and getting round the problem. But on a Commando all the special tools are available, and they're not that expensive, and they make the job much, much easier. As far as I'm concerned it's a no-brainer and I would strongly advise investing in the appropriate tools – and in some cases they are essential anyway, as with the clutch spring removal tool.
- Special tools can be an investment too, as my crankshaft pinion removal tool was actually bought a few years ago to work on my Tridents, and also fits Commandos – a good purchase.
- Sprag bearings (or sprag clutches as they are sometimes called) are just a very clever piece of engineering – they roll one way, but not the other.
- My cordless impact driver – the second best tool I ever bought (after the bike lift).
- One of the main differences between MkIII Commandos and earlier models is the primary chaincase/starter motor/gear change.

Chapter 11
Dismantling the gearbox

With the primary chaincase and timing case removed it was time to dismantle and remove the gearbox. See photo 11.1. Note that dismantling was made much easier by having already removed the footpeg, brake pedal, exhausts, clutch cable and right-hand support plate.

First of all I drained the oil by removing the drain plug from the front underside and then began to remove the outer casing. I removed the little inspection cap at the top of the outer casing (used to connect/disconnect the clutch cable), which gave me something to pull on, and, having removed the cover screws (which were incredibly loose), the outer casing came away. See photo 11.2.

With the outer cover removed, the inner cover was revealed. Note that on the MkIII the 'knuckle pin roller' on earlier models has been replaced with a 'spherical trunnion.' Apparently, the advantage of this is that the trunnion can be removed and replaced without having to first remove the inner cover and also allows the new gear change mechanism, which is at a slightly different angle then previous models, to line up with the trunnion. See photo 11.3.

11.1 Preparing to dismantle the gearbox – draining the oil.

Next, I removed the end of the kickstart return spring. See photo 11.4. However, I then realised that I still couldn't remove the spring, and I could have just left it in situ and removed it after the cover itself was off. I then dismantled the clutch release mechanism to allow me to get to the locking ring behind it. See photo 11.5. After this I put a punch mark in the casing in line with the cutaway in the lock ring, to ensure I could align the locking ring again on reassembly. See photo 11.6. Unfortunately, I didn't understand the manual instructions, and the punch marks should have been to align the release mechanism body with

HOW TO RESTORE NORTON COMMANDO

11.2 The outer gearbox cover removed.

11.5 Dismantling the clutch release mechanism.

11.8 Clutch release mechanism removed with the ball bearing behind it.

11.3 Inner gearbox cover revealed.

11.6 Marking the position of the release mechanism locking ring.

11.9 The mainshaft nut unscrewed.

11.4 Unhooking the end of the kickstart return spring with a pair of mini mole grips.

11.7 Using another little special tool to unscrew the locking ring.

the casing, not the locking ring. The clutch release mechanism is mounted at a slight angle so that the clutch cable has a totally straight run and it is this angle that needs marking. In my case this meant that when it came to reassembly I would have to spend some time realigning the clutch release mechanism with the cable hole.

Anyway, moving on, I then used another special tool (Don't you just love 'em!) to remove the clutch operating mechanism locking ring. See photo 11.7. Again, you could probably get away with not using the special tool but you would also probably damage the locking ring and make a horrible mess. Use the special tool – you know it makes sense! The mechanism was then released, and I removed it and the ball bearing behind it. See photo 11.8. The ball bearing is there as an interface between the clutch push rod and the operating mechanism: the clutch push rod rotates at engine speed, the operating mechanism remains stationary – the ball bearing is a simple way to connect the two without damaging either.

Removing the clutch operating mechanism revealed the gearbox mainshaft nut behind it, which is tightened to 70lb/ft torque and is usually Loctited as well, so can be a bugger to remove. However, I am the proud owner of a cordless impact driver (have I mentioned this before?!) and the nut was no match for that.

See photo 11.9 of the mainshaft nut loosened off. In order to do this, all that was required was to lightly lock the gearbox to stop the mainshaft from rotating too freely. In order to achieve this, all I did was clamp a pair of mole grips onto the gearbox sprocket. See photo 11.10. That was a sufficient impediment on the sprocket to stop the mainshaft from turning, and for the impact driver to do its work and loosen the mainshaft nut. Without the impact driver you need to lock the gearbox properly.

If you need to lock the gearbox properly there are several main methods:
• If the bike is still together, put it in gear and lock the back wheel with the rear brake or a lump of wood between the chain and rear sprocket.
• Loosen the mainshaft nut before fully dismantling the primary chaincase and lock the engine with the clutch locking tool.
• Wrap the final drive chain round the gearbox sprocket and jam the rest of it against the frame etc.
• Remove the cylinder head, barrels and pistons first and then insert a bar through the small ends of the conrods (with suitable protection) and lock the conrods against the tops of the crankcases.

DISMANTLING THE GEARBOX

11.10 Loosely locking the gearbox sprocket with some molegrips.

11.13 Gear cluster revealed.

- Buy a cordless impact driver. With the mainshaft nut removed, I removed the kickstart spring that was now easily accessible, and then the seven nuts that held on the inner cover, and pulled the inner cover away from the main gearbox housing. See photo 11.11. The kickstart shaft is also good to pull on when trying to pull off the inner cover. The cover came away complete with the kickstart shaft, which then pulled out from the inside when on the bench. See photo 11.12. Removal of the inner cover revealed the gear clusters in the main housing. Looking at photo 11.13, the mainshaft is at the top, the layshaft to the bottom and the thin gear selector shaft to the right.

At this point, I decided to remove the gearbox from the engine frames as I thought that from this point on it would be easier working with the 'box on the bench. I think I was right in that assumption, but alternatively you could remove the gearbox before dismantling it at all, or fully dismantle it in situ – the choice is yours!

Having removed the top and bottom gearbox bolts, I removed the gearbox from the engine frames by rotating the 'box slightly anti-clockwise; the engine frames have a clever diamond-shaped hole to allow this to happen. See photo 11.14. Brilliant! Now, apparently, the gearbox can be removed in this

11.11 Removing the inner gearbox cover with the kickstart shaft.

11.12 Inner gearbox cover removed.

11.14 Removing the gearbox from the engine frames.

HOW TO RESTORE NORTON COMMANDO

11.15 Unscrewing the selector shaft.

11.16 Selector shaft removed together with the first two gears.

11.17 Circlip removed from mainshaft behind gearbox sprocket.

manner on all Commandos, but as the models developed the hole became bigger, and gearbox removal became easier and easier. This means that on very early models, gearbox removal is more difficult, and you may even have to remove the rear engine bolts and lever the crankcases out of the way to gain sufficient clearance to remove the gearbox – but I am assured that it is possible on all Commandos!

With the gearbox on the bench, my first job was to remove the selector shaft, which screws into the rear of the casing and is unscrewed with a spanner on the end. See photo 11.15. Removal of the selector shaft and the first selector allowed the first of the gears to come away too. See photo 11.16.

After this, I removed the circlip from the end of the mainshaft, beyond the gearbox sprocket (see photo 11.17) which allowed me to withdraw the mainshaft, the remaining selector, and most of the remaining gears. I carefully placed the gears and selectors I had so far removed in order on the bench to photograph to help with reassembly. See photo 11.18.

Referring to photo 11.19, I was now left with a mainly empty gearbox housing apart from the layshaft and its final gear (bottom of photo), the mainshaft sleeve gear, which runs in the main bearing in the housing (top of photo) and the camplate (on right of photo). I tried to remove the camplate, but quickly discovered (after a determined effort) that, as with many such gearboxes, the mainshaft sleeve gear needs to be removed before the camplate can come out. I also found that for some reason the layshaft and its final bearing wouldn't come out either. I think they should have done, but they didn't want to move, so I left them there until the mainshaft sleeve gear was removed.

In order to remove the mainshaft sleeve gear I needed to undo the gearbox sprocket nut, and these are a total nightmare: tightened to 80lb/ft torque and no obvious way of locking the shaft. Note that this nut is also LEFT-HAND THREAD. In the past I have used the rear chain in a vice to lock the sprocket. See photo 11.20. Wrap the chain around the sprocket and put one end in the vice: as you loosen the nut, the sprocket is pulled up against the vice and locks solidly, allowing the nut to be undone. However, as I no longer had a vice that was securely bolted to my bench (I just have one now that I clamp to the bench when required, and then move out of the way again) I failed to loosen the nut using this method as the nut was so tight it merely dislodged the vice as I tried to loosen it. Hmm, plan B was required.

I was now the proud owner of a cordless impact driver (hurrah!) but I didn't have a socket large enough to fit the nut, so I went onto glorious eBay and bought myself one (easy, huh?) When the new socket arrived, I simply clamped the sprocket in the

11.18 Mainshaft and more gears withdrawn.

11.19 High gear (top of photo) preventing the layshaft (bottom) and selector camplate (right) from being withdrawn.

DISMANTLING THE GEARBOX

11.20 Trying to use my normal method of removing the gearbox sprocket nut by wrapping the chain round the sprocket and then locking it in a vice.

11.20a Removing the gearbox sprocket nut (LH thread) with my cordless impact driver and a vice.

11.21 The gearbox fully dismantled – the main bearing came out with the high gear.

jaws of the vice on the bench which provided enough lock to enable the impact driver to loosen the nut without problem. See photo 11.20a. Oh, cordless impact drivers, we salute you!

With the gearbox sprocket removed, together with the spacer behind it, I heated the casing and knocked the mainshaft sleeve gear through. In my case, instead of the mainshaft being knocked through the bearing, the bearing came out together with the mainshaft. In retrospect I shouldn't have heated the case first as later on I had to ask the engineers to pull the bearing off the mainshaft for me, as I had no tool that would do it. I was then able to empty the housing of the remaining parts. See photo 11.21. On the bottom left of the paper towel you can see the mainshaft sleeve gear with the main bearing still on it, and the empty hole in the casing where it fitted. Also note the mainshaft oil seal still in situ in the casing, together with the layshaft rear bearing below it.

My next task was to try and remove the rear layshaft bearing from the casing. The problem with this bearing is that it is a 'blind' bearing, meaning that there is no hole behind it. See photo 11.22. The only way to remove the bearing therefore, is to heat the casing and then encourage the bearing to simply fall out. So I heated the casing until it was quite hot and then banged the casing down on a lump of wood on the bench and the bearing suddenly popped out. See photo 11.23. The casing was now empty. At this point I found a casualty. One of the teeth was broken off the camplate quadrant gear. See photo 11.24. I would love to blame someone else,

11.22 The rear layshaft bearing still in the casing (the mainshaft bearing is already out).

11.23 The rear layshaft bearing removed.

11.24 Broken tooth on the camplate.

HOW TO RESTORE NORTON COMMANDO

11.25 Preparing to dismantle the inner cover.

but in this case I knew that I had broken off the tooth when I was messing about trying to remove the camplate before the mainshaft sleeve gear. Ho-hum.

I then returned my attention to the inner and outer gearbox covers, beginning with the gear change mechanism in the outer cover. See photo 11.25. I duly removed the mechanism from the cover, ready for checking and cleaning later. See photo 11.26. My final job was to drive out the inner mainshaft bearing by heating the casing and then driving it out with a suitably sized socket and a lump hammer. (See photo 11.27) The gearbox was now fully dismantled.

LESSONS LEARNT

- Punch mark the position of the clutch release mechanism relative to the casing, not the locking ring (!)
- Can't get enough of those special tools!
- Use a cordless impact driver to remove the gearbox mainshaft nut.
- Use a cordless impact driver to remove the gearbox sprocket nut (LEFT-HAND THREAD).
- The gearbox can be removed as a complete unit if required, or dismantled in situ.
- You can't remove the camplate without removing the mainshaft gear first – or you might break a tooth on the camplate if you try!
- The rear layshaft bearing is fitted blind and has to be removed by heat and banging the casing down.
- I have never yet taken a bike apart that the gearbox sprocket wasn't worn out on – and this one was no exception. Because the gearbox sprocket is usually such a bugger to replace, it often remains in situ long after it has worn to excess. Again, a sure sign of excessive wear is hooked teeth.
- It is always worth checking the number of teeth there are on the gearbox sprocket on your bike, especially those re-imported from the USA. Over there, they are pretty obsessed with how fast a bike accelerates and covers the standing quarter mile, not on top speed. USA bikes were therefore geared down to provide better acceleration – so don't just necessarily fit like-for-like, but according to your requirements. Gearbox sprockets range in size from 19 to 24 teeth with 20 being the standard size for the USA and 22 or 23 teeth standard for Europe (MkIII).
- Always take care when heating alloy casings as localised heating can change the properties within the metal and lead to premature failure. Try to heat cases uniformly where possible – like in the oven. Having said that I've never had a problem with a casing or wheel hub that I've heated with a blow torch.

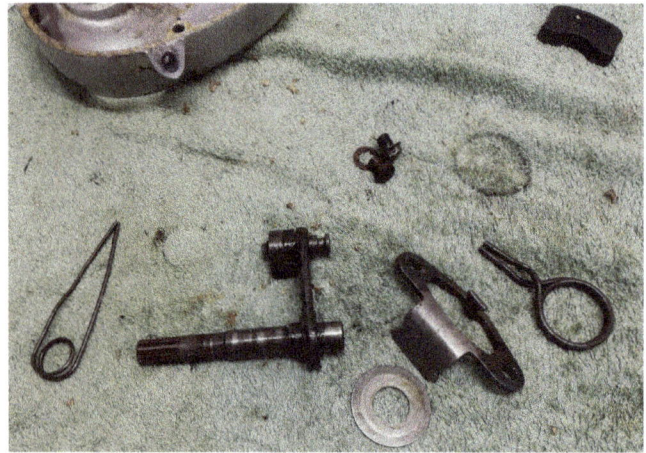

11.26 The gear selector mechanism removed.

11.27 Removing the mainshaft bearing from the inner cover.

Chapter 12

Removing the cylinder head

It was finally time to remove the cylinder head – something I'd been itching to do since day one. My first job was to fully remove the head steady. See photo 12.1. The main item of note in this case being that you shouldn't remove the adjusting locking nut on the cross bar. If you look at photo 12.1 again you can see the adjusting nut between the two springs, as fitted to MkIII models. This nut adjusts the exact amount of tension the head steady gives and is factory set. If it's too loose or too tight it can seriously affect engine vibration. I'm hoping to re-set mine anyway when the bike is finished and I can road test it – the only real way to re-set the tension accurately, if it has been altered, is by setting it roughly, and then running the bike and experimenting with different spring tensions.

I carried on removing the various parts of the head steady until the whole unit was off the bike and on the bench. See photo 12.2. Note that the adjusting nut is still in position and that the main plate of the head steady is attached to the head with Allen screws. With the head steady removed the cylinder head was ready to be dismantled. See photo 12.3.

12.1 Removing the head steady.

The first thing I did was remove the sparkplugs, which gave me quite a surprise as it was clear that the engine had only been running on one cylinder since it had been given a make-over. See photo 12.4 of a fairly normal plug, and one that was virtually as new with no signs of combustion having taken place. After this I removed the rocker box covers – two exhaust covers and one central cover for the inlet rockers. See photo 12.4a.

I then began to remove the ten cylinder head nuts and bolts that hold the head onto the cylinder barrels. The thing to note here is that there

59

HOW TO RESTORE NORTON COMMANDO

12.2 Head steady assembly removed.

12.3 Cylinder heads ready for removal.

12.4 Plugs removed to indicate that the engine was running on only one cylinder.

12.4a Tappet covers removed.

are, indeed, no less than ten nuts and bolts and you need to ensure that you have found and removed all of them before trying to separate the head from the barrels. The ten nuts and bolts are as follows:
• Four bolts in the top of the head, two either side of each sparkplug hole.
• Two nuts down inside the fins at the front of the head, just inside the exhaust rocker covers on either side – see photo 12.5.
• A nut below the rear of the head, in the centre under a few fins of the cylinder barrel.
• Two elongated nuts that run up through the cylinder barrel fins to either side of the front of the head – see photo 12.7.
• A single bolt at the front centre of the head, down inside the cylinder head – see photo 12.9. This bolt should be the last one to be removed.

I slowly went round, removing the cylinder head bolts and nuts. First of all I removed the four bolts from either side of the sparkplug holes and then I removed the two nuts down inside the fins inside of the rocker covers. I removed these with a standard ¼in Whitworth socket on a short extension. See photo 12.5. After this, I turned my attention to the nut at the rear of the head and the two elongated nuts to the front. In order to gain easier access to them I employed my special curved 'half-moon' ¼in Whitworth spanner as I couldn't get a socket onto them. Unfortunately, however, the spanner was no match for the tightness of the nuts (or my ham-fistedness) and simply snapped. See photo 12.6. Luckily, however, my straight (and much stronger) ¼in Whitworth spanner fitted okay and I was duly able to remove all three nuts. See photo 12.7 of the elongated nuts at the front of the engine being removed. When the elongated nuts were completely removed it became clear that the barrels had been resprayed black at some point – with the barrels in situ, hence leaving black stripes across the elongated nuts that run up between the fins. See photo 12.8.

All the nuts and bolts bar the centre front bolt had now been removed and I knew that once this final bolt was removed the head should be ready to lift away – aided by the force of at least one, and possibly two valves, exerted by the pushrods. The manuals recommend that the pistons are at TDC (top dead centre) position to enable as much force as possible to be exerted by the valve springs, to help the head come off. However, I simply couldn't undo the last bolt as I couldn't get a socket or box spanner to go on the head of the bolt, which is hidden away at the bottom of a long shaft on the top of the head. My standard ¼in Whitworth socket wouldn't even go down the hole the nut was in, and so I resorted to my old box spanner

REMOVING THE CYLINDER HEAD

12.5 Removing the two front cylinder head bolts.

12.6 Oops! My special 'half moon' Whitworth spanner was no match for the cylinder head nuts.

12.7 Removing the long cylinder head nuts with a standard spanner.

12.8 Long cylinder nuts removed from the front of the cylinder barrels – to reveal that the barrels were clearly spray-painted in situ at some point!

12.9 Finally managing to undo the central cylinder head bolt.

that I hadn't used for years, but whilst it went down the hole, that too wouldn't fit over the head of the bolt. I was stumped – there was something wrong. I called one of the parts specialists and it sent me an extra slim ¼in Whitworth socket designed just for this job. The socket was now thin enough to go down the hole, but, like the box spanner, still wouldn't engage with the bolt head!

I tried to look down the hole but the top rail of the frame was in the way, which made life difficult. I poked about down the hole a bit, blind, with a small screwdriver, but to no avail. Eventually, I employed my little telescopic mirror and a torch which, with some difficulty, finally allowed me to look down the hole. I could then see the problem – a small stone had at some point fallen down the hole and had managed to wedge itself between the bolt head and the side of the hole, preventing a socket or box spanner from going over the bolt head. I was then able to use my small screwdriver to prise away the stone, get the thin socket on the head and, by using various extensions and adaptors, undo and remove the final bolt. Hurrah! See photo 12.9.

With all the cylinder head nuts and bolts removed, the head was ready to be lifted off the barrels. The manuals state that the problem here is the pushrods, which are apparently too long to allow the head to lift away before it hits the top rail of the frame, so you are supposed to partially lift away the head, then disconnect the pushrods from their seats and push them right up inside the cylinder head: this gives enough room for the pushrods to clear the top of the barrels, and the head to come away with the pushrods. However, in my case I was quite lucky. Because the engine had dropped slightly in the frame due to my having accidentally removed the front isolastic mounting, I was able to simply lift the head from the barrels without worrying about the pushrods. The engine, being that bit lower, gave sufficient clearance for the pushrods to clear the top of the barrels without fuss. Every cloud …

Initial inspection of the head (see photo 12.10) revealed several things: firstly, it confirmed that the engine had only been running on one cylinder; secondly, that there was evidence of oil leaking down the valve guides; and thirdly, that at some point there had clearly been a foreign object rattling around in one of the combustion chambers, damaging both the head and the piston crown. If you look at photo 12.11 you can see a close-up of the damage to the cylinder head from the foreign object. Looking at the damage I would guess that it was maybe a small washer or similar. It was certainly something that was small enough to get in (maybe down a sparkplug hole), and small enough to be blown out of the exhaust valve at some point, or maybe fished back out by the PO

HOW TO RESTORE NORTON COMMANDO

12.10 Cylinder head removed to reveal evidence of oil contamination. Plus signs of a foreign body having been in one of the combustion chambers.

12.11 A close up of the left-hand combustion chamber showing damage from a foreign body.

12.12 Initial inspection of the head revealed a very badly worn valve stem.

12.13 Pistons show similar damage, oil contamination, and confirmation that the engine was firing only on one cylinder.

with a telescopic magnet when he started the engine and heard a terrible racket! (Anyway, there was no sign of the object still in the combustion chamber).

Looking at the top of the head I also noticed that one of the inlet valves showed signs of serious wear to the top of the stem where the rocker tip had worn through the case hardening and created a cavity. See photo 12.12. This confirmed my initial assessment that I needed to replace all the valves and valve guides as part of reconditioning work on the cylinder head.

Looking at the top of the barrels also confirmed oil leakage into at least one of the combustion chambers and showed the damage to the left hand piston crown caused by the foreign body. See photo 12.13. No matter what the condition of the cylinder bores I clearly required new pistons regardless. Having a piston that is as damaged as this is not a great idea. It could have minute cracks in it, or metal fatigue, that might lead to catastrophic piston failure at any time. Indeed, if only for peace of mind, the pistons required replacing (would you ride this bike knowing the piston had been damaged?).

My final job was to withdraw the pushrods from the cylinder barrels and keep them in the correct order as it's advisable to refit them in their original positions to prevent excess wear. Note that two push rods are short and two are long. This is because the Commando only has a single camshaft (unlike such models as the Triumph Bonneville/Trident that have two – one inlet and one exhaust) situated to the front of the crankcases, and that camshaft operates both the inlet and exhaust valves, so the inlet pushrods have to be longer as they need to cross diagonally through the cylinder barrels to reach the inlet rockers to the rear of the head. See photo 12.14.

Time to remove the barrels. I'm very glad to say by the time Norton came to make the 850 they finally strengthened the base of the barrels and added through bolts from the top of the barrels down into the crankcases so avoiding the possibility of the barrels fracturing around the

12.14 Push rods removed from the barrel – one long and one short on each side.

12.15 Using a thin spanner and an Allen key to remove the barrels.

bottom and parting company with the crankcases. (Remember that this is exactly what happened to my friend Alan's Combat!). This means that on an 850 there is a combination of cylinder base nuts and four through bolts that have Allen heads. See photo 12.15 of the through bolts and bottom nuts. Note that I used a special thin spanner to undo the cylinder base nuts. This is because the tops of the nuts are very close to the bottom fin on the cylinders and you can't get a normal ring spanner in there. The one I used is actually a special 'star shaped' one to fit Triumphs – but it works fine on Nortons too!

However, when I tried to undo the nuts to the rear of the cylinders I discovered that not even the special thin ring spanner would squeeze between the top of the nuts and the bottom fin and so I had to resort to using an open-ended spanner instead. Luckily, and much to my surprise, this worked okay and the nuts came loose. See photo 12.16. However, there wasn't enough room to fully remove the nuts from their

REMOVING THE CYLINDER HEAD

12.16 Using an open-ended spanner to remove the rear cylinder barrel nuts.

12.17 Barrels separated from the crankcases and extended nuts fully unscrewed as the barrels rise.

studs without hitting the bottom fin. So, with the through bolts removed and all the cylinder base nuts loosened, I was able to partially lift the head, and as I lifted it I was able to keep unscrewing the nuts until they were fully removed. See photo 12.17.

With the barrels removed I could inspect the pistons, both of which appeared to be in good condition with no signs of scoring or overheating etc. However, they were due to be replaced anyway because of the damage to the crown of the left-hand piston by the suspected foreign body in the combustion chamber. See photo 12.18.

I then inspected the cylinder bores, and they looked to be in quite good condition apart from rings of corrosion probably caused by standing without use for a long time. See photo 12.19. I hoped that I might get away with just having the bores lightly honed to remove the corrosion, without the need for a full re-bore. I planned to fully inspect them later.

It was also at this point that I became acquainted with the little stone that had got lodged in the front centre cylinder head recess, between the bolt head and the cylinder head, and prevented me from undoing the final bolt for so long. I realised that when I'd finally removed that bolt, the stone had fallen down the resulting hole and ended up in the corresponding bolt hole in the head. If you look closely at photo 12.19 again you should be able to just see the stone sitting in the bolt hole to the

12.19 Initial examination of the barrels revealed light corrosion from standing, but nothing too horrendous – maybe just need honing.

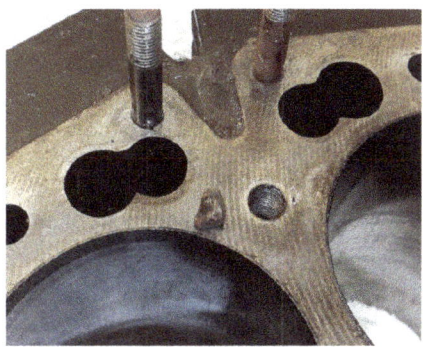

12.20 The little stone that caused all the problems when trying to remove the front centre cylinder head bolt.

front centre of the barrels. See photo 12.20 of the offending item after I fished it out. (Little b*****d!)

I then inverted the cylinder barrels to check the tappets (sometimes known as cam followers, or occasionally as valve lifters) and they seemed to be in very good condition with no signs of excessive wear from the camshaft. See photo 12.21. By cutting off the locking wire and unscrewing the holding plates I was then able to withdraw the tappets and carefully label them to ensure that they would go back in the same place during reassembly. Like other such parts (eg the pushrods), unless they require replacing, they should go back in the same position they came from, in order to minimise wear. As it was too early to decide whether they needed replacement or not, I labelled them so they were ready to be correctly refitted if, after proper inspection, replacement was deemed unnecessary. See photo 12.22.

I then returned my attention to

12.18 Barrels removed to reveal the pistons – they looked okay, but would require replacing due to the damage caused by the foreign body.

63

HOW TO RESTORE NORTON COMMANDO

12.21 Cam followers, or tappets, looking good and lock wired up.

12.22 Tappets clearly labelled to ensure correct reassembly.

12.24 Rocker shafts coming out – eventually!

from behind and need to be pulled out from their open end with a slide hammer or similar. I therefore duly bought the requisite special tool, in this case a slide hammer, and, after heating the head with my blow torch, the shafts slowly came out. See photo 12.23. However, they were a much tighter fit than I envisaged and were a bugger to get out.

There are other ways to remove the rocker shafts though, without using a slide hammer. One such way is to use an elongated socket that is of a slightly larger internal diameter than the rocker shaft. Put the end of the socket over the end of the shaft and then screw a long bolt into the shaft (which is internally threaded), through the body of the socket. Near the head of the bolt, have a nut and a washer large enough to sit on the top of the socket. After this, tighten the nut up against the end of the socket, and this will serve to pull the rocker shaft out, up through the inside of the socket.

But, as you know, I'm a big fan of special tools (and generally want to get on with things ASAP – but trying not to rush!) and so I bought the slide hammer and one-by-one the rocker shafts came out. See photo 12.24 of one of the inlet shafts removed, with its corresponding rocker on the bench.

With the rocker shafts and rockers removed, I began to remove the cylinder head, and to removing the rockers and valves. I quickly discovered that in order to remove the rocker shafts from the head I required yet another special tool! The rocker shafts are pressed into the head and need to be pulled out. The problem is that they are fitted blind and so cannot be tapped through

the valves with my valve spring compressor. See photo 12.25. I clamped the compressor over the valve and spring, then tightened the clamp up on the screw. When the screw was done up tight, I gave the clamp a little tap with a hammer and this freed the collets. I then continued screwing up the clamp until the collets were free to be removed from the tops of the valve stems.

When the valve springs were compressed I used my little telescopic magnet (seen ready and waiting on the left in photo 12.25) to remove the valve spring collets, and removed the valves one at a time. See photo 12.26 of one of the valves on the bench with its associated springs (inner and outer) etc. Note that the seating washer on the bottom of the large outer spring simply pulls off the spring. At this point I noticed some rather strange marks/damage to the top of one of the valve stems. I'm not sure what this was caused by and I've never seen it before. See photo 12.27. Also note that in order to remove the inlet valves I first had to remove the inspection cover stud which was in the way. I achieved this by using the time-honoured method of locking two nuts together on the thread and then unscrewing the stud by turning the lower of the two nuts which was prevented from turning by the upper nut. See photo 12.28.

The head and barrels were now ready to be vapour-blasted (also known as aqua-blasting) before being given a detailed examination as to exactly what work was required to recondition them and bring them back to tip-top condition.

12.23 Using a slide hammer to remove the rocker shafts.

REMOVING THE CYLINDER HEAD

12.25 Using a valve spring compressor to remove the valves.

12.28 Removing the inlet rocker cover stud by locking two nuts together.

- You need a very thin socket to reach the central front bolt, which should be removed last.
- Normally, to remove the head you have to unseat the pushrods and stuff them up inside the head as far as they'll go so they clear the cylinder barrels.
- 850 models have four through Allen bolts that go down through the barrels. (Hurrah!)
- Tappets are also known as cam followers – just to confuse everyone!
- Tappets are also known as valve lifters – just to confuse everyone even more!
- You never know what you're going to find in an engine until you get it apart – in this case a damaged combustion chamber.
- The rocker shafts are a tight interference fit in the head.
- Use a small magnet to remove those pesky little valve collets.
- I've not rebuilt an engine yet that didn't require new valves, valve springs and valve guides – and this one looks to be no exception.
- Vapour-blasting is also known as aqua-blasting (because it combines glass beads with water) – just to totally confuse everyone!

12.26 Valve and springs, etc, removed from the head.

12.27 Strange damage to the outside of the valve stems.

LESSONS LEARNT

- MkIIIs had a different head steady with adjustable springs added. If the adjustment nut is removed, the head steady tension will require resetting when the bike's on the road.

- There are no less than ten nuts and bolts holding the head on. As you remove them, lay them on the bench so you can count them and check that they're all off before trying to remove the head.

65

Chapter 13
Removing & dismantling the crankcases

With the cylinder head and barrels removed and dismantled, it was time to remove the crankcases from the frame. See photo 13.1. Note that I had deliberately left the pistons in situ in order to protect the con-rods. Conrods can easily be damaged by hitting the crankcase mouth, etc, and any nicks or scratches form weak points that can lead to conrods snapping! Not a great idea. To begin with I removed the bolt on the engine plates that is the central bolt for the primary chaincase by using two spanners to hold and unlock the nuts either side of the engine plates. See photo 13.2. After this, I withdrew the engine bolts that held the crankcases to the engine plates. See photo 13.3.

I then lifted the crankcase on the trolley jack so that I could insert a long screwdriver into the front isolastic mounting and then remove the long, rear isolastic bolt. See photo 13.4. With the rear bolt removed the engine plates were removed, complete with the rear isolastic mounting. See photo 13.5. The crankcases were now ready to lift out of the frame, and, with most parts of the engine already removed, it was an easy task to remove the screwdriver from the front isolastic mounting, and then lift the crankcases out and onto the bench. See photo 13.6. The frame was now empty with only the front wheel and forks still attached. See photo 13.7.

It was time to strip the crankcases. To begin with I removed the pistons from the conrods by removing the outer gudgeon pin circlip on each piston and then gently heating the pistons to allow the gudgeon pins to slide out. See photo

13.1 Crankcase ready to be removed from the frame.

REMOVING & DISMANTLING THE CRANKCASES

13.2 Removing the primary chaincase central bolt from the engine frames.

13.5 Engine frames removed.

13.6 The crankcase can now be lifted out quite easily and moved to the bench.

13.3 Removing the engine bolts.

13.4 Having lifted the crankcase slightly, a long screwdriver is inserted through the front isolastic mounting, whilst the rear isolastic bolt is withdrawn.

13.7 Frame now nearly stripped, apart from the front wheel and forks.

13.8. I already knew I was going to replace the pistons, but it's always good to remove them ASAP, both to prevent them from being damaged and to get them out of the way. After this I removed the front isolastic mount by undoing the engine bolts (see photo 13.9) and then removed all the remaining crankcase bolts in readiness to split the crankcases, not forgetting the two screws at the bottom. See photo 13.10. I then checked and double checked (as always) that I had removed all the crankcase bolts and prepared to split the crankcases.

Splitting the crankcases can

13.8 Removing the pistons from the conrods.

HOW TO RESTORE NORTON COMMANDO

13.9 Removing the front isolastic mount.

13.10 Don't forget to remove the two screws at the bottom.

13.11 Splitting the crankcases using my patent method.

13.12 Drive-side crankcase removed with the camshaft.

often be a bugger of a job as they frequently don't want to come apart, and there's little to push against to encourage them to let go. I therefore use my patent method of inserting a pry bar between the crankshaft and the inner crankcase face to open the cases. I've used this method many times and it works fine for me (but some mechanics will roll their eyes and shake their heads at such profanity!) Beginning with the drive-side case, I gently tapped a tapered pry bar (or large screwdriver in my case) down inside the casing between the crankshaft cheek and the casing and this will force the casing off. See photo 13.11. With the seal broken, the drive-side casing pulled away quite easily, together with the camshaft, leaving the inner race from the main bearing on the crankshaft. See photo 13.12.

An initial inspection of the camshaft revealed strange wear marks on every cam lobe, just off the top of each cam. See photo 13.13. I was pretty sure this meant that a new camshaft was required, but decided to seek more advice on the subject before making a final decision. (Just as well as it transpired that the camshaft was in fact okay). I also removed the crankcase oil filter at this point (see photo 13.14) and then dismantled it for cleaning (see photo 13.15), but it seemed pretty clean anyway.

After this, I removed the timing side crankcase, easing it off using the same method as above, although this side came off much more easily as there was no seal to break. See photo 13.16. I also realised that the large spacer for the camshaft was still in situ and needed to be bagged and tagged before it got lost. See photo 13.17. It is worth noting that different Commando models used a variety of different spacers and combinations of spacers on the camshaft – check in the parts catalogue for your model what your camshaft should have. Take copious photos of any spacers there, before removing them, whatever.

Next job on the agenda was the removal of the crankcase to primary chaincase oil seal. Note that Commandos have separate oil in the primary chaincases and so an oil seal is required to keep that oil separated

REMOVING & DISMANTLING THE CRANKCASES

13.13 Camshaft showing strange wear marks just off the top of the cam.

13.14 Removing the crankcase oil filter.

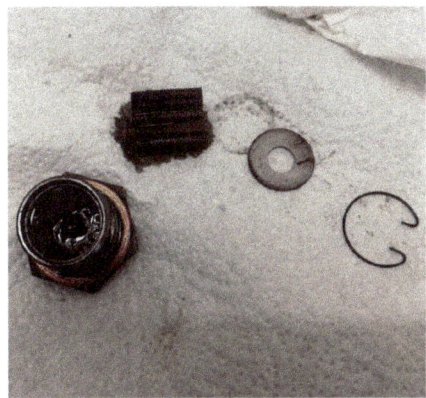

13.15 Crankshaft filter dismantling.

13.16 Timing side removed to reveal the crankshaft.

13.17 Taking care to save the camshaft spacer – only one on a MkIII.

from the engine oil in the crankcases. (This is unlike such as Triumph Triples and Twins which use the same oil in the crankcase and primary chaincase and so have no oil seal between the two).

It's also worth noting that this oil seal is the one most likely to be damaged by wet-sumping. If the bike's wet-sumped then there's so much oil in the crankcase that if the bike's started without draining the oil, the crankcase pressure can be very high, and the easiest way for it to relieve this pressure is by blowing the crankshaft oil seal. However, this might be a bit of an urban myth, as if you actually ask owners, very few have known this to happen.

Note also that if this seal is damaged or blown when the engine's in the bike that it can be removed by carefully screwing two or more self-tapping screws into it which will slowly push the seal out as the screws hit the metal behind it, and can then be pulled out with pliers – sure beats stripping the engine anyway! Note also that the MkIII has a circlip fitted to help hold the oil seal in place in order to try and prevent it being blown out. I removed the circlip (see photo 13.18) and this allowed me to then prise the seal out using my oil seal removal tool. See photo 13.19 –

as all oil seals should be replaced as a matter of course it doesn't matter how much you damage the seals on removal. (It would be a false economy to fully rebuild the engine and not replace the oil seals.)

After this I prepared to remove the main bearings from each crankcase. At this point I wasn't sure if I needed to change the main bearings or not, but they needed to be removed from the cases before the latter were vapour-blasted anyway – but I had to take care not to damage the bearings if they were to be reused. As ever, I removed the bearings by heating the cases with my blowtorch and then driving them out with a suitably sized socket and lump hammer. See photo 13.20. Without too much fuss both main bearings were out of the cases. See photo 13.21.

The crankshaft was now free and ready to be dismantled. See

13.18 Removing the circlip (MkIII only) in readiness to remove the drive-side oil seal.

HOW TO RESTORE NORTON COMMANDO

13.19 Drive-side oil seal removed.

photo 13.22. Note that the inner main bearing races are still on the crankshaft spindles. To begin with, I removed the conrods by undoing the big end bolts, pulling off the bottom section of the conrod, and freeing the whole rod. Note that the two halves of the conrod are clearly marked to ensure they go back together the right way round. See photo 13.23. I also marked each conrod to ensure that the correct one went back on the correct side. I gave the con-rods an initial check to see if there was any obvious damage or signs of them being poorly cast (swirls in the metal), but they seemed fine. I also checked that they weren't stamped with a double 'D' on the sides, as apparently this particular batch of conrods are known to be weak – mine weren't.

Initial inspection of the big end bearing shells showed that they were worn, but nothing major. They would be replaced as a matter of course anyway. See photo 13.24. I removed the small oilway plug in the

13.20 Driving out the drive-side main bearing.

13.22 The crankshaft ready for dismantling.

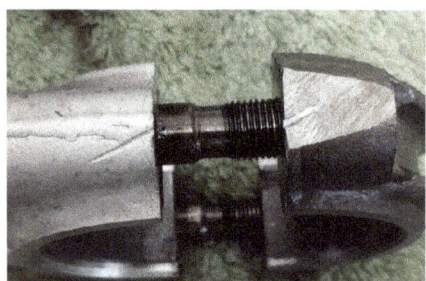
13.23 Big end caps and conrods are matched and marked accordingly.

13.21 Main bearing removed.

13.24 Big end shells show normal wear.

REMOVING & DISMANTLING THE CRANKCASES

timing side crank cheek (as seen in photo 13.22) as it's a bugger to get out, and I thought it would be easier to remove it now rather than later – although it turned out that I didn't need to remove it at all – see below. I then prepared to split the crankshaft in order to inspect and clean out the oilways inside it.

I punch marked the three sections of the crankshaft (left cheek, right cheek and flywheel) and with some difficulty, undid the various bolts holding the three parts of the crankshaft together. Most of the nuts could only be undone with an open-ended spanner, and as the nuts are very tight and Loctited, they didn't want to shift, but eventually they were all off. To my surprise, the hollow centre of the crankshaft was remarkably clean, and neither was there much oil in there. See photo 13.25. At this point, I realised that the oilway blanking plug I'd removed earlier only went into the hollow crankshaft centre, and as I'd split the crankshaft, which gave full access to the void, then the plug could have stayed where it was!

Note that dismantling the crankshaft and removing the oilway

13.25 Crankshaft dismantled – to reveal a very clean interior!

plug is a real pain of a job and can be entrusted to the engineers with all their special tools etc if required.

LESSONS LEARNT

• With most of the engine dismantled, it's pretty easy to lift the crankcases out of the frame and onto the bench – especially if you have a bike lift so the engine is at waist height.
• I recommend splitting the crankcases using a pry bar between the crankshaft and the casings – but some mechanics will raise their eyes to heaven.
• Protect the conrods from being damaged by the crankcase edges.
• Carefully check conrods for any sign of damage or poor casting. Conrods stamped with a double 'D' are suspect.
• Different models used a variety of camshaft spacers.
• The crankshaft oil seal separating the crankcase from the primary chaincase is subject to leaking, possibly exacerbated by wet-sumping, but can be removed in situ with a bit of ingenuity.
• Note that if the crankshaft oil seal fails, oil will leak into the primary chaincase and this then encourages the chaincase to leak and the clutch to slip.
• You don't have to remove the little oilway plug if you're going to split the crankshaft.
• Mark up the three sections of the crankshaft if you're going to dismantle it, to ensure it goes back together the right way round.
• It can be easier and more sensible to take the crankshaft to the engineers for dismantling and inspection – no loss of face.
• The hollow crankshaft centre will probably be full of oil and sludge – mine wasn't.

Chapter 14
Removing the front wheel, forks & yokes

With the entire crankcase safely out of the frame, it was time to remove the front wheel, forks, and yokes. To begin with I rearranged the straps securing the frame so that the rear one was tight enough to pull down the rear of the frame and lift the front wheel off the ground – high enough to enable the front wheel to be removed easily. See photo 14.1. After this, I removed the iconic Norton-Lockheed front calliper from the left-hand lower fork leg, which is where it was moved to on a MkIII, having previously been on the right, although I'm not sure exactly why – probably something to do with American legislation, I'm guessing. See photo 14.2. (Again, note that you should use the hydraulic pressure to drive out the rearmost piston before removing the calliper from the bike, otherwise it's very difficult to do so.) The calliper and short brake pipe were then set aside ready for appraisal – although I was pretty sure I was going to upgrade the calliper anyway (and yet the originals are so unique, iconic and beautifully styled). See photo 14.3.

After this, I removed the clamp bolt from the bottom of the right-hand fork leg (MkIII), which then

14.1 Frame repositioned so the front wheel is slightly off the bench and there is no tension from the straps.

enabled me to unscrew and remove the long wheel spindle nut from that side. With the nut removed I began to withdraw the wheel spindle, taking note of the positioning of the spacer between the wheel hub and the fork leg as I did so. See photo 14.4. With the wheel spindle fully withdrawn, the front wheel simply came away from the fork legs. See photo 14.5.

With the wheel removed, I turned my attention to the forks. First of all, I loosened the pinch bolts in the bottom yokes. See photo 14.6. After this I removed the fork top nuts from on top of the top yokes. See photo 14.7. When the nut was fully unscrewed I remembered that

REMOVING THE FRONT WHEEL, FORKS & YOKES

14.2 Removing the front brake calliper.

14.3 Front brake calliper removed and on the bench awaiting refurbishment.

14.4 Withdrawing the front wheel spindle – watch that spacer!

14.5 Front wheel removed from the forks.

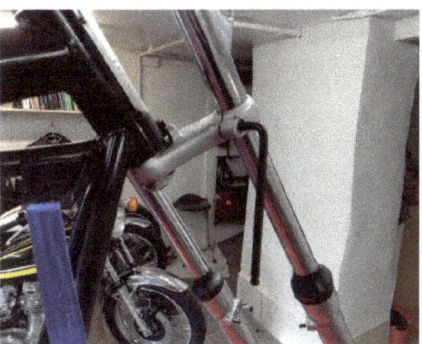

14.6 Loosening the clamps in the lower fork yokes.

14.7 One leg removed. Removing the fork top nut on the second fork leg.

14.8 Draining the damper fluid.

14.9 Removing the stem nut from underneath the lower yoke.

it was also screwed to the top of the damper rod inside the fork stanchion and I had to loosen the locknut on the rod to allow me to unscrew it and remove it fully. By twisting and pulling the stanchion, the fork leg then came out through the bottom of the yokes. See photo 14.7 again, showing one leg already removed.

I then took both fork legs to the bench, removed the little drain screws at the bottom of the lower fork legs, and drained the oil. See photo 14.8. I could have done this with the forks still on the bike, but I find it a bit easier this way, with less chance of the oil missing the drain tray.

Turning back to the forks, I undid the large stem nut underneath the bottom yoke, having first knocked back its locking tab. See photo 14.9. I then tried to separate the two yokes by tapping the bottom one down – but they didn't seem to want to come apart. Eventually, they did start to move, following some increasingly enthusiastic 'persuasion' with a lump hammer and the taper of a cold chisel between the bottom yoke and the headstock (don't tell anyone!). See photo 14.10. Note that as soon as they began to separate I was able to lift out the chrome headlamp ears and their washers/spacers. In this

HOW TO RESTORE NORTON COMMANDO

14.10 Lifting the top yoke away – eventually!

14.11 Drifting out the head races from the steering head.

photo, you can also see the alloy plate giving the date of manufacture riveted to the frame, as required in the USA.

With the yokes off, I removed the steering head races. These are two enclosed bearings, one in the top of the headstock, one in the bottom, with a long spacer between the two of them. This is similar to the way the wheel bearings are mounted. To remove them, I prised one end of the spacer out of line, just enough to get a drift onto the inner bearing race and drive it out, having heated the frame around it first. The spacer came out with the first bearing and it was therefore a lot easier to drive out the second bearing using a drift. See photo 14.11. If you look at photo 14.12 you can see the two sealed bearings on the bench together with the spacer tube and the top and bottom yokes.

Time to dismantle the forks. I clamped the lower legs in the vice – made easy on the left leg as I could use the calliper mountings in the vice. See photo 14.13. I removed the fork spring by undoing the locknut and spacer on top of the damper rod (see photo 14.14), which allowed the spring to come out. After this I used my oil filter removal tool to unscrew the fork seal retainer in the top of the lower fork legs. See photo 14.15. With the retainer removed the stanchion could be pulled out, together with the oil seal. I was able to use the stanchion rather like a slide hammer to push the oil seal out of the lower fork leg. See photo 14.16.

All that now remained in the fork leg was the damper and damper rod. As with virtually all forks, the damper is held in position in the lower fork leg by a bolt that goes up through the bottom of the fork leg. See photo 14.17. This bolt is often a complete pain to remove as not only is it quite inaccessible, but the damper often turns with the bolt and you have to try and insert something down inside

14.12 Head races and yokes removed.

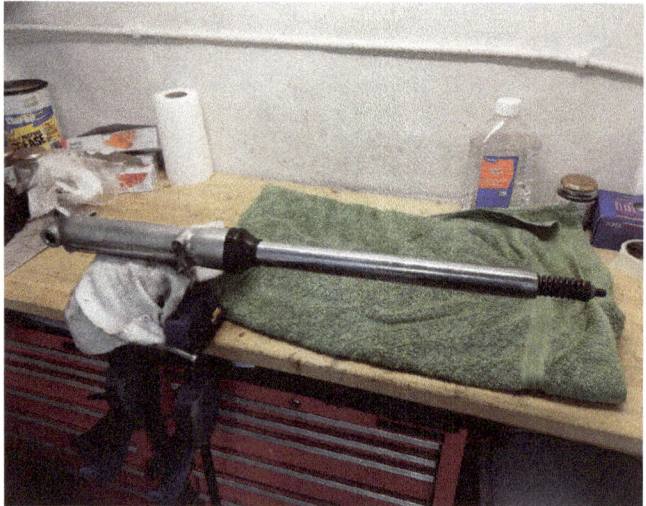

14.13 Left-hand fork in the vice ready for stripping.

14.14 Removing the nut from the top of the damper rod to allow the spring to be withdrawn.

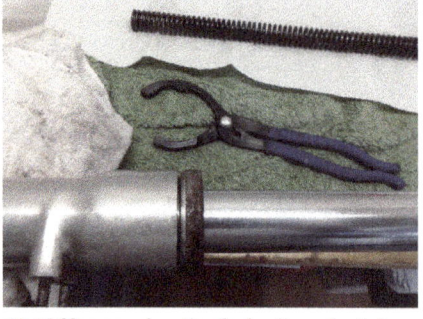

14.15 Unscrewing the fork oil seal retainer with a pair of large grips.

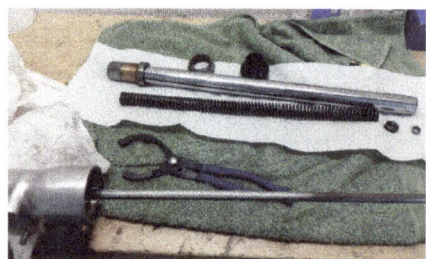

14.16 With the retainer removed, the stanchion can be pulled out with the oil seal. Only the damper and damper rod remain in the fork leg.

REMOVING THE FRONT WHEEL, FORKS & YOKES

14.17 Bolt up inside the fork leg, securing the damper assembly.

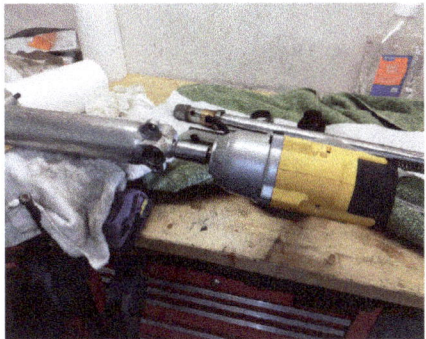

14.18 Removing the damper securing bolt with the cordless impact driver.

14.19 The damper removed together with its fibre washer in the bottom of the fork leg.

14.20 The damper rod is now unscrewed from the damper and the fork is fully dismantled.

the fork leg to jam the damper and stop it turning (I have a very long screwdriver bought for this very purpose in my case). However, I have a brand new champion – a cordless impact driver! Using the impact driver the bolt came out straight away without having to lock the damper. See photo 14.18. The damper then came out of the top of the fork leg. One damper came out together with its fibre washer, the other one came out leaving the washer stuck at the bottom of the inside of the fork leg and I had to remove it by using the aforementioned long screwdriver to dislodge it. See photo 14.19.

The final task was to unscrew the damper rod from the damper, and the fork legs were now fully dismantled and ready to be set aside awaiting full inspection and restoration where necessary. See photo 14.20.

LESSONS LEARNT
- Ensure the front wheel is well clear of the ground to make removal easier.
- Commandos used unique 'clamshell' brake callipers made in partnership with Lockheed – and they look great – but you also want great, modern brakes: dilemma!
- Don't forget to use the hydraulics to push out the rear piston before removing the calliper if you intend to overhaul the calliper.
- The fork top nuts screw into the top of the stanchions and are also screwed onto the damper rod.
- The stem between the two yokes is held in the top yoke, not the bottom yoke as on most bikes, with the stem nut being at the bottom.
- The steering head races are proper sealed bearings, not loose ball bearings as on most machines.
- A cordless impact driver really does make short work of so many jobs that are usually a nightmare.
- If the damper rod turns when trying to remove its mounting bolt, shove something down the fork leg to jam the damper and stop it from turning.

Chapter 15
Dismantling the wheels

The next job was to dismantle the wheels ready for refurbishment. First up was the front wheel, and I removed the disc (left-hand side on my MkIII) with my cordless impact driver. See photo 15.1. I then inspected the wheel bearings and how they were fitted. The left-hand bearing had a series of grease seals in front of it, see photo 15.2, and the right-hand bearing had a large circlip holding it in place (MkIII). See photo 15.3. Between the two bearings, inside the hub, is a spacer shaft. See photo 15.4. Normally, the spacer shaft has a collar on one end to hold it central, and you can then reach in and push the end without the collar out of line so you can get a drift on the bearing and drive it out, as with the steering head bearings. However, on this bike the spacer shaft didn't want to move out of line at all. Eventually, I managed to shift it just enough so I could get a drift on the inner edge of the left-hand bearing (see photo 15.4 again) and, with the help of some heat, drive out the bearing, together with its grease seals. The spacer shaft then came out, and it was then relatively easy to drive out the right-hand bearing – once I had removed the large

15.1 Removing the disc with the cordless impact driver.

15.2 Left-hand wheel bearing and grease seals.

15.3 Right-hand bearing and circlip.

DISMANTLING THE WHEELS

15.4 Levering the spacer tube out of the way enough to get a drift on the inner edge of the left-hand bearing.

15.5 Both bearings driven out. Note the spacer that goes between the bearings.

15.6 Bearing grease seals and circlip.

15.7 Tyres removed – at last!

15.8 Shock absorber assembly inside the rear wheel hub.

15.9 The lock ring removed with a punch and hammer.

retaining circlip! See photo 15.5. I think on earlier models there is a locking ring rather than a circlip to hold the bearing in place.

What I then realised was that, for some reason, the spacer shaft on these wheels had a collar at both ends, making it very, very hard to lever the spacer shaft out of the way to drive the first bearing out. If you look at photo 15.5 you can see the spacer shaft behind the wheel with its two collars. I'm not sure what Norton were thinking about here (when the wheel spindle is inserted, it naturally lines the spacer shaft up so there's no need for two collars). I think they were just having a laugh.

I then collected the three grease seals from the left-hand side; two metal plates and a felt washer, and the large circlip from the right-hand side, and bagged and tagged them. See photo 15.6. Note that, in my case, both bearings looked good and were packed with quite fresh grease. However, I'd already decided to change them regardless, for peace of mind.

I then set to work on one of my least favourite jobs – removing the tyre. By using three tyre levers in sequence, eventually it came off, together with the inner tube, and I was ready to begin removing the spokes. See photo 15.7. Hate that job!

After this, I turned my attention to the rear wheel and looked at the shock absorber assembly in the large, left-hand side of the conical hub (MkIII). See photo 15.8. Most bikes of that era had some form of shock absorber system fitted to them to slightly soften the power delivery from the engine to the back wheel and avoid mechanical damage to the power train. Some bikes (like the Trident) had shock absorbers inside the primary chaincase, on the clutch shaft, but others, like Norton (and Kawasaki), situated them inside the rear hub. They usually consist of a series of small hard rubbers between the drive and the rear wheel, and, apart from the very early models, the Commando has them too.

See Chapter 6 for more information on the different rear sprockets and hubs used in earlier models.

The shock absorber cover is held on by a central locking ring which has peg holes in for removal. Not having the special tool required to fit the locking ring (what?!) I used a hammer and a small, flat-headed punch to unscrew it. Apparently some of these were left-hand thread, but I'm not sure which. Mine was right-hand thread – but if yours won't undo then it may be that it's a left-hand thread. See photo 15.9 of the locking ring removed.

With the locking ring removed, the shock absorber cover simply lifted away, and as it did so, all the rubbers simply fell out. With the shock absorber assembly removed it was time to drive out the bearings. The manual states that in order to remove the bearings you need to re-insert the wheel spindle from the right-hand side. The wheel spindle head then rests on the end of a special bearing sleeve (like the spacer shaft for the front wheel, but different as it goes through the larger right-hand bearing, but butts up against the inner race of the smaller left-hand bearing). The manual states that if you then hammer on the end of the wheel spindle, it will serve to knock the left-hand bearing out via the bearing sleeve. If you look at photo 15.10 you can see the wheel

77

HOW TO RESTORE NORTON COMMANDO

15.10 Rear wheel spindle inserted from the disc side ready to drive out the left side bearing.

15.11 Having failed to drive out the left side bearing, using the bearing sleeve to drive out the right-hand bearing – ouch!

end of the bearing sleeve didn't take too kindly to being hit with a drift. Anyway, this method finally worked and the right-hand bearing was finally removed, together with the bearing shaft. See photo 15.12.

It was then quite an easy operation to drive out the left-hand bearing, together with its oil/grease seal, now that the right-hand bearing and the bearing sleeve were out of the way. See photo 15.13. With the bearings and sleeve on the bench, I tried to work out what on earth had gone wrong, and why I hadn't been able to drive out the left-hand bearing by knocking on the wheel spindle. Then it suddenly hit me … I hadn't removed the large spacer on the right-hand side of the bearing sleeve!

There is a large spacer that goes over the bearing sleeve on the right-hand side. See photo 15.14. I should have removed this spacer before trying to drive out the bearings. By leaving it in situ, when I knocked on the end of the wheel spindle, instead of the bearing sleeve pushing on the left-hand bearing, the spacer meant that I was pushing against the right-hand bearing, and all I was doing by hammering on the wheel spindle, was pushing the right-hand bearing inwards, against the shoulder of the hub – and that meant it wasn't going anywhere. Doh!

A simple error like failing to remove the large spacer had led to a whole lot of grief and potential

15.12 Right side bearing driven out with the bearing sleeve.

15.13 Both bearings removed – trying to work out why the left-hand bearing wouldn't drive out.

damage. I should have stopped hammering on the wheel spindle when the bearing wouldn't move, had a break, and then had a proper look at what was happening. Instead, I barged on like a bull in a china shop, and was lucky not to cause more serious damage. There's a lesson in there somewhere.

Note that I didn't remove the wide bearing from the inside of the

spindle inserted and ready to be knocked through from the other side so as to drive out the left-hand bearing.

Unfortunately, however, the manual does not allow for mechanical ineptitude on the part of the operator (me). I inserted the spindle into the bearing sleeve and tapped on the end of the spindle; nothing. I tapped harder on the end of the spindle; nothing. I gave the end of the spindle a great clout and heated the hub at the same time; still nothing. There was no sign of the bearing moving one iota. Hmm.

I then decided to try and drive out the right-hand bearing instead, using the bearing sleeve to push that bearing out. The bearing sleeve has a collar on it, which will push out the bearing if you can manage to get a drift onto the end of it. I somehow managed to move the bearing sleeve slightly out of line so I had a small edge exposed, sufficient that I could get a drift onto it and begin driving out the right-hand bearing. See photo 15.11. Note that the inner

15.14 Eureka! The left side bearing wouldn't drive out as some dummy (!) had left the spacer on the end of the shaft.

DISMANTLING THE WHEELS

15.15 Both tyres removed.

15.16 Removing the spokes from the rear wheel rim and hub.

15.17 Removing the spokes from the front wheel rim and hub.

rear sprocket, as I knew that I would be replacing both the sprocket and the bearing with new items. Had I have wanted to do so, the bearing is driven out after removing the circlip that holds it in position.

Anyway, moving on. After another struggle, the rear tyre was removed (I try to occasionally do jobs I hate, rather than giving them to someone else to do, as each time you do the job you get a bit better at it). With both tyres off and the wheel bearings removed, I began to undo the spokes. In the past, I have simply cut the spokes off with an angle grinder as they've been completely rusted in. However, in this case, the spoke nipples were all free and so I unscrewed them with the aid of a cordless drill/screwdriver, and managed to save the spokes for posterity, and felt all the better for it. See photos 15.15 and 15.16. The hubs were now free and ready to be polished and rebuilt with new rims.

LESSONS LEARNT

• Drive out the front wheel bearings by dislodging the spacer shaft at one end.
• Norton decided to fit two collars on the front wheel spacer shaft, one at either end. This makes it very difficult to move it out of the way to knock the first bearing out – I'm not sure why.
• The shock absorber assembly is situated inside the rear hub (on most models – very early models had no engine shock absorber at all!).
• The locking ring for the shock absorber assembly can apparently be either left or right-hand thread, depending on model.
• Remove the large spacer from the bearing sleeve before trying to knock the left-hand bearing out!
• Sometimes it pays to follow your own advice. If things aren't going right, down tools, leave the workshop (preferably overnight) and come back refreshed to look at the problem with fresh eyes. Don't keep hammering!

Chapter 16
Chroming, polishing, painting & parts

So, the bike was now fully dismantled and it was time to get parts sent off for vapour-blasting, polishing, chroming and powder-coating, which was a priority due to the long lead time on such work. I therefore assembled all the parts that required finishing, ready to send them off. See photo 16.1 of most parts assembled ready to be sent away.

Note that I had made the following decisions about refurbishing parts:
• I like a bit of bling so I sent all my exterior engine and gearbox casings to be polished (I sometimes do this myself, but the metal finishers can always get a better shine than I can, and it's a messy job so I let them do it! – I have included a guide on alloy polishing in the next chapter, for those who want to do this themselves).
• Liking a bit of bling, I elected to have a few parts chromed or polished that weren't originally, eg: I had the top yoke polished and chromed along with the sidestand, the bottom yoke 'flash chromed' (chromed without first having been polished, so giving a duller finish – for reasons of cost and the risk of having maybe too much bling!), and I also had the alloy instrument brackets highly polished (which were originally matt black).
• In the end, there were some parts that I elected to replace rather than have re-chromed, as they were in poor condition, and it was cheaper to buy new replacement parts in excellent condition than re-chrome

16.1 Parts assembled ready for chroming, polishing and painting.

ones that were dented or badly rusted, eg: the headlamp shell – although you have to be careful, as some parts like this can be of poor quality, with thin metal and dodgy chrome.
• I decided to have my frame, swinging arm and engine plates, etc, powder-coated. I like powder-coating because it is very hard, it

CHROMING, POLISHING, PAINTING & PARTS

16.2 Parts back from vapour blasting and powder coating.

16.3 Chromed and polished parts being sorted and stored in their correct location.

vapour-blasting, remove any bits of old gasket, as the beads in the blasting process will simply bounce off it and just leave a gooey mess.
• Make sure that any engine casings are completely dismantled prior to taking them to be cleaned – no bearings etc. The only exception to this are phosphor-bronze plain bearings for the camshaft etc. They can stay in, as long as they're not actually blasted directly. Always check with the blast cleaners.

In my case, I made one fairly basic error, simply because I was in a rush to get things done, and I was lazy. I should have taken more time to mask off the parts of the frame etc that I didn't want powder-coating beforehand. As it was I didn't do this fully and ended up with twice the work later on, trying to remove unwanted powder-coating. I can still hear my mother's admonishment ringing in my ears whenever I tried to take a shortcut over something or other: "Lazy people take the most trouble!" She was always right. Before getting the frame powder-coated, you should mask off any areas that you don't want to be coated, including the front and rear engine mountings, isolastic mounting points and swinging arm mounting points. Don't forget that powder-coating can be up to about $1/16$in thick, and will cause all sorts

gives a nice finish and is less prone to being scratched or chipped than normal paint. However, there are a number of owners and restorers who prefer spray painting to powder-coating. One problem with powder-coating is that it is pretty thick, and so you have to mask off any mating faces before painting. If you don't then parts won't fit together when they come back, and if you do manage to fit them, the thick paint between them will slowly break down and leave the joint loose. Also, if powder-coating does chip, it can let water in and parts can start rusting underneath the paint. The choice is yours.
• I sent my parts for vapour (aqua) blasting rather than bead blasting as it is a much gentler process with less chance of damaging the alloy.
• Before sending engine casings for

16.4 Taking photos of parts before sending them off for plating and polishing.

HOW TO RESTORE NORTON COMMANDO

of problems if it's applied in the wrong places. There is an excellent article about this in the technical section of the Old Britts website, giving comprehensive details about masking off a Commando frame before powder-coating. In my case, I didn't bother masking everything I should have done, and had to grind parts of it off later. Not great.

See photo 16.2 of some of the parts back from being aqua-blasted and powder-coated, and photo 16.3 of some of the parts back from being polished/chromed and being sorted back into their correct storage places. At this point note that I took labelled photos of all the small parts I sent off for chroming and polishing so that when I got them back I had at least some chance of remembering what they were and where they went. See photo 16.4 as an example. If you send off 30 small parts, including little brackets and nuts and bolts, for chroming, I can guarantee that you'll have no idea as to what goes where when a mixed pile of assorted bits returns – unless you have photos for reference.

I had also decided to have my wheels rebuilt for me, rather than try and rebuild them myself. I keep telling myself that I ought to learn to rebuild my own wheels as it'd be very satisfying and save me some money, but I don't really trust myself enough to have a go. I'm sure I could rebuild them – but how good they'd be is another matter! I therefore sent the wheel hubs off to have them rebuilt with polished hubs, stainless spokes and stainless steel rims. The original rims both required rechroming so I thought I might as well fit new stainless rims and be done with it. I decided on stainless steel rims, rather than alloy ones, just to retain more of the original look of the bike. The advantage of alloy rims

16.5 So, that's over £500-worth of stainless fasteners!

is that they are lighter, so reducing unsprung weight[1] and they give a bike more of a sporty look – but they are more easily damaged.

I'm a big fan of stainless steel so at this point I also ordered a complete set of stainless steel fasteners for my bike from Middleton's – at a cost of over £500! The set duly arrived, looking good (see photo 16.5). Stainless steel is expensive, so £500 worth doesn't look much. Not only that but there were still many bolts that I had to buy separately; rear wheel spindle, isolastic bolts, gearbox mounting bolts and studs, ignition coil brackets, etc which took the total cost to nearer £700 just on stainless fasteners by the time I'd finished.

I also planned to send my tank off for repainting after I'd cleaned out the inside and sealed it, but after approaching various painters I decided to strip it myself and take it to my local paint shop and have them do it. It meant I was saving quite a bit of money and I knew the local paint shop very well and they do a really good job (they sprayed my E-Type!).

I also intended to either have a go at refurbishing my rev counter and speedo myself, or send them off for some professional TLC. However, I discovered that my clocks were made by the French company Veglia and apparently you simply can't buy parts for them – not even the faces – so they simply couldn't be serviced or restored. I could have had the bezels removed and maybe chromed them and had new glass put in, but that was it. I don't really like the look of these particular clocks anyway (heresy!), so in the end I decided to buy some classic Smiths clocks, which I really like the look of, for not much money – and the problem of refurbing the clocks was gone! (Or so I thought, until I found that the replacement clocks didn't fit.)

Around this time (and after I'd checked most parts more thoroughly) I also began to order most of the parts I knew I needed for the bike, as well as paying a pre-booked personal visit to one of

---

[1] Unsprung weight is any weight on a vehicle that comes before the suspension – so on a motorcycle that would be the lower fork legs, mudguard, brakes and wheels on the front, and wheels, rear sprocket, and rear brake, on the rear.

Now, for whatever reason, the lower the unsprung weight, the better a vehicle will hold the road, so reducing unsprung weight is always a good thing. Hence fitting alloy rims will not only give you a general weight saving, it will also serve to reduce unsprung weight as alloy rims are lighter than steel ones.

Anything that reduces unsprung weight is a bonus, which is why the legendary Jaguar Independent Rear Suspension, as fitted to E-Types etc, sports in-board discs and callipers after the suspension, and so massively reduces unsprung weight (but makes it a bugger to get to the callipers!)

Note, therefore, that by fitting such as twin discs to your bike, whilst you may well improve the braking, you will be increasing the unsprung weight and adversely affecting road holding.

CHROMING, POLISHING, PAINTING & PARTS

the main parts suppliers to buy parts in person. I bought such things as my new clocks and a new headlamp shell (as mentioned above); new primary chain, rear chain and sprockets; new uprated clutch plates; new mudguards; an uprated front brake assembly; Tri-spark electronic ignition; new pistons; new big end shells; new valves and new guides; a full gasket and seal set; an upgrade for the starter motor; new carburettors; new rear shocks; new wheel bearings; a gearbox refurb kit; and new cables – about £4000 worth of parts in all! (Yes, £4000!) Hopefully there wouldn't be too many more bits to buy after this (there were – the total cost of parts and services came to over £8000, all told). I did this so that I'd have as many parts I knew I needed as possible at the start of the rebuild, so that I wouldn't be waiting for parts to arrive in the middle of the rebuild – always infuriating! I also had the money at that point, so good to use it wisely before I just wasted it!

Note that most of the work listed above will be covered in detail in later chapters, but it's a good idea to get as much sorted before the rebuild as possible. Also note that how your bike is finished is entirely up to you, the owner. Some owners might want to restore their bikes as close to original as possible, others may want to create a café racer or even a custom bike. Others may wish to go for an 'oily rag' restoration, which I've always taken to mean refurbishing parts, such as the engine, but without cleaning them or restoring them, so you end up with a reliable bike but one that still retains its patina. But what you do is entirely up to you. Don't listen to the naysayers who tell you, "You didn't want to do that" – yes, you did, that's why you did it, it's your bike.

As part of this, note that you therefore need a plan at the start of the restoration as to how your bike is going to look when finished so you can prepare accordingly. You may well change the plan as the restoration progresses, that's quite normal, but at least have a plan to begin with.

LESSONS LEARNT

- I try to get all my chroming and painting etc done, and as many parts as possible bought, before I begin the rebuild, so that everything is ready and you can work at your own pace and not have to wait for parts, etc.
- When you take your parts to the chrome platers or painters etc have a chat with them and discuss exactly what you want doing, and the various options available, to avoid any ambiguity.
- Completely strip engine cases of all removable parts – apart from plain bearings.
- Preferably mask off the parts of the frame and engine plates that don't want to be powder-coated before having the frame painted – or make a rod for your own back.
- Take labelled photos of all small parts before taking them to be chromed etc. When they come back (sometimes several months later) in one big pile, you won't have a clue what some of them are.
- If there are some parts you already know you need, buy them now – sometimes you have to order them and wait a few weeks for delivery: that can be infuriating in the middle of a rebuild!
- Veglia clocks, who needs them?
- Stainless steel – we love it!
- It's your bike, do it how you want.
- Lazy people take the most trouble.

Chapter 17
Polishing engine casings & other alloy parts

Okay, so I thought I would include a chapter on how to polish casings to a mirror finish. However, on the Commando I didn't polish them myself, but had the chrome platers do it, for several reasons: they can get a better finish than I can, it's a dirty job that you should ideally do outside (not good if the weather's bad), and they could do it quickly. But I thought I would include this chapter on how to polish alloy engine casings, etc, taken from a previous manual I wrote on restoring a Kawasaki Z900 (What? Japanese?! Not a British classic? Yes, my first Japanese restoration – and I was very impressed by the engineering). Although it obviously deals with the Z, the techniques for polishing Commando alloy are exactly the same. Apologies to those who are easily offended.

One very arduous, laborious yet particularly satisfying job is polishing the various alloy parts on the bike. There is a big debate in the restoration world as to how shiny and polished your engine, etc, should be. All I can say is that that's entirely up to you, and I'm just going to give some guidance on how to achieve a highly polished finish if you want one. End of.

All-in-all I spent at least a week solid polishing various alloy parts. It's a real pain of a job, but if you want a nice shiny engine then it needs to be done. There's one simple basic rule: The more work you put in, the better the finish that comes out.

If you want to achieve a really highly polished finish to your alloy engine casings then the only way is by using some kind of buffing machine. Hand polishing alone simply won't do it (or rather it can be done, but it takes an awfully long time and a huge amount of work!). To achieve a polished finish on parts such as

17.1 Polishing wheel, buffing mops, and grit mops.

POLISHING ENGINE CASINGS & OTHER ALLOY PARTS

crankcases and cylinder heads (that you can't get on a buffer due to their convoluted shape) you'll need a variety of mildly abrasive brushes and some wet and dry emery cloth.

For a real mirror finish you need a polishing wheel with a variety of mops (see photo 17.1). I use a converted bench grinder that I then hold in the vice (I used to clamp it direct to the bench but the mountings weren't up to it). I then have five different polishing mops, although I usually only use four of them. The most abrasive mops I have are two grit mops of 150 and 240 grade (similar to emery cloth). The 150 grade is only used on really rough castings that have a very uneven surface from the casting process and have never been polished before. So in most cases I don't use the 150 grit mop at all – it's just too coarse and you can easily do more harm than good.

The next grade down is the 240 grit mop (on the left in photo 17.1) which is still pretty coarse and only used for parts that are too uneven for just polishing. I use the 240 grit on any parts never previously polished, plus any parts that have been vapour-blasted, plus any parts with deep scratches or dents that are too deep to polish out. Note that if you vapour-blast any parts they will come out rough even if they were polished previously and you will need to begin the polishing process with grit mops. However, if you can get away without vapour-blasting parts already polished then the whole job is much easier and you can begin with polishing mops. See photo 17.2.

After the 240 grit is the first of the polishes, the grey polish and mop. Using the grey polish should leave you with a pretty shiny piece of metal. After this is the medium green polish, using this achieves a very good shine. See photo 17.3. Finally comes the last polish, the blue polish with the softest mop. See photo 17.4. (NB: See note below).

My technique is as follows:
• Screw the grit mop onto the buffer (if required) remembering that they are all left-hand threads.
• Apply grit sparingly to the grit mop (use a sisal mop that is closely stitched and therefore very hard). Be aware that grit is very abrasive and

17.2 One leg after being polished with a fine 240 grit.

17.3 One leg after polishing with a grey polish and then with a medium (green) polish.

17.4 Final polish with a soft blue mop.

you can easily do more harm than good if you're not careful. Apply grit frequently but sparingly to the mop.
• After finishing with the grit mop (if required) go on to the polishing mops, beginning with the coarsest first. Harder sisal mops are stitched, and the more stitching the harder the mop. Apply polish frequently but very sparingly – if you start getting polish residue on your work the chances are you've got too much polish on the mop. Use harder mops to begin with and work your way down to the softer mops.
• Only use a mop for one grade of polish – don't use different grades on the same mop – I mark all of mine so they don't get mixed up.
• Don't push too hard – if the buffer slows right down you're pushing too hard.
• There will always be some polish residue left over and this can be removed either with French chalk that comes with most polishing kits, or with white spirit, or when you give the piece a final hand polish with Solvol Autosol.

The good news is that every time you polish something you get a little better at it (like most things) and as a general rule if you don't get a decent shine after using the grey polish, the work might need more work with a fine grit first.

Don't forget that what you're doing is slowly getting rid of uneven/cast finishes by slowly cutting down the roughness with successively finer polishes. Consider that the highly polished surfaces on your engine started life with a cast finish like crankcases and are only shiny due to careful polishing.

I'm certainly no expert but I can get a decent finish on most parts after a few engines' worth of practice. Even now, I know that the professional polishers (at the chrome platers) can still produce a way better mirror finish than I can. (It's a bit like trying to teach yourself plastering if you've ever tried that: you get better at it each time, but it's a long learning curve and you'll probably never be as good as the pros). Having said that polishing alloy parts to a wonderful shine is one of the really rewarding jobs on a bike – but also one of the most time-consuming and dirty – note that I try to do my polishing outside whenever possible to stop the workshop getting covered in thick black dust. See photo 17.5

The second type of polishing (for those who want it) is to try and polish parts that can't be buffed due to their odd shape and size, eg crankcases, cylinder barrels and cylinder heads, and for these I use a cordless drill with a variety of fine bristled flap brushes combined with a selection of wet and dry emery cloth. I use fine bristled flap brushes (not steel brushes as these are too abrasive; I occasionally use brass brushes but I find these hard to source and they

HOW TO RESTORE NORTON COMMANDO

17.5 Preparing to polish the head and other parts.

17.6 Various abrasive mops for cleaning and polishing parts that can't be buffed on the wheel.

17.7 Wet and dry emery paper graded 240 to 2500 grit.

17.8 Cylinder head before polishing.

17.9 Cylinder head polished with abrasive wheels and emery cloth.

17.10 Final finishing with Autosol.

can be a bit too aggressive as well), and I have a wide selection of shapes and sizes for different jobs. See photo 17.6. Together with the flap brushes I have a selection of wet and dry emery cloth from 240 down to 2500 grit which I always use wet. See photo 17.7.

To begin with, I use the cordless drill and the flap wheels as far as possible, and then finish the work with wet and dry to remove the scratches left by the flap wheels. The level of finish is dictated by how much graft I put into the finishing with the wet and dry. The higher the grade of emery cloth the higher the level of finish, but you need to work your way up slowly from 240 to 2500 grade – and this takes a lot of graft. Luckily, although I like a bit of shine on my

POLISHING ENGINE CASINGS & OTHER ALLOY PARTS

17.11 Crankcase polished with abrasive wheels and emery cloth.

17.12 Cam cover buff polished.

17.14 Dremmel with wire brush and flap wheel attachments.

17.13 Buff polished clutch cover.

17.15 Parts being washed in a jam jar of white spirit.

cylinder heads etc, I don't like too much, so there often isn't a great deal of graft with the emery cloth to be done. Hurrah! See photos 17.8 and 17.9. After all of this, I finally finish the job off with Solvol Autosol to remove any light scratching left by the emery cloth and leave the work with a lovely deep finish. See photo 17.10. There are a few photos showing some of the casings polished using different methods: 17.11, 17.12 and 17.13.

I also use a Dremmel multi-tool with a variety of bits for such as nuts and bolts and hard-to-reach nooks and crannies on occasions. I used small sanding flap wheels, stainless steel brushes and brass brushes, but the flap wheels are pretty abrasive, the stainless brushes tended to leave the metal quite dark and the brass brushes wear out quickly, so beware. See photo 17.14.

I also have a selection of jam jars for de-greasing nuts and bolts etc before detailed cleaning and polishing. I just put the nuts and bolts in the jar together with some white spirit and give it a good shake for a couple of minutes. See photo 17.15. It works great – but some heavy nuts and bolts being violently shaken in a glass jar? Yes, I do have some 'incidents'! I think I should invest in a plastic container or similar!

LESSONS LEARNT

- How much alloy you polish is up to you – some love it, some hate it (but as I always say: it's your bike).
- The easiest way to obtain a mirror shine is by mechanical buffing – you can do it by hand but it'd take an awful lot of time and effort.
- Use grit to begin with if the surface is poor or cast – but be careful.
- Compare the finish on a Commando cylinder head with that on a Kawasaki of the same age!
- Use polish on the mop sparingly but frequently.
- If it doesn't shine with the grey polish it isn't right.
- Polish left on the job – too much polish.
- The mop stalling on the buffer – too much pressure.
- The quality finish is directly proportional to the amount of effort you put in.
- Use wet and dry to obtain a polish on parts that can't be buffed – but be prepared to graft!
- Practice makes perfect.
- Glass jars and nuts and bolts aren't the best combination!
- Polishing is at once one of the most frustrating yet rewarding jobs on the restoration.
- Sometimes you just say, "Oh, sod it!" and take it to the specialists and have them do it for you.

Chapter 18

Reassembling the crankshaft & crankcases

Now, finally, the good part! It was time to begin reassembly! Hurrah! Now all the parts had been cleaned and refurbished, it was time to begin slowly reassembling the bike with beautifully clean and new or refurbished parts. Heaven!

Note that before I had taken the crankcases to be vapour-blasted I'd scraped off all the old gasket myself, as vapour-blasting won't remove it. See photo 18.1. At this point I also noted that all the threads in the cases that required a high torque setting were helicoiled with thread inserts. See photo 18.2. At first I thought they'd been stripped by a PO (previous owner) but on further investigation it turns out that these were done at the factory as the inserts proved to be stronger than the original alloy! I'm not sure what this says about the quality of the aluminium alloy Norton used, but it makes sense. You learn something new every day.

With the crankcases back from the blast cleaners I gave them a very thorough clean with soap and water, paying particular attention to the oilways and any threads. See photo 18.3. The vapour-blasting process uses small glass beads (like

18.1 Scraping off the old gasket.

grains of sand) and they get into every nook and cranny and sit there. It's very important to ensure they're completely removed as otherwise they'll cause havoc inside the engine.

NB: At this point it's worth noting that I previously cleaned a pair of Kawasaki crankcases in the dishwasher, but there was something about the alloy in them that reacted with the dishwasher tabs and formed a hard black crust all over the cases, including inside the threads. As a result I had to have the cases blast cleaned again to remove the black crust and use a tap to clean out all the threads in the cases – over 100 on that engine! As a result I'm now

REASSEMBLING THE CRANKSHAFT & CRANKCASES

18.2 The threads in the crankcases that required a lot of torque all had thread inserts.

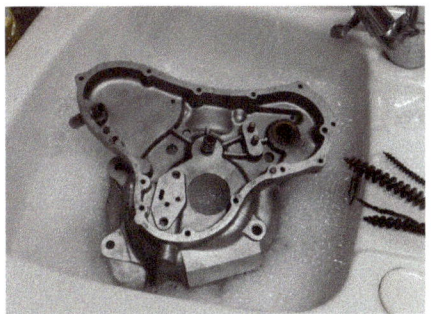

18.3 Thoroughly washing the crankcases on their return from vapour blasting.

very wary of using the dishwasher to clean cases, as clever and exciting as it may sound.

Next up were the main bearings. A lot has been written about the roller main bearings in Commandos – and for good reason. Apparently, some of the early bearings failed very quickly. There is a belief that this was due to the long, cylindrical bearings being too cylindrical and uniform in shape, and that Norton then changed to Superblend bearings, made by FAG in Germany, which were slightly barrel-shaped, with a curved profile, and that this cured the problem. However, it would appear that the Superblend bearings aren't actually barrel-shaped; it's just that they have a bigger radius on the corners of the bearings that stops them from digging into the bearing casings, which was apparently the cause of the original problem. Whatever the case, these Superblend bearings work well. It's also worth noting that the very early Commandos had altogether different main bearings, but I believe that these can also be replaced with the Superblend ones.

Now I had to decide whether or not to replace the main bearings in my engine. Normally, I would replace them as a matter of course, because if they fail you have to completely strip down the whole engine again to replace them. However, my existing ones seemed to be in good condition: they rotated freely but without any discernible play, and the inner races that were still on the crankshaft looked to be in very good order, and new ones are very expensive at over £50 each. I therefore decided to reuse my existing bearings. To be honest I'm not sure if this was a wise decision (only time will tell), and I would normally advise anyone to replace the mains as a matter of course. I would only reuse existing ones if they appear to be in very good condition, and are genuine FAG ones, as in this case.

With some misgivings, I therefore prepared to refit the mains into the crankcases, where they are an interference fit. The easiest way to achieve this is to expand the crankcases and shrink the mains. I therefore put the crankcases in the oven (best done when certain people are out for the day!) to get them hot so they expand, and, conversely, put the mains in the freezer to get cold and shrink. See photos 18.4 & 18.5. After this I coated the outside of the mains with bearing seal (see photo 18.6) before dropping them into the hot crankcases. They went in easily due to the heating/cooling procedure. See photo 18.7. Note I ensured that each bearing went back into the same side it came out of – and

18.4 Heating the crankcases in the oven ready to refit the main bearings ...

18.5 ... whilst cooling the bearings in the freezer.

18.6 Coating the outside of the bearing to prevent it from spinning in the casing.

18.7 Both main bearings fitted in their respective cases.

the right way round! Using existing bearings means that they **must** go in the same position they came out of, as otherwise they are prone to rapid wear and failure.

With the crankcases ready I turned my attention to the crankshaft. I had already taken the crankshaft to the engineers to confirm my own appraisal that the big end journals were fine and that they didn't need re-grinding. And so it proved. It's always good to get a second opinion about such matters as you don't want to get such a basic decision wrong! The engineers therefore merely polished the big end journals to ensure they were completely smooth.

I then thoroughly cleaned out the oilways and screwed in a new blanking plug (see photo 18.8) before beginning to loosely assembling the three pieces of the shaft together, ensuring that the punch marks I'd made on disassembly all lined up. See photo 18.9.

Whilst I had been at the engineers I had also asked for their advice on how to torque the studs that hold the three pieces of the shaft together. The manual says that the studs should be tightened to 30lb/ft (25lb/ft on earlier models) but I could see straightaway that there was no way I could get my torque wrench onto the nuts to torque them up. Unfortunately, they were as nonplussed as I was. We agreed that probably the best method was to torque up one of the nuts that was accessible to 30lb/ft, feel how tight that felt with normal spanners, and use that as a guide for all the other nuts. So that's what I did. See photo 18.10 of an accessible nut being torqued up as a guide.

I then duly used a combination of sockets, ring spanners and open-ended spanners to tighten the crankshaft nuts to what I hoped was 30lb/ft of torque. I also used Loctite on all the nuts. See photo 18.11. To be honest, I'm not sure if there is a way of torquing the nuts on the crankshaft using a torque wrench – but if there is, I don't know about it!

With the crankshaft assembled, the next job was to ensure that there was some end float present on the crankshaft, when in the crankcases. End float just means that there is a little side-to-side free play, about 10 to 20 thou is recommended on a Commando. The end float is necessary to ensure that the crankshaft can turn freely in the cases at all times without seizing, but also without too much end float, which can cause problems with the con rods, the primary chain and timing case gears.

I therefore loosely assembled the crankshaft in the crankcase, as detailed below, but without sealant or the camshaft etc, so I could check for end float by pushing and pulling the crankshaft sideways, before assembling the crankcases properly. My end float appeared fine, seemingly being between the 10 thou and 20 thou play stipulated by Norton. You should measure end float with a dial gauge on the end of the crankshaft, but I just did mine by feel. Note that shims are available if there is too much end float on the crankshaft.

I then removed the crankshaft from the cases and filled the oilways and large cavity in the crankshaft with oil so that on initial start-up the big ends etc wouldn't be starved of oil. To do this you have to squirt oil down the main oilway until the crankshaft is full of oil and it begins to flow out of the oil holes in the big end journals. In order to do this I emptied all the assembly lube out of its squeezy container and refilled it with engine oil. I then stood the crankshaft vertically and squeezed oil down the oilway through the timing side crankshaft. See photo 18.12. However, I soon realised that I had done this far too early in the assembly process, and it just led to oil going everywhere every time I turned the crankshaft over, and I had to drain the oil back out again. The oiling of the crankshaft should be left until the crankcases are about to be inserted back into the frame.

After this, I inserted the new big end shells into the bottom of the con rods. See photo 18.13. Note that one of the shells has a hole in it which lines up with the oilway in the con rod, whilst the bottom shell is blank – don't get them mixed up! I then ensured the following:

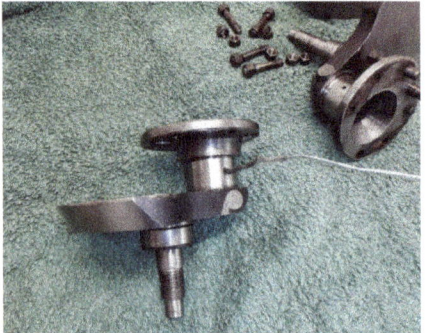
18.8 Thoroughly cleaning the oilways in the crankshaft.

18.9 Beginning to reassemble the crankshaft.

18.10 Tightening one of the studs to 30lb/ft for reference.

18.11 Tightening all the studs on the crankshaft to what was, hopefully, 30lb/ft.

REASSEMBLING THE CRANKSHAFT & CRANKCASES

18.12 Filling the crankshaft void with oil.

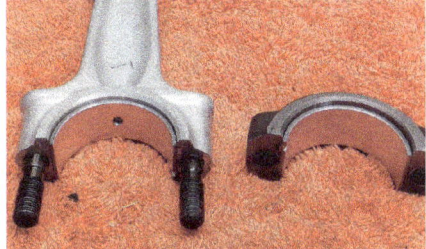

18.13 New big end shells fitted – with the holed one in the conrod.

18.14 Oil draining back out of the crankshaft as the big end nuts weren't right.

- That I had the correct two halves of each con rod and that the marks made at manufacture lined up with each other.
- That I had the correct con rod for each side of the crankshaft. I had marked them on dismantling – it's best to always ensure that things go back in exactly the same position as they came out.
- That the oilway that exits each con rod just above the journal was facing outwards on both con rods (Most of the oil in the crankcase comes out of these holes in the con rods – oil is pumped at high pressure down the crankshaft and exits through these small oilways in the con rods, spraying oil onto the sides of the crankcases and therefore the main bearings. If the oilways on the con rods face inwards, the oil is sprayed towards the centre of the crankcases and doesn't go to the main bearings – potential disaster!
- That I never reused big end nuts. They are self-locking nuts and once used, they lose their self-locking ability and can come undone – and you really don't want that to happen!
- That the new big end shells and crankshaft journals are liberally smeared with assembly oil to avoid oil starvation on start-up.

I then clamped the con rods round the big end journals ensuring all was as prescribed above, and began tightening the big end nuts up on the big end bolts. But, hang on, there was something wrong! For some weird reason the new big end nuts wouldn't run freely down the big end bolts, and tightened up (or galled) halfway down the threads. They were so tight that the nuts had already reached their torque setting of 25lb/ft before they had even got to the con rod! I was completely befuddled as to the reason behind this. I swapped the new nuts for the old ones and they were absolutely fine. Bizarre, I'd never had this happen before. I therefore had to take the con rods off again and try and find out what the problem was.

I rang the suppliers to be told it was something I was doing wrong, but they finally agreed for me to send the con rods, big end bolts, and big end nuts to them for investigation. The suppliers found that indeed the entire batch of big end nuts supplied to them were faulty and were returned to the manufacturer. I was then supplied with new big end nuts and new bolts that worked properly, and the new big-end nuts ran down the threads on the new big end bolts easily. However, in completing all this, oil from the crankshaft went everywhere, and I drained the oil back out of it. See photo 18.14.

I knocked out the old big end bolts from the con rods and replaced them with the new ones. Note that the heads of the big end bolts are offset so that they don't turn in the con rods when tightening the big end nuts. See photo 18.15.

The problem with the big end nuts could have been a complete disaster! Imagine if the nuts were only slightly too tight – I would probably have used them, but they would have given me a false torque reading. When the torque wrench read 25lb/ft the nuts would have actually only been at about 15-20lb/ft torque as they were tight on the bolt. 'Luckily' mine were so bad there was no way they could be used.

I could then refit the con rods to the crankshaft and torque the

18.15 Note the eccentric top to the big end bolts.

91

HOW TO RESTORE NORTON COMMANDO

18.16 Fitting the big ends and locking with loctite.

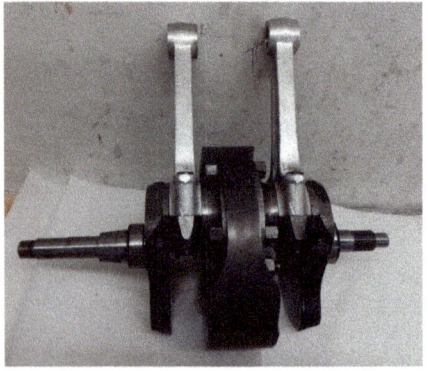

18.17 The crankshaft assembled and ready to go in the crankcases.

big end nuts as normal. See photo 18.16. Note that I also Loctited them for good measure. The con rods were now fitted and the crankshaft assembly was complete. See photo 18.17. I immediately checked that each con rod rotated freely on its journal with no tight spots etc. Note also that I decided not to refill the crankshaft with oil at this point, as it simply kept leaking out if the crankshaft was tilted – which at this point it often was. I decided to add the oil just before the crankcases were put back into the frame.

It was now time to reunite the crankshaft with the crankcases for the second and final time. In order to facilitate this, I had to stand the crankshaft upright. I found that a glass tankard I had was ideal for this. See photo 18.18. I have to admit that I'm quite proud of that tankard, which was given to me as a prize when one of my Tridents was awarded best T150 at Beezumph, the annual get together of the TR3OC (Trident and Rocket 3 Owners' Club) a few years ago. See photo 18.19. I don't generally do concours type events, but it was all part of the Beezumph event, and I have to say it was a great honour to receive it.

With the crankshaft in the vertical position, and the main bearing race liberally covered in assembly oil, I slid the timing side crankcase onto it. Note that the side of the crankshaft with the longer shaft is the drive side! (It'd be easy to get the crankshaft round the wrong way!) See photo 18.20. With the timing case in position, I prepared to fit the timing pinion on the crankshaft. See photo 18.21 of the pinion with spacers etc. First of all, I slid the backing plate and spacer on, followed by the Woodruff key. See photo 18.22. Note that the shortened end of the Woodruff key goes towards the spacer. I then pressed the crankshaft pinion onto the shaft using a long socket of a suitable internal diameter. See photo 18.23.

After this, I prepared the drive side casing for fitting. To begin with I cleaned the crankcase oil filter. See photo 18.24. I then assembled it and fitted it to the crankcase using a new copper washer. Note that I also Loctited the threads, not for fear of it coming undone, but to help keep it oil tight. See photo 18.25.

18.18 Holding the crankshaft vertical using my winner's trophy – note the manual!

18.19 I'm very proud of this award.

REASSEMBLING THE CRANKSHAFT & CRANKCASES

18.20 Lowering the timing side crankcase onto the crankshaft.

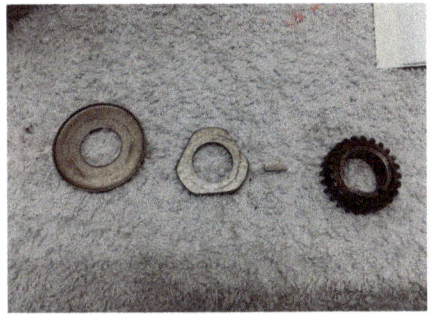

18.21 The timing pinion ready to go back on the crankshaft.

18.22 The back plate, spacer and Woodruff key in place. Note the flat on the Woodruff key faces the spacer.

18.23 Tapping home the pinion with a long socket.

I prepared to fit the camshaft. My camshaft had strange wear marks on the lobes that I'd never seen before, and I thought it must require replacing. (See Chapter 13). However, I took it down to one of the specialist suppliers who examined it and informed me that it was fine, as Commando camshafts often show this type of wear, and it was perfectly normal and not harmful – I hope they were right! I therefore prepared to fit the camshaft to the crankcases by slipping the single spacer (MkIII) onto the timing side, with the curved side facing the worm drive. See photo 18.26. Don't forget that different models use different spacers and you need to ensure that the correct spacers are fitted to your particular model. I then liberally coated the camshaft ends and the phosphor-bronze bearings in the crankcases with engine assembly oil, and slid the camshaft into the timing side case. After this I coated the mating surfaces of the crankcases with Wellseal and let the sealant go off for a few minutes. See photo 18.27.

I slid the drive side crankcase onto the crankshaft (not forgetting to generously cover the main bearings with engine assembly oil) and tapped them together. See photo 18.28. After this I inserted my new stainless steel crankcase bolts and screws and the crankcase was assembled! I immediately rotated the crankshaft to ensure that all was well and there were no tight spots that would have signalled a problem.

18.24 Cleaning the crankcase filter.

18.25 Crankcase filter reassembled and ready to be screwed back into the drive side crankcase.

18.26 The camshaft collar is in position – curved side to the tacho drive (MkIII).

18.27 The camshaft slotted into position and the crankcase faces smeared with Wellseal.

HOW TO RESTORE NORTON COMMANDO

18.28 The two halves of the crankcase being slid together.

18.29 The crankcase assembled!

18.30 So this is a matched pair?

18.31 Not quite a match.

Note that you have to protect the con rods whilst doing this as they can easily be damaged by hitting the crankcase mouth – and small chips and scratches on a con rod can start stress fractures and lead to a con rod snapping – not a great idea. In my case the crankshaft turned smoothly and easily. Hurrah! See photo 18.29.

One item of note, however, was the fact that the two halves of the crankcases clearly didn't line up. See photos 18.30 and 18.31. Initially I was puzzled – were these not a matched pair? Maybe one case had been replaced at some point? But then I remembered that the casings are both stamped underneath with the same number to identify them as a matched pair (In the factory the cases would be line-bored together to make a matched pair and then stamped with the same number so if they were separated for further machining etc they could easily be reunited later on). It slowly dawned on me that these were in fact a matched pair. I was stunned. Here were the crankcases from a Norton Commando 850 MkIII, flagship model of the Norton empire, an engine that'd been in production for nearly 20 years – and this is the best they could come up with? A pair of crankcases that didn't even line up with each other – not even close. I really don't know what to say. Was this the pinnacle of British engineering? Or is this a sobering reminder of why the once great British motorcycle industry collapsed – with production quality like this, the only real question is why the motorcycle industry didn't fail earlier. (Don't forget that, by way of contrast, we made Concorde, a supersonic aeroplane in the mid 1960s!)

LESSONS LEARNT
- Remove old gasket before taking engine parts for blasting.
- Norton used to insert helicoils in its crankcases from new.
- Thoroughly clean crankcases after blast cleaning – but be careful of using a dishwasher!
- Commandos need to have proper Superblend main bearings fitted, which don't fail anywhere near as often as the earlier ones.
- The crankshaft should be bolted together and torqued up to 25 or 30lb/ft – but how do you do this?
- Crankshaft end float should be between 10 and 20 thou.
- You need to fill the crankshaft with oil before use to avoid oil starvation – but don't do it too early!
- Fit the con rods with the oilways facing outwards.
- If something doesn't feel right, check it and sort it – don't ignore it!
- Never reuse big end nuts.
- Sometimes the customer is actually right!
- Always use engine assembly oil on all bearing surfaces. Do not use ordinary engine oil as this is too thin and will run off before the engine is started.
- Don't forget to fit the camshaft!
- Check that everything turns smoothly at every stage, don't wait until everything's back together.
- British motorcycle engineering? I sometimes sadly shake my head in disbelief.

Chapter 19
Fitting the crankcases & isolastics

With the crankcases assembled, it was time to prepare the frame to accept them. This involved restoring the isolastics, preparing the frame and engine plates, and fitting the centre stand.

To begin with I dismantled the isolastics. See photo 19.1 of the rear isolastics removed from the engine plates and partially dismantled, and photo 19.2 of the front isolastics removed and fully dismantled. Note that, as mine is a MkIII, the isolastics are of the later type which means that the rubbers are all bonded together as one mounting, and that the isolastics are adjusted using a Vernier system (screwing up and unscrewing the end cap). This is unlike earlier models, which had separate pieces of rubber in the isolastics, and used shims to adjust the end-float. The good news is that I believe all earlier models can be converted to the later system without modification – a definite bonus.

If you look at photo 19.2 again, you can also see that the fixed end cap is removed from the isolastic shaft by unscrewing the small grub screw that locks it to the shaft (see bottom right in the photo) and that these later systems also use different washers behind the end caps, which are apparently much superior to the earlier types. They are easily distinguishable as they are red in colour, as opposed to the earlier white ones.

When they were dismantled, I inspected the old isolastic units to see if they required changing. The

19.1 Removing the rear isolastics.

19.2 Front isolastics dismantled.

HOW TO RESTORE NORTON COMMANDO

front one was fine, but the rear one was shot. See photo 19.3 showing the old unit at the top and the new unit at the bottom. The old one looks okay, doesn't it? That's what I thought, too, until I asked Les Emsley at Norvil Motorcycles for his advice and he told me to look down the isolastics side on, and if they were no longer round, then they needed replacing. If you now look at photo 19.4 of the isolastic unit viewed end-on you can see just how worn it is, with one side almost half the size of the other.

However, before I could go ahead and fit the units into their brackets I realised that I had to remove some of the powder-coating from around the edges of the brackets. See photo 19.5. This was because the isolastics have a cap that fits over the ends of the brackets and with the thick powder-coating in place they wouldn't fit. Not only this, but, more importantly, they would have given a false reading when the isolastic end-float was set and then, as the powder-coating on this area crumbled, the isolastics would have become very loose and caused all sorts of problems. I therefore ground the coating off using a small flap wheel on a Dremmel, and then painted the bare metal with Hammerite to prevent it from rusting.

After this I inserted the isolastic units into their brackets by thoroughly cleaning the inside of the brackets and then employing my secret weapon: soap. I used soap to lubricate the rubbers and allow them to slide in. Soap can be good in these situations as it is very slippery, but then dries out afterwards allowing the rubbers to sit tight, unlike oil which stays liquid and slippery – but don't use liquid soap as this doesn't dry. With the isolastics in place, I put the caps on, followed by the red washers and then the end caps, and tightened the grub screw in the end that is fixed. After this I tried to fit the rubber gaiters over the ends – what a nightmare! As fitting the isolastics had been easy, fitting the rubber gaiters was hard. Anyway, eventually (and I mean eventually) I got them all on, after I developed a bit of a knack with the aid of a couple of screwdrivers. See photo 19.7. At this point I realised that I should either have polished my old end caps or bought new ones as they were very visible. I had previously thought that the rubber gaiters would cover them completely, but as the old gaiters were damaged, I couldn't tell how much they covered, and the end caps were indeed quite visible. As a result I polished them up as best as I could whilst in situ. Note that the adjustable side of the isolastics goes on the right at the front, and on the left at the rear – not sure why, but that's what the manuals say.

After this I removed the powder-coating from all the other important mating surfaces. First of all I ground the coating off the inner frame brackets for the isolastics (see photo 19.8) and then off the bolt holes on the engine frames where they mate with the crankcases. See photo 19.9.

19.3 New and old rear isolastics.

19.4 Crushed rear isolastics.

19.5 Removing the powder coating from the edges of the mountings.

19.6 Inserting the isolastics into the mountings.

19.7 Isolastics fully fitted.

FITTING THE CRANKCASE & ISOLASTICS

19.8 Powder coating removed from frame brackets.

19.11 How to fit the main stand spring.

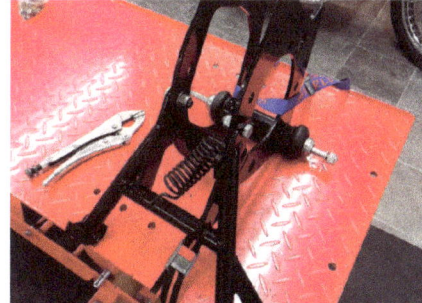
19.12 Strapping down the engine frames and stand to fit the main spring.

19.9 Removing the powder coating from the engine frame mountings.

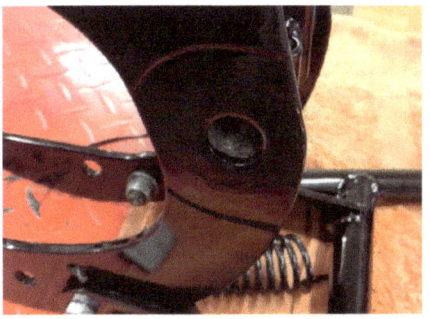
19.10 Powder coating removed from the swinging arm mounting on the engine frames.

19.13 Engine in the frame with front isolastics attached.

Finally, I removed the coating from around the swinging arm mountings. See photo 19.10. Note that I repainted all the exposed metal with Hammerite before fitting.

My next job was to fit the centre stand – and the centre stand spring. I soon realised that this was to be no easy task as the spring was very, very strong, and when in place there was a big gap between the bolt holes on the stand and those on the engine plates. See photo 19.11. I tried various ways of fitting the three together, levering and pulling and twisting, both with the stand on and off the frames, and with increasing levels of brutality, and therefore the risk of damage to both myself and the parts. After half-an-hour of wrestling it was time to stand back, leave the workshop and come back to it fresh the next day.

Overnight I'd had a think and came up with a cunning plan. I bolted the stand to the engine frames and then strapped both of them to the bike lift. With them securely strapped down I used a pair of mole grips (very tightly clamped!) to pull down the spring, and engage it in the hole in the stand. See photo 19.12. Hurrah! It was only after doing this that I remembered I'd bought a special spring-stretching tool for this very job! I'd forgotten all about it and used mole grips instead.

It was time to fit the crankcases into the frame, so I bolted the front isolastic mounting to the crankcases, protected the frame with towels (easy to remove afterwards) and then lifted the assembly into place, loosely inserting the front isolastic bolt from the timing side. (See photo 19.13.) I then slid the engine plates into position, loosely inserting the rear isolastic bolt. After this I began to insert the engine bolts with the help of various screwdrivers to lever and cajole as necessary. See photo 19.14. As I did this I realised that I had used the wrong (slightly longer) bolts to mount the front isolastic bracket, and the remaining bolts were just too short. I therefore spent quite a time swapping bolts to get them in their correct positions. The engine was now back in the frame! See photo 19.15. Hurrah! Note that lifting the crankcases into the frame was quite easy as the crankcase without the rest of the engine wasn't too heavy, and being able to move the cases at waist height from the bench to the frame on the lift meant that no bending was required.

HOW TO RESTORE NORTON COMMANDO

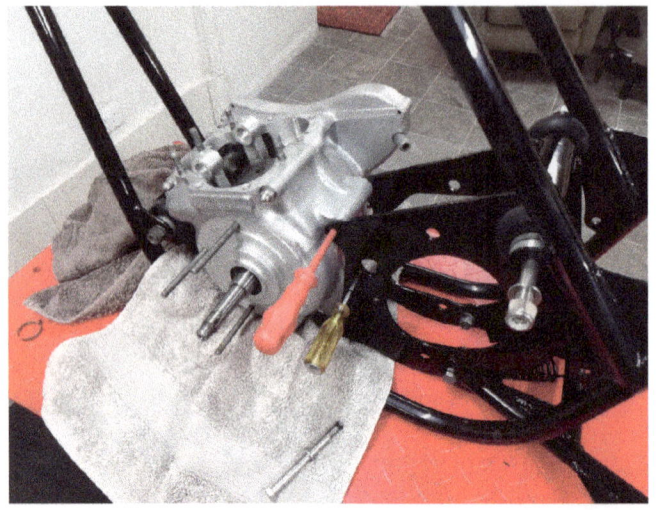

19.14 The engine frame slid into position and being bolted up.

19.16 Oh, no! Centre stand bolts inserted the wrong way round!

19.15 Engine in the frame!

Oh dear. I was celebrating too soon. I suddenly realised that I had inserted the bolts holding the centre stand on the wrong way round – the bolt heads should be on the inside, not the outside, as I had it. See photo 19.16. With the bolts round this way they interfered with the spring on the centre stand. I was now faced with the problem of removing the bolts whilst the spring was under high tension, and now fitted in the frame. Hmm. After a bit of thought I came up with cunning plan No 2. I strapped the front of the frame to the end of the bike lift, and the centre stand to the rear of the lift. I then tensioned the straps until they were just taut, which I hoped would mean that when a bolt was removed from the stand, the stand wouldn't move either way – and so it proved!

I was very pleased with myself and changed the bolts round easily. Result! However, as has happened many times before, my celebration was short lived. I realised that as the stand actually mounts on two collets that run through the frame and stand, I could have removed the bolts without having to strap anything down; the collets would have held the stand firm! The bolts only serve to hold the collets in position and stop them falling out! Pride comes before a fall.

With the engine and centre stand now fitted correctly, I set the end-float on the isolastics. In order to do this I had to find something that would fit in the holes in the turning end of the unit to allow me to turn it either way, to both tighten and loosen it. I eventually found a punch that would just about

fit. I turned the end until it was tight, ensuring that there was no free play in the unit and then slackened it off until there was a six thou gap between the cap and the red washer, which is the correct setting – this equated to turning the end cap through about 1½ holes. See photo 19.18. Note that to check the gap I had to prise the rubbers back slightly. I then repeated this operation with the rear isolastics. See photo 19.19. I then torqued up both isolastic mounting bolts to 30lb/ft and I will re-check the end-play again after about 100 miles or so. Note that you shouldn't check them with the bike on the main stand (which is attached to the engine plates) but with the bike either on its wheels, or preferably with the frame supported on a block of wood/trolley jack etc, or just sitting on the bench, as in my case.

After this I looked to the swinging arm. I had taken this down to be vapour-blasted and powder-coated, but I had forgotten to remove the rubber oil seals first! The blast cleaners therefore duly returned the swinging arm to me for oil seal removal before it could be powder-coated. As the oil seals sit behind the top-hat bushes, I heated the swinging arm and used a suitably sized socket to drift the bushes out. See photo 19.20.

The bushes and the oil seals that sit underneath them came out relatively easily, and the bushes looked to be in good condition, and could be reused, whilst the oil seals would be replaced as a matter of course. See photo 19.21. I also inspected the swinging arm itself to discover that there was evidence of a saw mark on one of the bearing houses. See photo 19.22. I think that

FITTING THE CRANKCASE & ISOLASTICS

19.17 Strapping down the frame and stand in order to swap the stand bolts.

19.18 Setting the isolastic end float on the front mounting.

19.21 Bushes and oil seals removed.

19.19 Setting the isolastic end float on the rear mounting.

19.22 Damaged swinging arm housing.

19.20 Driving out the bushes from the swinging arm.

19.23 Driving in the new bearings and seals.

may have been caused by some PO having sawn a split in the old bush in order to remove it, and got a little carried away. No real harm done, anyway.

When the swinging arm was back from the powder-coaters I inserted the original bushes with new oil seals. See photo 19.23. This was slightly harder than removing them, as you have to drift them in from the inside of the swinging arm – I used an old socket extension bar as a drift, which I keep for just such situations.

However, when I came to fit the swinging arm onto the engine plates it just wouldn't go on – it was too narrow. Remember that I had already removed the powder-coating from around the bushes, so it wasn't that, but there was no way that the swinging arm would go on, and I ruined the new oil seals trying to force it into position. I therefore removed the bushes again and inspected the new oil seals, comparing them with the originals (never throw anything away until the bike is 100 per cent finished). I twisted the rubber seals to reveal the metal plate inside them so I could measure the thickness. As I thought, the metal of the new seals was that bit thicker than the originals, and it was these, sitting behind the bushes, that made the swinging arm too narrow to fit. See photo 19.24. If you look closely, the new seal on the right is visibly thicker than the original on the left.

I therefore ordered new oil seals, and in the meantime I used my bench grinder to shave a few thou off each inner edge of the swinging arm. See photo 19.25. When the new seals arrived I fitted them to the swinging arm with the bushes and the swinging arm slid perfectly over the engine plates.

I prepared to fit the swinging arm by gathering the requisite parts and liberally coating them with 140w oil. Commando swinging arms are designed to have 140w oil in them, and not grease. Earlier models have grease nipples fitted to them so that fresh oil could be pumped in, but so many owners pumped grease into them by mistake, causing the swinging arm bushes to seize, that on MkIII models they simply stopped putting grease nipples on. I had

HOW TO RESTORE NORTON COMMANDO

19.24 Old and new seals were different thicknesses.

therefore wondered how the bushes were lubricated, if you couldn't pump oil in. The answer was simple: Norton inserted several felt pads into the ends of the bushes and these hold enough oil to lubricate the bushes. I soaked the felt pads in 140w oil (bought from eBay) and liberally coated all the other parts with oil before fitting them. See photo 19.26.

I then slid the spindle into position, through the bushes (see photo 19.27) and then secured it in place with the two cotter pins (MkIII). See photo 19.28. These were later covered with rubber bungs. Note that the cotter pins have fibre washers under them to prevent any oil draining out past them.

I then inserted the first of the four felt pads into position (two on either side) that were impregnated with oil. See photo 19.29. With all the felts in place I inserted the convex end caps. See photo 19.30. These caps need to be hammered in the middle until they turn concave, when they expand slightly and seal the hole they're in (like core plugs on a car engine). If you look at photo 19.30 again you can see that I've started to hammer them in, but not hard enough. I later discovered that they were weeping oil slightly and that I needed to really hammer the centres much harder until they turned fully concave, at which point they sealed properly.

My final job was to fit new rear shock absorbers. The obvious

19.25 Grinding down the inside edges of the swinging arm brackets.

19.28 The two cotter pins inserted, as per the MkIII.

19.29 Inserting the oil soaked felts into the spindle centre.

19.26 Preparing to fit the swinging arm.

19.27 Inserting the swinging arm spindle.

19.30 End plate inserted and semi-fitted.

FITTING THE CRANKCASE & ISOLASTICS

19.31 Swinging arm in place with new Hagon shock absorbers fitted.

choice was new Hagon shocks. They look like the originals, but are far more capable. There are alternatives, such as modern shocks, which work really well, but they look rather anachronistic for my money. Alternatively, there are shocks that are cheaper and look original, but don't work too well. For my money, the Hagons are the best of both worlds. See photo 19.31. Isolastics and swinging arm fitted.

LESSONS LEARNT
• Preferably mask off areas of the frame, isolastic mountings and engine plates that are critical mating surfaces before taking them to be powder-coated.
• If you don't mask the above areas, be ready to spend time grinding off the paint afterwards.
• Adjuster on the right for the front isolastics and on the left for the rear.
• The MkIII uses better and much more user-friendly isolastics than earlier models, and these can be retro-fitted to earlier Commandos.
• If you're facing an impossible job in the workshop, stop work, walk away, and come back to it fresh the next day, when it'll all magically come together without a problem.
• The bolts on the centre stand are fitted from the inside outwards.
• Three of the crankcase bolts are very slightly longer than some of the others – these go through the thick engine plates.
• Stainless steel bolts, etc, are available to replace virtually every fastener on a Commando.
• Pride comes before a fall.
• New swinging arm oil seals appear to be thicker than the originals.
• Commando swinging arms are lubricated with 140w oil – not grease!
• MkIIIs don't have grease nipples on the swinging arms, to prevent owners from pumping grease in by mistake.
• Commando shocks were apparently set at that acute angle by the designers, in order to echo and emphasise the forward slant of the engine.

Chapter 20
Rebuilding the front forks & front wheel

With the crankcases in the frame it was time to get the rest of the frame ready to continue the rebuild, and that meant getting the bike secured on its main stand with the front wheel in position. So, my next job was to rebuild the front forks.

Starting with one leg, I screwed the inner damper rod into the damper tube. See photo 20.1. I fitted a new fibre washer onto the end of the damper tube and added some low strength Loctite to the threads of the bolt that secures the damper tube to the fork leg. I added the Loctite not to prevent the bolt coming loose, but to help prevent it from leaking – another line of defence after the fibre washer. See photo 20.1a. I then inserted the damper tube into the lower fork leg and bolted the two together. See photo 20.2. I was worried that the damper tube would turn along with the bolt as I did this, but I realised I could get a spanner onto the top of the damper tube and hold it firm that way. As a result the damper tube was firmly tightened.

I then turned my attention to the fork stanchion and slid a new oil seal onto it to replace the original. See photo 20.3. Note that there were two bushes at the bottom of the stanchion

20.1 Preparing to insert the damper rod into the damper tube.

20.1a Fibre washer fitted, and the bolt Loctited.

REBUILDING THE FRONT FORKS & FRONT WHEEL

20.2 Tightening the nut holding the damper into the bottom fork leg.

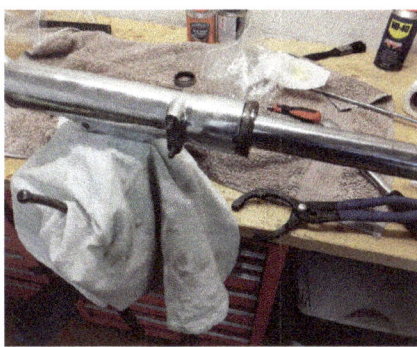

20.5 Tightening the seal retainer with adjustable grips.

20.3 Replacing the front fork oil seal.

20.6 Fork spring inserted and then held in position by a spacer and nut on the inner damper rod.

20.4 Preparing to drive home the fork seal by screwing in the seal retainer.

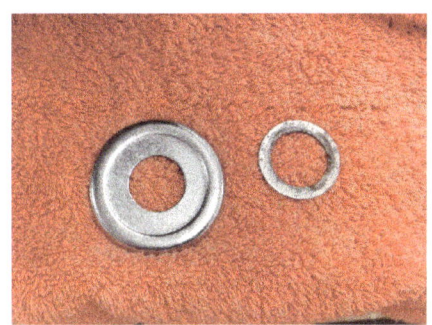

20.7 Two washers to go underneath the top yoke, the one on the right next to the bearing.

that I had not replaced; the phosphor-bronze one that sits in the top of the lower fork leg, and the bush at the bottom of the stanchion. These are known to wear, but they seemed fine in my case and so I decided that there was no need to replace them. If I had needed to do so then the phosphor-bronze one just slides off the top of the stanchion, and to remove the steel one there is a large circlip underneath it, holding it on.

I slid the stanchion into the lower fork leg and prepared to screw the seal retainer into the top of the fork leg. See photo 20.4. Screwing down the seal retainer serves to push the oil seal down and seat it properly, and I tightened it fully with my oil filter grips. See photo 20.5. With the stanchion in position I inserted the fork spring (as it's uniform in shape it can go in either way up) and held it in position with a spacer and nut on the top of the damper rod. See photo 20.6. I also inserted a new drain screw at the bottom of the leg, together with a new fibre washer and Loctite on the threads. After this, I slid a new dust cover (gaiter[1]) down the stanchion to cover the seal retainer (which is why they weren't polished), and the fork was ready to be fitted to the yokes. I then repeated the operation for the second fork.

With the forks completed, I turned my attention to the fork yokes. I prepared to insert the top yoke down through the head bearings (that I'd previously inserted by gently heating the frame and cooling the bearings – don't forget to fit the tube spacer between them). The main thing is to remember to fit the two washers/spacers underneath the top yoke. See photo 20.7. Note that the smaller washer goes underneath the larger one, next to the bearings. I put the top yoke in the freezer to shrink it as much as possible and then slid the stem down through the bearings. See photo 20.8. Note the condensation on the top yoke from the freezer.

---

[1] Note that the short black dust covers are listed as gaiters for the American market, and the long 'concertina' type ones that cover the whole stanchion are referred to as home market ones. I prefer the short ones as I think they look so much better and aren't prone to splitting like the long ones, although they don't protect the exposed sections of the stanchions as much.

HOW TO RESTORE NORTON COMMANDO

20.8 Ice cold top yoke inserted through the head races.

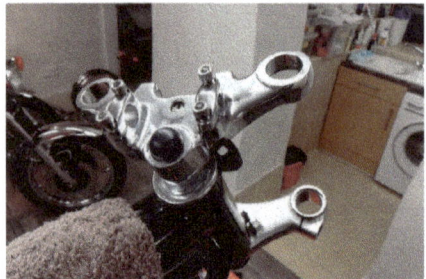

20.9 Bottom yoke loosely bolted onto fork stem.

I loosely screwed the bottom yoke onto the bottom of the stem, followed by the handlebar clamps and the rubber bung in the top yoke. See photo 20.9. Note that I had the top yoke chromed and polished and the bottom yoke just flash chromed (chromed, but not polished first – it's much cheaper and the bottom yoke's not that visible). I like a bit of bling. I was nearly ready to insert the forks, but first I had to remove the mudguard mounting studs from the fork legs. See photo 20.10. I had to do this as I realised that, as part of my stainless steel fasteners pack, I had been supplied with short bolts to replace the studs completely, rather than just stainless nuts to go on the existing studs, and as the studs are UNC thread on both ends, rather than UNF, I didn't have any spare stainless nuts to fit them. I removed the studs by the usual method of locking two (non stainless steel) nuts together and then unscrewing them; they all came out easily – not always the case!

Before I could fit the forks I had to get the frame ready to accept them. At this point, the frame was still sitting on its bottom, and I needed to get it up on its centre stand. I enlisted the help of my neighbour, Rob, and we started by tilting the frame towards the drive side and refilling the crankshaft with oil. Remember I'd tried to do this previously, but failed as the oil kept coming out every time I moved the crankshaft; the idea was that this time the oil would stay put. I used the same method as before, filling my engine reassembly lube squeezy bottle with engine oil and squeezing it into the crankshaft. I think it worked okay, although later on I found that I could prime the engine with oil by simply turning the engine over on the starter anyway, so I'm not sure that this operation is strictly necessary. See photo 20.11. After that, with Rob's help, we put the bike

20.11 Filling the crankshaft full of oil – again!

up onto its main stand and strapped it down so that the headstock was up in the air, giving enough height to fit the front forks and front wheel as easily as possible. See photo 20.12.

I inserted the first fork stanchion up through the bottom yoke, not forgetting to then slide on the headlamp ear, before inserting it fully home. See photo 20.13. Don't forget that I'm not rebuilding the bike completely standard but adding a few bits and making a few alterations to suit me (it's my bike!). One such alteration is to fit aftermarket headlamp ears, as fitted to many café racers of the era. I just don't like the original, fully enclosed ones: they're

20.10 Removing one of the mudguard studs using two nuts locked together.

20.12 Bike on the centre stand with rear strapped down to raise the front end.

REBUILDING THE FRONT FORKS & FRONT WHEEL

20.13 Inserting the stanchions through the yokes – don't forget the headlamp ears!

With the forks in situ, I then added the required grade and amount of suspension fluid: 150ml of 20W fluid per leg, in this case. I used my trusty measuring jug 'borrowed' from the kitchen some years ago and never returned (no, she still doesn't know!) and having measured out the correct quantity, I poured it into each fork leg. See photo 20.15. Note that as the spring and damper tube are in the way, you can only pour a little fluid in at a time, as otherwise it'll overflow. I poured in about 25ml at a time, leaving a couple of minutes between each addition for the oil to seep down.

The forks were now ready to accept the front wheel.

20.15 Measuring 150ml of 20W fork oil for each fork leg.

functional but are a bit too 'pipe and slippers' for my liking. I think it'll look good when it's all together – we'll have to wait and see!

I loosely fitted the new stainless steel front mudguard and stainless steel stay – all with stainless steel fittings, of course! (It's great that you can buy virtually every nut, bolt, fastener and bracket for a Commando in stainless these days.)

See photo 20.14. Everything was only loosely fitted as I still had to fit the front wheel, and then ensure the fork action was sorted and straight before tightening everything. (Only after the bike is finished and I have pumped the front suspension up and down a few times to get everything properly lined-up, will I finally tighten all the bolts on the front forks and front wheel.)

20.14 Forks and mudguard loosely assembled ready to accept the front wheel.

LESSONS LEARNT

• I tend to add low-strength Loctite thread sealant to any thread that might potentially leak oil (eg engine drain plugs, fork drain seals, pressure relief valve, etc) as an extra defence against leaks.

• You can stop the damper tube from turning when tightening the bottom bolt with a spanner on the top (but you can't use this method to *remove* the bolt, as the nut on top of the damper just unscrews).

• Chromed yokes? Aftermarket headlamp ears? Stainless steel fittings? It's your bike: do it how you want it.

• Don't forget the washers underneath the top yoke, or the headlamp ears.

• Long or short gaiters? The choice is yours.

• Don't fully tighten the front suspension until after the bike is completed and bounced a couple of times to straighten everything out.

Chapter 21
Refitting the front wheel & front calliper

With the forks in place it was time to rebuild and then fit the front wheel. I had sent the wheels off to be rebuilt with stainless spokes and rims, and they had returned, looking good, although they had taken longer than expected and I was a bit disappointed in the finish of the rims, which looked rough where the rim had been joined. Anyway, they were back and ready to be assembled.

To begin with I needed to fit new wheel bearings. To do this I followed the standard practice of heating the hub and cooling the bearings before inserting them. When I had done this I inserted the right-hand bearing by driving it home using a suitably sized socket. See photo 21.1. Note that the new bearings are both sealed units that don't require greasing throughout their lifespan.

With the right-hand bearing in place I inserted the bearing spacer (see photo 21.2) before driving home the left-hand bearing, at first with a soft lump hammer (see photo 21.3) and finally with another socket of the correct size.

I finished fitting the bearings by inserting the three-piece grease seal into the left-hand side. See photo 21.4. Although probably not strictly necessary anymore when using sealed bearings, it's still a good idea to fit it as it prevents water and brake dust from getting to the bearing. See Chapter 15 on dismantling the wheels for the order of how the seal fits (Yes, I forgot to take a photo before inserting it!) I then inserted the retaining circlip (MkIII only) on the right-hand side of the hub. See photo 21.5.

It was nearly time to take the wheels down to Manhattan Motorcycles, my good local motorcycle shop (too few and far between these days), to have the tyres fitted and wheels balanced (I hate fitting tyres, and as I needed to have the wheels balanced anyway, it was a good excuse to combine the two). Before I did that I needed to clean the 'new' tyres. The previous

21.2 The wheel spacer inserted.

21.1 Inserting the right-hand wheel bearing.

21.3 The left-hand side bearing inserted.

REFITTING THE FRONT WHEEL & FRONT CALLIPER

21.4 Inserting the three-piece grease seal onto the left-hand bearing.

21.5 Inserting the retaining circlip onto the left-hand bearing.

21.6 Stamp showing the date of tyre manufacture – week 16 of 2015.

21.7 Removing the manufacturer's stickers from the tyres.

21.8 Large rim weights look awkward.

21.9 Spoke weights look better – still not too happy, though.

owner had clearly had brand new tyres fitted, along with a new exhaust system, immediately before laying the bike up and selling it on to my friend and occasional bike importer, Frank, from whom I bought it. The tyres were so unused that they still had the stickers on from the manufacturers!

Looking at the four-digit date stamp on each tyre, the tyres were made in 2015. Every new tyre manufactured has to have a date stamp, usually shortly after the word 'DOT' on the sidewall. In my case the date stamp was 1615. See photo 21.6. The first two digits tell you the week the tyre was made, and the last two which year it was made. So this tyre was made in April (week 16) 2015. As I write it's currently December 2018, so the tyres are completely unused, but already 3½ years old. This shouldn't be a problem as tyres are usually okay to use for at least five years after manufacture. (On usable tyres, the rubber secretes a sticky substance which, when warmed up, keeps them soft and supple – as the rubber gets older, regardless of use, the rubber dries out and hardens and the sticky substance is no longer secreted when warm; not good news for motorcyclists!) Anyway, the tyres still had the manufacturer's label on them and I had to remove this unholy sticky mess with the aid of a heat gun. See photo 21.7. I then took the wheels and tyres down to the shop for fitting and balancing.

NB: With both wheels having 19in rims, there's not a lot of tyre choice out there, and what there is tends to be quite skinny (100/90-19) but the bikes were designed to run on these. If you want a slightly fatter back tyre, you can change the rim to an 18in, for which there is a much greater tyre choice available, but the wheel is that bit smaller. That's a matter of personal preference, but the choice is there. (I have an 18in rear on one of my Tridents which it looks good, and riding it, you wouldn't notice the difference.)

However, the bike shop then rang to say that the wheels were both considerably out of balance and required a lot of weights to get them into balance and that there were so many weights they were quite unsightly. See photo 21.8. They therefore recommended that I opt for spoke weights that are more traditional and slightly less unsightly. I agreed to this, and the wheels did indeed look better than before. See photo 21.9. However, I'm still rather annoyed that these are clearly not very good rims as they shouldn't have needed so much weight to balance them in the first place. Also, if you look at the left-hand side of photo 21.9 again, you can see the poor quality of the finishing of the rim where the two ends were joined – which is where the weights were required on both rims. Not great.

Anyway, the wheels came back with the tyres fitted and balanced, and I prepared the forks to accept the front wheel by fitting the front mudguard and the mounting bracket and calliper for the uprated front brake I'd chosen. See photo 21.10. I'd decided to go for a Norvil set-up with large floating disc and APP calliper. This would later be combined with an uprated master cylinder from Andover Norton, which I hoped would

HOW TO RESTORE NORTON COMMANDO

21.10 Fitting the uprated calliper and mounting bracket to the fork leg.

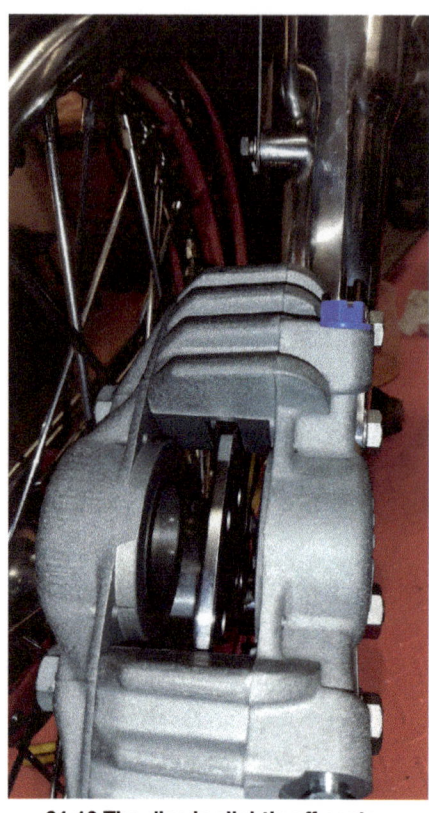

21.12 The disc is slightly off centre.

give me much improved braking, combined with decent looks. (In my case the latter is as important as the former – I'm a bit of a poser!)

My next job was to fit the new, snazzy looking floating disc to the front wheel. See photo 21.11. This was harder than it sounds as the mounting holes on the new disc didn't quite align with the studs on my wheel, and I had to carefully enlarge a few of the holes with my Dremmel to get the whole thing to mate up, but eventually it was on. Note that I also put a bit of grease on the grease seal on this side of the wheel as the grease seal turns with the wheel, but the spacer that sits inside it when the wheel's fitted, does not. I therefore greased it so there was no friction between the two.

With the frame pulled quite far down at the back, so as to lift the forks as high as possible, I loosely inserted the wheel, guiding the disc into the calliper as I did so, and loosely inserting the wheel spindle and spacers. Note that the spacer with the long extension goes on the disc side. However, as soon as the wheel was in place, it was clear that the disc was very slightly off-centre in the brake calliper. If you look at photo 21.12 you might be able to tell that the calliper is running too far to the outside of the calliper – but it's hard to see as I couldn't take a photo straight-on as the tyre was in the way. Anyway, I tried to see if I could insert a brake pad into the smaller gap, to the outside, but couldn't – the gap was just too small.

I therefore removed the calliper and its rather large and slightly clumsy mounting plate (required to take the replacement calliper and larger disc) and used three good quality washers to space the mounting bracket out slightly, and then reassembled it. It worked! The disc and calliper were now exactly central to one another. I prepared to fit the new brake pads and put a little copper slip grease on the backs to help prevent brake squeal. (There's nothing worse than brake squeal to turn you right off your fantastic new brake conversion!) See photo 21.13. The new pads then slotted perfectly into the new calliper. See photo 21.14.

The front wheel was now loosely in position, complete with new brake calliper. I fully tightened the

21.11 New disc mounted on the hub – eventually!

21.13 Slightly grease the rear of the disc pads to prevent squeal.

REFITTING THE FRONT WHEEL & FRONT CALLIPER

21.14 Disc centralised and pads inserted.

front wheel spindle to check that everything was turning smoothly and freely, and not catching or binding anywhere – all good, phew! – and I then slackened off the wheel spindle again. Note that I hadn't tightened anything fully up at this point as the forks weren't properly settled and correctly positioned yet – the whole thing (including the mudguard, which can affect the fork action) would be fully tightened later on.

I loosened off the strap holding the rear of the frame down so that the front wheel was lowered to sit on the bike stand, after which I re-tensioned the two holding straps. The bike was now secure and solid and capable of withstanding the rigours and stresses of a rebuild without falling off the lift – hopefully! See photo 21.15 of the bike now with front wheel and forks in situ. Looking good!

LESSONS LEARNT

• Don't drive a bearing home on the inner race if you can possibly avoid it. Try to find a drift or socket that will press on the outer race.
• Good local bike shops are, unfortunately, all too rare these days.
• Tyres are stamped on the sidewall with the week and year of manufacture, shortly after the word DOT, using a four-digit code.
• Newish tyres secrete some kind of sticky goo when warm that keeps them soft and pliant – the older a tyre gets, the less it secretes the sticky goo, and the harder it gets.
• Cheap wheel rims – not great.
• Disc brakes won't work properly if they're not lined up straight to begin with.
• I always slightly grease the rear of brake pads to try and reduce the possibility of brake squeal.
• Don't fully tighten the front suspension yet as it needs to be fettled first.
• Later on I modified the rather clumsy calliper mounting plate so it didn't look quite so slab-like. See chapter 38.

21.15 Front wheel and front forks in place.

Chapter 22
Fitting the timing case

Time to fit the timing case to the crankcases. To begin with, I finally discovered why the bike had wet-sumped so badly before I dismantled it. It turned out that the anti-drain valve (which is like a piston in a cylinder) had seized in the bottom of its shaft. See photo 22.1. What I initially thought was the bottom of the shaft was, in fact, the top of the seized anti-drain valve. The valve has a small spring underneath it that is supposed to push it out, but the valve had jammed in its shaft, and the spring wasn't strong enough to free it, and it was so seized, in fact, that it had survived being polished at the metal finishers! Apparently, this is quite common and can be alleviated to some degree by fitting a stainless steel valve to replace the original, which I duly purchased. However, fitting a stainless valve doesn't necessarily cure the problem, as I was to discover later. (See Chapter 38.)

In order to remove the stuck valve I used my small air compressor. There is a small oilway that runs to the back of the valve, and this is perfect for driving out the valve. See photo 22.2. Just a quick blast of compressed air and the valve was free. I was then able to fully remove the valve and its spring from the casing. See photo 22.3.

Time to sort the valve timing. Setting the valve timing on a Commando is pretty straightforward, and as long as you double-check everything, there are no nasty or tricky bits. To begin with I highlighted the timing marks with Tippex, to make them stand out clearly. I then loosely dry-assembled the various sprockets to ensure I knew exactly what should go where. If you look at photo 22.4 you can see the pinion on the crankshaft (bottom left) turned so that its timing mark lines up with the timing mark on the idler sprocket above it. Note that the timing mark on the idler sprocket is already painted red at the factory (when the chain is fitted this timing mark is very difficult to see). There are then two further marks on the idler sprocket and camshaft sprocket, which will be used when the timing chain is fitted.

22.1 Non-return valve jammed down inside the timing case.

22.2 Using compressed air to force out the valve.

22.3 Non-return valve removed from the timing case.

FITTING THE TIMING CASE

22.4 Camshaft sprocket.

Before fitting the timing assembly I needed to fit the timing chain tensioner, which (needless to say) is slightly different for a MkIII model, with the front and backplate being the same, unlike on earlier models. See photo 22.5.

With the tensioner in place, I looped the timing chain round the sprockets and fitted them in position. See photo 22.6. Note that there should be ten chain PINS between the sprocket timing marks (don't say five links, as that can be slightly confusing). Also note how difficult it is to see the timing marks between the crankshaft pinion and the idler sprocket with the chain in situ. I also Tippexed the chain with a ten pin gap between the two marks, just to make doubly sure that everything was set correctly.

When I was satisfied that everything was timed correctly, I tightened up the nut on the camshaft sprocket and the worm drive (left-hand thread) for the oil pump that goes on the end of the crankshaft. In order to do this I locked the engine by passing a long screwdriver through the gudgeon pins on the pistons, which jammed against the top of the crankcases that I'd previously padded. See photo 22.7. Note that I'd rather prematurely fitted the pistons (this is covered in the next chapter), and it would have been easier to lock the engine without the pistons in place – but they did help to protect the con rods. Also note that there are no torque figures given in the manual for either the camshaft sprocket or crankshaft nut. I therefore took advice from the experts, and tightened the camshaft nut up to about 20lb/ft and the oil pump drive worm gear up to about 35lb/ft (left-hand thread), putting Loctite on both. (Having completed this I belatedly realised that I had a special tool (!) to support the idler shaft during this operation, as there is quite a bit of stress put on it, but I forgot to use it – without apparent damage to the shaft.)

Another thing to note is that as the camshaft sprocket on a Commando can only be fitted in one position on the camshaft, the valve timing is fixed and cannot be fine-tuned. On Triumph Tridents, for example, there are three keyways on the camshaft sprocket and with the aid of careful measurement of the crankshaft and the valves, the valve timing can be altered slightly to provide optimum valve timing (as opposed to the generic standard factory setting, which is often a few degrees out). However, there is no such provision on Commandos (because there's only one camshaft that drives both the inlet and exhaust valves, so they can't be altered independently) so that makes life a lot easier, if not quite as accurate.

I then looked at the oil pump. My first impressions were that the pump was in good condition – I pushed, and pulled, and twisted the main driveshaft, but it showed no play at all, suggesting that all was well, without any excessive wear. However, I still wanted to dismantle the pump to double check that everything was okay (and also because this is supposed to be a manual, I thought I'd better cover it!) But I immediately discovered that the four screws holding the pump together were locked with double punch marks and showed no signs of wanting to let go. See photo 28.8. After some pondering I decided that discretion was the better part of valour and left it as it was.

Two points of note vis-à-vis the pump though: to remove the pinion on the top of the pump, replace the pump in the timing case – the pinion will then engage with its worm drive on the crankshaft, allowing the nut holding the pinion in place to be removed without the pump turning. Also, apparently most wear occurs between the cogs of the pump and the two end plates, and

22.6 Cam chain assembled with ten chain rollers between sprocket marks.

22.7 Locking the engine with a screwdriver through the gudgeon pins to tighten the sprockets.

22.5 Cam chain tensioner assembly.

HOW TO RESTORE NORTON COMMANDO

22.8 Oil pump assembly screws locked with punchmarks.

22.10 Priming the crankcases with engine oil.

22.11 New stainless steel anti-drain valve.

this can be removed by grinding the plates flat, if required (when you've got the pump apart!). Also, some owners believe that wet-sumping can either be eliminated, or at best reduced, by fitting a new oil pump. This is because the oil has to drain through the pump, and if it can't get through the pump, it can't wet-sump. I'm not so sure about this myself, as why did Norton feel the need to fit an anti-drain valve if they didn't need to, and all my bikes have wet-sumped regardless of a new oil pump or not. But it's something to consider.

I prepared to refit the oil pump using a gasket used dry (you don't want to accidentally block the oilways with gasket goo) and a new rubber oil seal over the short outlet pipe. See photo 22.9. This little round oil seal is essential. Without it oil is just pumped into the crankcases instead of under high pressure to the crankshaft, so it's always worth replacing, no matter what – and you should doubly check that it's still in place when the timing cover is fitted, as it's easily knocked off.

I then prepared to bolt the pump to the casing using the two mounting bolts, which gave me a big dilemma – to use the two washers on the bolts or not? I knew that on earlier models you definitely fit the bolts without washers

22.9 Oil pump with new oil seal fitted, and washers on mounting bolts.

– but this was a MkIII. There is more than some confusion as to whether or not washers should be fitted on MkIII models. When I dismantled the bike, washers were fitted, the parts catalog lists two washers, the workshop manual says don't use washers. Confusing. After consulting the experts I decided to fit the washers, but no-one was quite sure whether I should or shouldn't, so if you're in the same position, it may well be worth taking advice. I then tightened the bolts up to the required torque (slightly lower for the Mark III) and the oil pump was in place. Let's hope it stays there!

After this I poured some engine oil into the crankcases. I usually do this when rebuilding an engine – it's not in the manuals, but I think it helps on first start-up. By already having some oil in the crankcases it means that there is at least some in there to splash about and lubricate everything. I added the oil at this point so I didn't forget to do it later on, and while I still had full access to the crankcase tops. See photo 22.10.

I replaced the original anti-drain valve with a stainless steel one, as recommended. See photo 22.11. However, on testing it I found that it still jammed in the casing when fully depressed and I spent some time lightly sanding and polishing the casing and the valve, until it slid smoothly. (Although it still jammed. See Chapter 38.)

Turning to the timing case, I inserted the two new oil seals – the main one that fits around the end of the crankshaft, held in place with a circlip, and the oil seal that fits around the end of the camshaft. The crankshaft seal has the closed side uppermost (facing you), and the camshaft seal has the open side uppermost (open side always goes towards the oil – but you have to think about the crankshaft seal a bit, and where the oil is coming from!). See photo 22.12.

I also removed the little bung, which I'd made with tissue to stop the oil I'd primed it with from coming out, from the end of the crankshaft. See photo 22.4 again. Now, this was a really bad thing to do – blocking up any oilway is not good practice at all. You can easily forget to remove it on assembly, or, if you do remove it, some of it might break off and get left behind in the oilway. Either way, it's a bad idea. I had oil starvation to one of the camshafts on my E-Type once, for just this reason, and it took me over a year to find the problem! That was a year of total frustration as I took different bits of the engine apart, spent loads of money, and couldn't enjoy driving the car, all because of a bit of tissue in one of the oil feed unions. So, remember: do as I say, not as I do!

FITTING THE TIMING CASE

22.12 Timing case with two new oil seals in place.

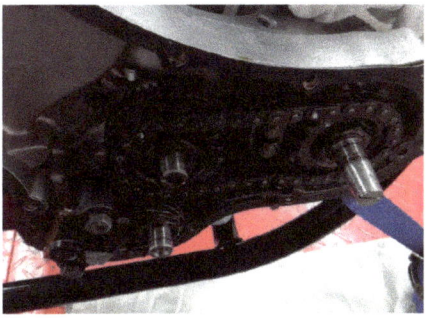

22.14 Tool in place to protect the points oil seal.

22.15 Oil pressure release valve cleaned and ready for assembly.

22.13 Wellseal and gasket applied, ready to fit timing case.

22.16 Timing cover and oil pressure release valve fitted.

I then applied Wellseal to both mating faces and put the main gasket in place along with the special round rubber seal on the outside of the oil pump. See photo 22.13. I then screwed my special tool into the end of the camshaft, which allows the camshaft oil seal to slide into place without damaging the lip, as it goes on lip side first, and can be easily damaged by the end of the camshaft. See photo 22.14. I then presented the cover to the crankcase, ensuring that neither the oil pump anti-drain valve or the oil pump rubber seal became dislodged in the process, and screwed it on (on a MkIII all the screws are of the same length).

With the cover in place, I cleaned and prepared the oil pressure release valve for refitting, using new copper washers (see photo 22.15), and then fitted it to the timing case – once again smearing the threads with Loctite to try and avoid leaks, and torquing it up to the prescribed 25lb/ft.

The (highly polished) timing cover and oil pressure release valve were now in position! It was beginning to look like an engine again! See photo 22.16.

LESSONS LEARNT

• The anti-drain valve can seize in the casing.
• The timing chain should be set with ten pins between the two timing marks (some people talk about links, but I think that's a bit confusing).
• It's not a great idea to fit the pistons before fitting the timing case – unless you're a bit of a numpty.
• Fit the oil pump with washers or without on a MkIII? Not sure.
• I recommend pouring some engine oil into the crankcases so there's already oil in there at start-up.
• Don't forget to fit the circular rubber oil seal to the outside of the oil pump.
• Don't forget to fit the oil seals in the timing case, together with the anti-drain valve (MkIII).
• I would recommend using the small special tool to help you fit the camshaft oil seal – it's difficult to fit the seal and not damage its lip.
• When the timing cover's fitted you know you're on your way!
• I think that it is pretty straightforward to upgrade an earlier model to a MkIII timing case, complete with anti-drain valve, if so desired. This is the easiest and least controversial way to fit an anti-oil drain valve to a Commando in order to prevent wet-sumping. See Chapter 38 for more on this.
• You should never block an oilway, even only temporarily, as otherwise you're courting disaster – I know from bitter experience.

Chapter 23
Fitting the cylinder barrels

Time to fit the cylinder barrels. (Note that I had already fitted the pistons at this point, but I'm covering the fitting of them in this chapter.) (Also note that if yours is a MkIII and you're planning on refitting the original airbox, then do so before refitting the barrels.)

Having previously checked the cylinder barrels for wear (see below), I had ordered a new set of standard pistons, as I needed to replace the one damaged by a foreign body in the combustion chamber, and pistons should be replaced as a pair unless they are exactly the same make and type. It would have been very risky to try and reuse the original, damaged piston, as although it showed little sign of wear, the damage caused by the foreign body in the combustion chamber could have weakened it and it might have suddenly broken up – not good. So, if only for peace of mind, I bought a new pair, together with new piston rings.

To begin with I checked the packaging, which showed where each set of rings should be inserted on the piston. See photo 23.1. I then carefully fitted the piston rings onto the pistons, beginning with the bottom one – the oil ring. I was very pleased to discover that the oil rings in this case were two-piece items with the main ring sitting over the top of a separate spring. On previous occasions I've been supplied with three-piece oil rings, with two thin rings sitting either side of a corrugated spring, and they can be hard to fit – and on more than one occasion I've had one of the thin rings un-seat itself during fitting, damaging itself or, worse still, scoring the cylinder wall, which meant I suddenly required (another) re-bore – and another new set of larger pistons and rings! Not great.

As I fitted the rings I checked each one for anything that suggested they had to be fitted a particular way up, and, sure enough, the second compression rings had a stamp on them saying 'TOP' so they had to be fitted with that side to the top. See photo 23.2. The other rings could be fitted either way up. Note that I fitted the rings to the pistons by hand, carefully opening each one with my fingernails and then sliding it down the piston until it was in the required groove. It was only after I'd finished, that I remembered I'd recently treated myself to a pair of piston ring pliers that are made specifically for this job. Still unused in the tool cupboard! Doh!

Note that I had carried out a variety of checks on the piston rings and pistons before fitting them, but

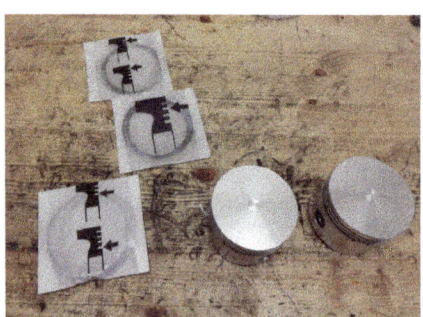

23.1 New pistons and piston rings; the wrapping shows which groove they go in.

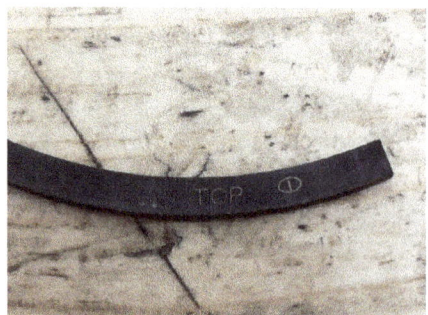

23.2 Some rings are marked as to which way up they go.

FITTING THE CYLINDER BARRELS

23.3 Inserting gudgeon pin circlips with the barrels covered.

there was still one very important check that I should have done, but forgot! Bugger! Any ideas? Answer in the 'lessons learnt' section below.

With the rings in place I fitted the pistons to the con rods. Before fitting the pistons I double checked that it didn't matter which way round the pistons faced (been there, done that!), but as there were no depressions in the piston crowns to avoid the valves, or arrows on the piston crowns, in this case I decided that it didn't matter, so they could go on facing either way. Having also checked that it didn't matter which way round the circlips went (sometimes they have a flat and a rounded side, and the flat side faces inwards) I fitted a circlip in one side of each piston (which would be the inner side of the piston, when fitted). After this, I liberally coated the gudgeon pins, con rods and pistons with assembly lubricant, and then gently heated the pistons and con rods to ensure the gudgeon pins could slide freely in them. I then slid the gudgeon pins through the pistons and con rods and checked that the pistons swivelled freely on the gudgeon pins, with no tight spots. All was okay.

I then prepared to fit the outer circlips. Before doing so, I stuffed a rag down inside the crankcase opening to stop any errant circlip from dropping down inside the cases. See photo 23.3. It's bad enough if a circlip does ping off whilst you're trying to fit it, as they tend to vanish into the fifth dimension and cause a frustrating delay while a new one is ordered, but if you're not sure whether it's gone down into the crankcases, it's worse! As you can never find a circlip that's pinged off, if you don't cover the crankcases then you're never quite sure if it's gone down there or not, and you might spend many happy hours with a magnet, fishing around in the cases to see if it's in there. Been there, done that, too! I also rotated the circlips so that the gap in them didn't align with the cutaway on the pistons.

With the pistons and rings fitted it was time to fit the cylinder barrels. After I had the barrels blast cleaned and powder-coated I checked the bores for wear to see if a re-bore was required. Note that I did this after I'd had the barrels cleaned and painted, because the cleaning/painting process is rather harsh and wet, and if you have the barrels honed or re-bored first, they can come back from the cleaners/painters needing another re-bore!

To begin with I used my internal bore gauge to check the bores for true. See photo 23.4. Cylinder bores tend to wear unevenly; from side-to-side, and from top to bottom, due to the way the pistons are turned by the crankshaft. As a result, bores can become oval and cone shaped, with the bores wider at the bottom than the top, and wider front to back than side-to-side. By using a bore gauge I was able to ascertain that there was very little difference in the readings from all sections of the bores and that therefore the cylinders weren't worn to excess.

I carefully checked the bores for any damage or scoring, but there was only minimal scoring evident. I therefore decided that I only needed the barrels honed, and not re-bored. I decided to take the barrels to the engineers to be honed as, although I have a honing tool that fits in my cordless drill, the engineers can hone them much better than I can. I was also able to confirm with them that a re-bore wasn't required in this case. Note that if you don't have a bore gauge you can just take your barrels down to the engineers and get them to measure everything for you, and get their expert opinion on what work needs doing. I also now ask the engineers to hone my cylinders, rather than doing it myself, as I used to. It's very important to get the correct grade of honing done on the barrels. Pistons using older style piston rings, like ours, need a coarser hone than modern, lighter piston rings. I would recommend about a 180 grit hone, as opposed to finer 'plateau honing' for newer style rings. It's very important to discuss this with your engineers – and piston ring suppliers, if necessary – before going ahead with any honing (you don't want to spend ages rebuilding the engine, only to find that it's smoking a bit because you didn't have the barrels honed properly).

With the barrels back from being honed, I cleaned them thoroughly as they were dirty from being blasted, painted and honed. First and foremost I cleaned the bores themselves as they invariably come back from the engineers honed, but not cleaned, and the bores are always full of iron filings. I cleaned them by squirting WD40 down the bores and then wiping them with paper towel. After this I used my set of oilway

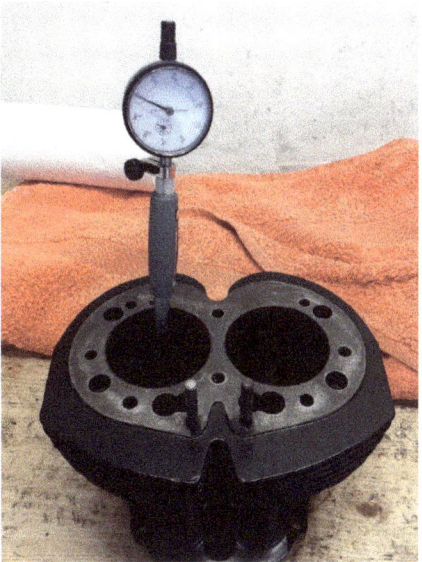

23.4 Checking the barrels for wear.

23.5 Cleaning the pushrod tubes.

23.6 Cleaning the oil drain.

cleaning brushes to thoroughly clean out the oilways. I began with the pushrod tubes (see photo 23.5), and then continued by cleaning out the oil drain passage that runs down through the barrels from the cylinder head. See photo 23.6. Note that although most oil in the cylinder head runs away down the pushrod tubes, the oil on the inlet side of the head is trapped, and so this extra drain passage is provided for that purpose and must be kept clear.

With the barrels thoroughly cleaned, I checked the tappets (cam followers) for signs of excessive wear or damage, but they all looked fine. I had carefully labelled them during the dismantling process so I knew which one went where. If you are to reuse such items it's important to replace them in the same place they came from as otherwise wear can be accelerated, sometimes alarmingly. See photo 23.7 of the tappets being inserted into the barrels having coated them first with assembly lube. When all four were in situ, I fitted the locating plates and secured them with the appropriate screws smeared with Loctite, before adding locking wire, for added security, as per the manual. See photo 23.8.

My next job was to prepare the pistons to accept the barrels. I needed some way to hold the pistons upright and still, and I found an old piece of dowel that seemed to fit the bill. I cut this into two short lengths and trial fitted them under the pistons: they were just the right size. See photo 23.9. At this point I also rotated the piston rings so that the gaps were all where they should be according to the workshop manual. Top ring with gap to the front, second ring with the gap to the rear, and the oil ring with the gap to the side, but not directly in line with the gudgeon pin. See photo 23.9 again. I was rather surprised at this, as I was taught to never have the ring gaps in line with either the front or rear of the piston – but every day in the workshop is a school day.

I made the final preparations to fit the barrels by coating the mating surfaces with Wellseal and fitting the piston ring clamps. These should be fitted tightly, but not so tightly that you can't move the clamps. See photo 23.10. I then lightly oiled the pistons below the piston rings with engine oil, and left the top section of the pistons, and the cylinders, dry. This was to help the piston rings bed in. Note that there are various different recommendations for how much oil to use, and where to smear it, when refitting pistons, but that's the way I've always done it, and it works okay for me. You need

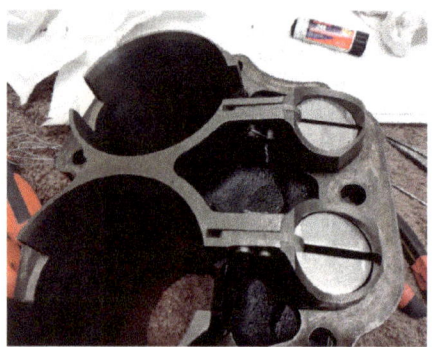

23.8 Tappets fitted and screws lock-wired together.

23.9 The pistons held in position with dowels, and the piston ring gaps aligned as per the manual.

23.7 Fitting the tappets.

23.10 Piston ring clamps on and Wellseal applied.

FITTING THE CYLINDER BARRELS

23.11 Barrels lowered, but the conrods were jammed in the crankcases.

23.12 An extra dowel at the front to hold the pistons central. Piston ring clamps being removed.

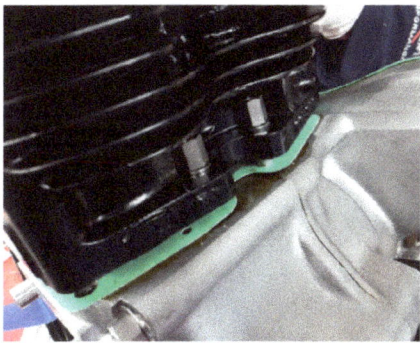

23.13 Screwing on the rear cylinder base nuts before the barrels are fully down.

the piston rings to bed-in by scraping against the cylinder walls – too much lubrication will prevent this from happening.

When all was ready I put the cylinder base gasket in place, re-inserted the dowels under the pistons, and prepared to fit the barrels. As usual on these occasions, I called upon my friend and neighbour, Rob, to help with this procedure. I always think it's best to fit barrels with the aid of another pair of hands – even if you don't need them, it's good to have someone there 'just in case,' and it makes the whole job a lot easier.

We duly lifted the barrels onto the pistons and tapped them down. All seemed well, and the piston rings went into the barrels without incident. However, as I tried to remove the dowels from under the pistons in order to lower the barrels fully, I realised that the engine was locked solid and wouldn't turn. I couldn't work out what the problem was, but it was clear that the engine was somehow completely locked and I couldn't turn it either way. This also meant that I couldn't remove the dowels that were now firmly jammed under the pistons. See photo 23.11. I had no alternative but to abandon the attempt and remove the barrels to see what the problem was. With the barrels (and piston ring clamps) removed, the engine was immediately free, and it was clear that the con rods had been jamming against the inside of the crankcase, pushed forward by the weight of the barrels. I therefore added a third piece of dowel, in front of the other two and resting against the crankcase studs, to hold the pistons more centrally, thus keeping the con rods away from the crankcase mouth, and we tried again, this time successfully. See photo 23.12.

With the piston ring clamps and wooden dowels removed we continued to tap the barrels down, but stopped before they were fully home. It's important to note that you have to start the nuts on the rear barrel studs before the barrels are fully down as otherwise there's not enough room between the stud and

23.14 Torquing the cylinder barrel Allen bolts.

117

HOW TO RESTORE NORTON COMMANDO

the bottom fin on the barrel to get the nuts in. See photo 23.13.

With the barrels then tapped fully home I did up the various nuts holding the barrel to the crankcases and, this being an 850, I also inserted the four long Allen through bolts that run from the top of the barrels down into the crankcases. These are there to avoid the barrels cracking at the bottom and lifting off the crankcases! (Those bolts should be called 'Alan bolts'!) They were then torqued down to 25lb/ft as per the manual. See photo 23.14. I was then also supposed to torque down the cylinder base nuts to between 20 and 25lb/ft – but I didn't. I have two torque wrenches, a large one (of which I'm very proud as I inherited it from my father) and a small one for accessing difficult to reach areas. Neither would fit onto the base nuts. How is one supposed to torque up a nut that you can't get a torque wrench onto? No idea, so I didn't. I used a ring spanner and my 'mechanic's sense' to tell me when the nuts were at about the right torque, and that was it. Is there a tool that can torque these nuts up accurately? Possibly, but I don't know of it.

Whatever the case, the barrels were now fitted and looking good. See photo 23.15 of the engine beginning to look like an engine! Hurrah! Note that the first thing I did (even before tightening the nuts/bolts down) was to slowly and carefully turn the engine over to check that all was well and that there was no stiffness or scoring of the barrels that

23.15 Cylinder barrels in place.

would have indicated an unseated or damaged ring. I turned the engine over (backwards) by temporarily fitting the rotor nut to the drive side end of the crankshaft and turning the engine over on that. Although the nut tightens on the shaft as you do this, it came off easily enough with the impact driver when I needed to remove it.

LESSONS LEARNT
- Check piston rings for the order they go on the piston, and to see if they need to be fitted a certain way up.
- The pistons on a Commando can be fitted either way round (or at least the ones I used – check all pistons with the manufacturers if in doubt).
- Cover the top of the crankcases with cloth before fitting the gudgeon pin circlips to avoid a circlip pinging off and going down inside the crankcases. Also don't have the circlip gap at the bottom and check if the circlips have a flat and rounded side, if so, flat side out.
- The gap in the piston rings should be turned to the following positions: top ring gap to the front, middle ring gap to the rear, oil ring gap to the side but not in line with the gudgeon pin.
- And the check I forgot to complete? I forgot to check the piston ring gaps! Piston rings should have a gap of the correct length between their two ends – too large a gap and the ring won't work very well, too small and the ring won't have enough room to expand when hot, and can badly score the barrels or seize the engine completely! Now, new rings are supposed to be pre-gapped to the correct dimension – but we all know that such things aren't always as they're supposed to be, and you should check every part before fitting, regardless. To check the gap on piston rings you should slide them down inside the cylinder bores, and measure the gap between the two ends. If it's too small you should then file the end of the ring down until it's right, and if it's too big then send the rings back to your supplier. See

23.16 How piston ring gaps should be checked.

photo 23.16. I completely forgot to do this and I can only hope that the manufacturer were as good as their word and that the gaps were correct. Fingers crossed! The correct piston ring gaps on a Commando are as follows: top ring 10-12 thou, middle ring 8-12 thou. Oil ring, no gap specified.
- Hone barrels to about 180 grit and don't over-lubricate the cylinder bores and pistons before refitting, to ensure the piston rings bed-in properly.
- When fitting the barrels, the con rods can jam in the crankcases if they're not in the centre of the crankcase mouth.
- Start the nuts on the rear crankcase studs before the barrels are fully down.
- Torque the cylinder nuts down to the settings specified in the workshop manual – how? No idea.
- You can turn the engine over backwards with the rotor nut on the end of the crankshaft – but make sure you know how you're going to undo it!
- Note that if you're planning to refit the original airbox on a MkIII, then now's a good time to do it! There's a lot of talk about the horn being one of the first things to fit on a Commando, but if you want to put the airbox back into a MkIII then do it before the cylinder barrels are on, as otherwise, at best, it's a nightmare, at worst, it's impossible!

Chapter 24
Refurbishing & refitting the cylinder head

It was time to reassemble and refit the cylinder head. When the head was back from the vapour-blasters I gave it a very thorough wash in the sink, repeatedly flushing it out to ensure that it was completely free of beads from the blast cleaning process. I then checked it for anything that required work, and indeed, there were a couple of jobs that obviously required doing. To begin with there was a broken fin that needed mending (see photo 24.1) and I also needed new valve guides. On removing the head it was clear that oil had been leaking down the valve guides into the combustion chamber, and when I checked the guides they were indeed clearly worn. NB: At this point also check such things as sparkplug threads and exhaust manifold threads, and the combustion chambers, for cracks, etc, in case they require work, too.

To check valve guides for wear, firstly remove the valves from the head with a valve spring compressor (see chapter 12), and then loosely slide the valve back into the guide. When the valve is nearly fully home, try rocking it from side-to-side; if there's any play at all, then the guides need replacing. Guides tend to wear more than other engine parts as the action of the rockers on the tops of the valves pushes them sideways as well as downwards, and this wears out the guides. I therefore sent the head off to engine guru Dave Smith for the fin to be mended and new guides to be fitted. I could have had a go at replacing the guides myself, but experience has shown me that it's just a heck of a lot easier to get someone else to do it for you!

I also bought new valves, as a matter of course, even though they actually showed little wear on their stems, unlike the guides. But if you're fitting new guides, it's always wise to fit new valves as well to avoid rapid wear. I made sure I sent the new valves off with the head so that Dave could properly cut the valve seats to fit the new valves, and subsequently grind the valves in for me.

As part of my checking of the head, I couldn't help but notice the poor quality of the casting. It really looked like someone had cast the head in their garden shed. This head had been cast by Norton for over 20 years, I think, and yet the standard of casting was rudimentary at best. Look at photo 24.2 showing the

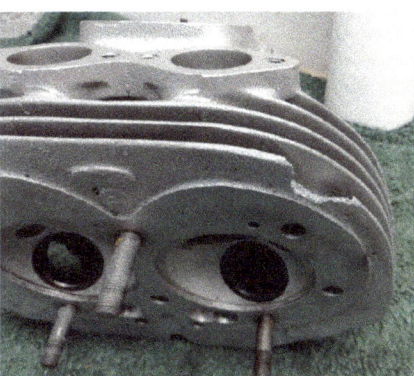

24.1 Head required broken fin to be mended and new valve guides.

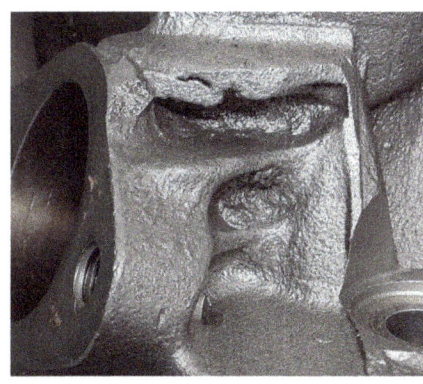

24.2 Poor quality casting.

HOW TO RESTORE NORTON COMMANDO

standard of finish of part of the head – and I could easily have posted at least another ten pictures. I do have to shake my head at this – even the cylinder heads on my Triumph Tridents are smooth and shiny, and yet this Commando one is rough beyond belief. This was the flagship model produced by Norton and they sold them looking like this? Words fail me. Have a look at the photo of my Kawasaki cylinder head in Chapter 17 by way of comparison.

Anyway, when the head came back from Dave's with the new guides fitted and the broken fin looking like new, I set to work giving the head a thorough clean. To begin with I checked that the drain hole from the inlet rockers, which goes down through the barrels, was clear. See photo 24.3. I then cleaned out the oilways that go from the central rocker feed to the ends of the rocker shafts. See photo 24.4. With everything thoroughly cleaned and checked, I set about reassembly.

Before refitting the valves, I checked the free length of the valve springs, and these were shown to be shorter than they should be, and I therefore bought a replacement set. See photo 24.5. Note that there are two springs on each valve, an inner and an outer one. If you look at photo 24.6 you can see the new valve and springs on the left, waiting to be fitted, and the old ones on the right. I duly fitted the two inlet valves without problem, once again using a combination of a small screwdriver and my telescopic magnet to seat the collets round the top of the valve

24.4 Cleaning the oil feeds to the rockers.

24.5 Measuring the valve spring free length.

stems. I also fitted the two new valve stem seals to the tops of the inlet valve guides, making doubly sure the lips on the seals were properly engaged with the groove in the valve guide.

However, when I prepared to fit the exhaust valves, I discovered an extra part that hadn't been previously fitted to the inlet valves – a heat insulating fibre washer. If you look at photo 24.7 you can see the fibre washer just above the tip of the screwdriver. This washer goes on first and sits under the base plate for the springs. So the question was, should there also be a fibre washer on the inlet valves? After a bit of checking, the answer was yes. I therefore had to order two new insulating washers and take the inlet valves apart again ready to accept them. I then discovered that the fibre washers wouldn't fit over the tops of the valve stem oil seals and these would have to be removed first, but I couldn't get them off without destroying them. I therefore had to now order two new valve stem oil seals! Damn! Four days wasted! Anyway, eventually the new seals arrived and I fitted the new heat insulating washers, and then the new oil seals. See photo 24.7a showing one of the new fibre washers and oil seals in place.

Now the question arises as to why these insulating washers are required underneath the valve spring plates. What are they insulating? The only thing they can protect would appear to be the valve springs – but why? My only conclusion is that while they are heat insulating, that

24.3 Cleaning the drain hole in the head.

24.6 New valves and springs ready to be fitted.

REFURBISHING & REFITTING THE CYLINDER HEAD

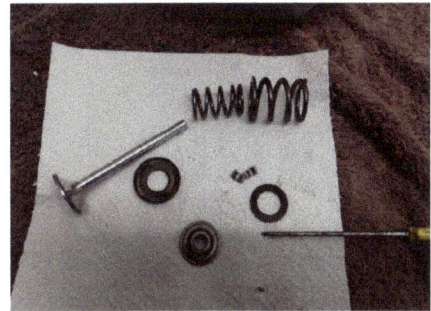

24.7 What's this above the screwdriver? An insulating washer.

24.9 Heating the head to 150 degrees.

24.7a Insulating washer now in position underneath the valve springs, and replacement valve stem seal fitted.

24.8 Worn rocker shafts.

24.10 Inserting the new rocker shafts into the head – oilway opposite to the one in the rockers.

24.11 Inserting the rockers with their washers, as the rocker shafts are inserted.

is just a coincidence, and they are in fact used to protect/cushion the cylinder head from the valve springs – they're strong enough to do the job without breaking up. Whatever the reason they are apparently required, maybe to just slightly shorten, and therefore stiffen, the valve springs.

With the valves in place I prepared to fit the rocker shafts and rockers. I inspected the shafts and deemed them to be in need of replacement as they showed signs of excessive wear. See photo 24.8. When the new shafts arrived, I heated the head in the oven to around 150 degrees to expand it, and put the shafts in the freezer to shrink them. See photo 24.9. I then began to drive the rocker shafts into the head. See photo 24.10. On a Commando, the oilway on the rocker shafts should face outwards, towards the valves. Look again at photo 24.10. This means that the oil hole in the rocker shaft does NOT align with the oilway in the rocker itself. If the two oilways aligned, then the oil would come out of one hole and go straight down the other. By ensuring that the oilways do not align, the oil coming out of the rocker shaft is forced to squeeze out round the rocker and rocker shaft, and lubricate them effectively under pressure.

I inserted the rockers in position as I hammered the shafts home. The rockers go in with a plain washer on the outside, then the rocker, and then a Thackeray washer (springy, spiral affair) on the inside. See photo 24.11 of the Thackeray washer in the process of being inserted. I then knocked the rocker shafts almost fully home. Before they were fully home I engaged a special tool I'd bought from Norvil to ensure the shafts were in exactly the right position. See photo 24.12.

The rocker shafts have to be inserted with the two slots in the end of the shaft exactly horizontal. The reason for this is that the oil feed to the rockers comes into the shafts through a drilling that lines up with one of the slots. If the slot was rotated, the oilway would be blocked by the shaft – disaster! Look again at photo 24.4, where you can see the oilway to the rockers being cleaned. It's also for this reason that the inner cover plates for the rockers (see photo 24.14) have two tabs on them, to ensure that the shafts are in the correct place to begin with, and to then prevent them from turning in use.

HOW TO RESTORE NORTON COMMANDO

24.12 Aligning the rocker shafts with a special tool.

24.14 Preparing to fit the rocker shaft caps.

24.13 Driving the rocker shafts to just below the surface of the head with a socket.

Could I have got away without using the special tool to line the rocker shafts up? Probably, but who needs an excuse to buy another special tool? Anyway, it certainly made the job of rotating the rocker shafts into exactly the right position very easy. When they were correctly aligned, I drifted them fully home, with the aid of a socket of the correct size, as is my want. See photo 24.13. The shafts should be driven in until they are just below the level of the surrounding cylinder head – if they sit proud, the end plates won't seal properly, and if they're too far in the little tabs on the cover plates won't engage with the slots in the shafts and might allow the shafts to rotate in use and block off the oil supply.

NB: There are two slots on the end of the rockers shafts, rather than just the one required to allow the oil through, as on other Norton models the rocker shafts are fitted 180 degrees round, with the oilway facing inwards.

With the rocker shafts in position, I then prepared to fit the end caps. See photo 24.14. These are a rather bizarre and seemingly excessive collection of gaskets and plates, but they will hopefully do the job – without leaking! I was now beginning to reap the rewards of my full stainless kit from Middleton's, and I soon had the shiny new stainless plates and bolts in place and looking good. See photo 24.15.

Having done all this, I belatedly remembered that I'd previously bought some mushroom-headed tappet adjusters to replace the originals. See photo 24.16. I like mushroom-headed adjusters as they are far kinder to the tops of the valve stems and to valve guides. They are also so much easier to adjust than the originals as they use an Allen key to adjust them, rather than that horrible little square nut on the top of the originals that no spanner known to man seems to fit. But, I had, of course, forgotten to fit them.

No problem, though, as I could easily replace the originals with the mushroom-headed ones with the head assembled – or could I? It suddenly dawned on me that whilst the original adjusters could be screwed in from the top, the mushroom adjusters could only be screwed in from underneath the rockers, due to their shape, and the valves were in the way. I managed to get three of the four adjusters in – just – but the fourth adjuster didn't want to know. See photo 24.17. I therefore had no alternative but to once again remove the valve to provide enough clearance to screw the new adjuster in. See photo 24.18. I then had to replace the valve again afterwards; some people never learn.

With the head now finally(!) finished, it was time to fit it onto the barrels. To begin with I checked that the holes on the cylinder head gasket lined up correctly, especially the small oil drain hole. See photo 24.19. Note that it appears the gasket can be fitted either way up as it lines up both ways. I also decided to use Wellseal on the head gasket as I'm a great fan of it, and my argument is the usual: "Why not?" I think it will help stop any oil leaks and won't hurt anything; others may tell you different. The main problem that I find with composite gaskets is that they require re-tightening several times during the running-in period, and the first re-tightening needs to be done very soon after starting the bike for the first time; having ridden no more than 10 or 20 miles.

I then jammed the pushrods up inside the head as far as they would go. See photo 24.20. Note that I ensured the pushrods went

REFURBISHING & REFITTING THE CYLINDER HEAD

24.15 Cylinder head with rockers and valves fitted.

24.20 Push rods jammed up inside the head to enable them to clear the barrels.

24.21 Head half-fitted with the pushrods successfully inserted in their tubes.

24.16 Original and mushroom-headed tappet adjusters.

24.18 Removing the valve to enable the mushroom-headed adjusters to be fitted.

24.22 Top of the pushrods are eased onto the rocker shafts – at the back of the photo.

24.17 Trying to fit the mushroom-headed adjusters, but the valve stems are in the way.

24.19 Pistons at TDC and gasket trial fitted to ensure the small oil drain hole on the left is not obstructed. Note gasket can fit either way up.

back in the same position as they'd been removed from. I noted that there were singular wear marks on the bottoms of each pushrod, that corresponded to wear marks in the top of the tappets, and if they had been swapped round, the resulting wear would have been quite excessive. In fact, I nearly changed the pushrods and tappets due to the wear on their mating surfaces, but in the end I decided they were okay.

I lifted the cylinder head above the barrels and eventually managed to insert the pushrods into the pushrod tunnels and rested the head on the cylinder barrel studs. See photo 24.21. Note that the pushrods have no option but to seat themselves in the cups on the tappets in the bottom of the pushrod tunnels, so no need to worry about that aspect. I then pushed the head until it was almost fully down, before engaging the tops of the pushrods with the balls on the rocker shafts. See photo 24.22. If you look to the rear of the photo you can see the inlet pushrod engaging with the inlet rocker. I used a small screwdriver to poke about and engage the pushrods.

The next job was to bolt down the head. I gathered together the various new nuts and bolts in preparation. See photo 24.23. Note that the slightly shorter bolt goes in the centre front hole of the head, and the four longer ones go each

HOW TO RESTORE NORTON COMMANDO

24.23 Stainless cylinder head nuts and bolts ready to be fitted.

24.25 Setting the tappet clearances to six thou inlet and eight thou exhaust.

side of the plug holes. The larger of the three nuts goes to the centre rear without a washer, and the two smaller ones to either side of the central bolt in the front. The two long nuts go up through the fins on either side of the cylinder barrels towards the front without washers. The two smaller nuts either side of the front central bolt should be torqued to 20lb/ft and the others to 30lb/ft and should be tightened in the sequence dictated in the manual. So far, so good.

The first little problem was how to fit the small nuts to either side of the centre bolt to the front of the head, as they are fitted down inside the head and kept falling out of the socket I was using to fit them. The answer was to jam the nuts lightly in the socket with tissue paper which allowed them to be started on the stud without falling out of the socket, after which the tissue paper could easily be removed. See photo 24.24. The second problem was, as with the cylinder barrels, how to torque down the nuts that couldn't be reached with a torque wrench. The answer, as

24.24 Holding one of the upper cylinder head nuts tight in the socket with tissue, so it can be fitted inside the head without falling out.

for the cylinder barrels, was to use a ring spanner and then set them to as near as I could judge was the correct torque. I really don't know how else to do it.

Another problem then manifested itself. I had forgotten to run the four outer cylinder head bolts down the threads in the barrels before fitting the head to check they were all okay – and mine weren't. I was kicking myself. If you have new bolts it's always wise to check that they run smoothly in the threads before fitting. In my case, I had to screw the bolts in and out several times to free the threads before finally tightening them. The problem (apart from running the risk of damaging the threads) is that you can't get a true torque reading. If the bolts are already tight in their threads, when they're tightened to their torque of 30lb/ft they'll only actually be tightened to say 20lb/ft. It's important to have the bolts running smoothly.

Anyway, after much ado, the head was finally on and I adjusted the tappet clearances on my new Mushroom-headed adjusters – six thou on the inlets and eight thou on the exhausts. See photo 24.25. Access to the tappets is very

good at this point so it's an easy job – especially with mushroom-headed adjusters fitted. My only concern was that there wasn't much clearance left between the adjusters and the valve stems – even when screwed fully up there was only just enough clearance to give the required gap. If the gap closes with wear I'll be in trouble. I think this has been caused by two factors: firstly, the valves have been re-cut and so protrude further up, out of the head than they did originally, and also I'm using mushroom-headed adjusters, which give slightly less clearance. Fingers crossed the gaps get bigger with use, not smaller! (Fortunately, they did!)

I then fitted my beautifully polished rocker covers. I used Wellseal just on the cylinder head and not on the cover, as I knew I'd be taking them off to check and re-adjust the tappets after a few miles. However, I soon realised that the gaskets were much bigger than the rocker covers and stuck out quite a bit. See photo 24.26. I therefore used a Stanley knife to trim the excess gasket off which made the whole thing look a lot better. See photos 24.27 and 24.28. Note that I should have dry fitted the gaskets

REFURBISHING & REFITTING THE CYLINDER HEAD

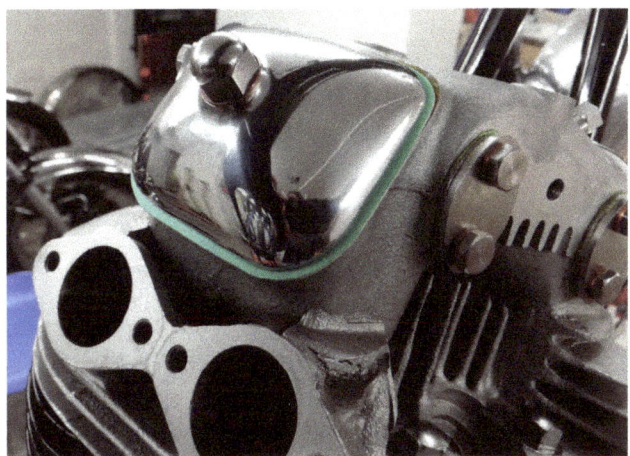

24.26 Fitting the rocker covers reveals a large expanse of unwanted extra gasket.

24.27 Gasket trimmed and the head looks good.

24.28 Gasket trimmed from the rear cover, too.

24.29 It's beginning to look a lot like an engine.

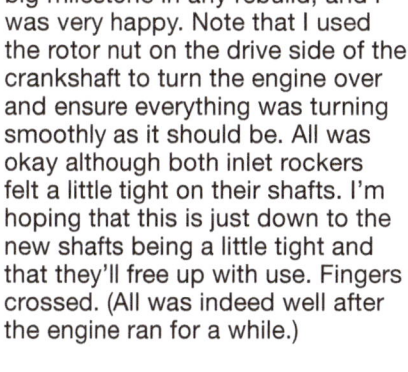

and covers first, which would have enabled me to remove the gaskets and trim them with a pair of scissors, which would have been much easier.

The cylinder head was now fitted! Hurrah! See photo 24.29. Getting the cylinder head on is a big milestone in any rebuild, and I was very happy. Note that I used the rotor nut on the drive side of the crankshaft to turn the engine over and ensure everything was turning smoothly as it should be. All was okay although both inlet rockers felt a little tight on their shafts. I'm hoping that this is just down to the new shafts being a little tight and that they'll free up with use. Fingers crossed. (All was indeed well after the engine ran for a while.)

LESSONS LEARNT
- If you can find a good specialist, use them. Try not to entrust work that requires an excellent finish to your local engineers.
- Check for valve guide wear by rocking the valves in the guides.
- It's wise to replace the valves as well as the guides if the latter are being replaced.
- The quality of the finish on Commando cylinder heads – are you kidding me?
- Valve springs tend to need replacing as they've spent most of their lives under compression, running or not.
- On MkIIIs there's an insulating washer underneath the valve springs.
- Double check the valve guide oil seals are properly seated.
- If you want to fit mushroom-headed tappet adjusters, do so before fitting the rockers to the head.
- When you re-cut valve seats, the valve stems move nearer the rockers. It may mean that the valve stems need cutting down to allow sufficient clearance.
- How do you torque down the inaccessible nuts on the cylinder head? No idea.
- Check threads before fitting parts together.
- If re-using parts such as the tappets and pushrod tubes, ensure they go back in the same places they came from, to avoid accelerated wear.
- Dry fit all parts first to check all is well – and to trim down gaskets if needs be.
- Happiness is a fitted cylinder head.

Chapter 25
Rebuilding the gearbox

With the cylinder head fitted, it was time to rebuild the gearbox. To begin with, I inspected all the component parts for signs of wear or damage etc. I looked at all the gears to see if there were any worn or chipped gears, or worn engaging dogs, especially on first gear, but all was well. Next up were the mainshaft and layshaft themselves – I checked them for straightness, as they can bend, and ensured that all gear cogs ran and slid smoothly on them. Finally, I checked the selector forks for wear, and, indeed, one needed replacing – see below. Note that I was replacing (or upgrading) all the bearings as a matter of course anyway, which I'd always recommend, but if you aren't, they will need checking carefully, especially the rear layshaft bearing.

With everything checked, my first job was to fit the mainshaft bearing and uprated layshaft bearing to the rear of the gearbox shell. I fitted an uprated rear layshaft bearing, which was a roller bearing rather than the original ball bearing, and therefore much stronger. The original bearings are an acknowledged weak spot and so fitting an uprated bearing is highly recommended. As usual, I shrunk the bearings in the freezer and heated the gearbox shell in the oven to expand it. I then coated the mainshaft bearing with sealing lock as the original one came out very easily and I didn't want this one to start spinning in its housing. See photo 25.1. Both bearings went in easily due to the heating/cooling procedure. See photo 25.2.

I then fitted the oil seal to the rear of the mainshaft bearing (innards towards the oil, don't forget). See photo 25.3. I prepared to fit the camplate plunger by cleaning it and fitting a new spring and washer. See photo 25.4. I then loosely screwed the plunger into the gearbox shell. I didn't insert it fully (with Loctite) at this point, as I wanted to check that I could change gears by hand, and with the plunger fully inserted, it makes it very hard to turn – so at this point it was only half screwed in. You

25.2 Mainshaft and uprated layshaft roller bearing fitted with 'top hat' centre fitted.

25.1 Preparing to fit the mainshaft rear bearing with bearing seal.

25.3 Oil seal fitted to rear of mainshaft bearing.

REBUILDING THE GEARBOX

25.4 Preparing to fit the camplate plunger with a new spring.

25.6 Quadrant fitted to side of gearbox, and 'top hat' inner race taken out of layshaft bearing.

25.8 Checking the indexing of the camplate quadrant.

25.5 Inserting a new spigot into the camplate.

25.7 Camplate fitted in fourth gear position and quadrant aligned with stud on the casing.

can see the plunger half inserted in photo 25.11.

After this, I inserted a new central spigot into the camplate. See photo 25.5. This was required as I'd accidentally (stupidly) managed to break one of the teeth on the spigot when dismantling the gearbox (see chapter 11). To remove the old spigot and insert the new one, I had to heat the camplate with my blowtorch (I had to use localised heating so as not to heat the spigot as well). I also needed to support the camplate as fully as possible to avoid bending it whilst hammering the spigots in and out. I checked the camplate afterwards and it seemed to have survived okay.

Note that my new, uprated layshaft bearing had a removable 'top-hat' inner race, and at this point I slid it out, ready to fit it to the end of the layshaft. I also fitted the quadrant to the wall of the casing. See photo 25.6. After this I fitted the camplate to the casing wall (both it and the quadrant have 'O' ring seals on the shafts). I fitted the camplate in fourth gear position with the camplate plunger engaged in the fourth gear indent. See photo 25.7. (At this point I should have still left the plunger only half inserted so as to make moving the quadrant and camplate far easier.) As I fitted the camplate, I aligned the inner top edge of the quadrant with the stud on the gearbox shell to 'index' the gears so that the gears would change correctly with the gearlever. I then loosely fitted the inner cover to check that the quadrant was indexed properly. See photo 25.8. If you can move the camplate round with a screwdriver and the quadrant doesn't foul the inner cover, then it's okay.

However, although I thought I'd checked this properly, I clearly hadn't, and later on I was to discover that I couldn't select all the gears as I hadn't indexed the quadrant properly and had to rebuild the gearbox all over again. How I failed to realise that the gears wouldn't all select at this point, I don't really know. I think that maybe it was a case of wishful thinking that if the gears wouldn't all locate I could put it down to not being able to move the quadrant properly – it is stiff if you have already fully inserted the camplate plunger, which is why it shouldn't be fully screwed in until the end.

Thinking that the gearbox was successfully indexed (Hah! That'll teach you to count your chickens!) I fitted the mainshaft gear sleeve in the mainshaft bearing. Once again I gently heated the gearbox casing (bearing in mind that the mainshaft oil seal was now in place) and cooled the gear sleeve before tapping it home using the shaft of a hammer to knock onto the sleeve. See photo 25.9. After this I prepared to fit the new gearbox sprocket to the rear of the sleeve. I replaced the old one as it was worn, and was a standard US spec one with 20 teeth, giving greater acceleration but not very relaxing cruising, and so I replaced it with a 21-tooth sprocket – more normal in Europe. If you look at photo 25.10 you can see the new sprocket on the left, and the old one on the right. If you look closely at the old sprocket you can see that the

25.9 With the camplate already fitted, I inserted the mainshaft gear sleeve in the mainshaft bearing.

127

25.10 New and old gearbox sprockets.

teeth are hooked, a sure sign that it's worn out.

I fitted the spacer through the oil seal on the mainshaft, and then loosely fitted the sprocket, with a view to tightening the gearbox sprocket nut to its required very high torque of 80lb/ft after the gearbox was fitted to the bike. See photo 25.11. This was a bit of a schoolboy error. I would normally have tightened the gearbox sprocket at this point by putting the old chain round the sprocket, clamping the chain in a bench vice, and effectively locking it sufficiently to allow the nut to be tightened. (See Chapter 11 on dismantling the gearbox).

However, I knew that my occasional vice, clamped to the bench, wasn't up to the job and that I'd have to take it to a friend's and use their vice. So, rather than do that, I thought I could tighten the sprocket on the bike by using the chain on the rear wheel to lock the gearbox. Unfortunately, I'd forgotten about the gearbox mainshaft. When that's fitted you can't get the socket (which I'd bought specially!) on the nut and so can't torque up the nut properly. See below. I should have tightened the gearbox sprocket up there and then. Damn. A real schoolboy error.

I'm also slightly unsure as to which way round the sprocket nut should be fitted. Note that the sprockets are dished – see photo 25.10 again – and so it makes more sense for the nut to be fitted chamfered side towards the sprocket so as to fit more snugly against the sprocket.

Anyway, blissfully unaware of my mistake at this point, I continued with the gearbox rebuild. I checked the selector forks for wear and realised that one of them was showing signs of excessive wear. If you look at photo 25.12 you can see the worn selector on the left. I duly ordered a replacement. At this point I also set the neutral indicator switch (MkIII). To do this I screwed the switch in and used an electrical tester to determine when the switch was inserted enough to operate. See photo 25.13. I did this at this point as it's a total faff trying to do it when the gearbox is in, especially as the wires are attached to the switch and get right in the way. It's also difficult to then seal the switch with Loctite, and to set it correctly so it works but doesn't interfere with the gear change, as can happen if the switch is screwed in too far.

Having generously lubricated everything with assembly lubricant, I fitted the third and fourth gear to the layshaft and then slid the 'top-hat' inner bearing race onto the end of the layshaft (on the left-hand end of the layshaft in photo 25.14), and inserted it into its bearing, together with the mainshaft, the mainshaft third gear and new selector fork. See photo 25.15. This was then followed by the second gear and second selector. See photo 25.16. Note that as mine is a MkIII it has the later second gear cogs fitted with a slightly

25.13 Setting the neutral indicator switch.

different ratio to earlier models and the gears have circular grooves cut into them, to differentiate them from the earlier ones and prevent accidental mismatching. Note that the mainshaft gear has the marks on the underneath, so can't be seen in this photo.

With both selectors in place, I could insert the selector shaft. It's important to seal the thread with Loctite to prevent leaks, but best to apply the Loctite to the selector shaft thread in the gearbox shell, rather than the shaft itself, to stop the selectors being contaminated with very sticky Loctite as the shaft is inserted through them. See photo 25.17 of the Loctite being applied to the gearbox shell. The shaft was then inserted and screwed into position. See photo 25.18. Finally, I slotted the first gear cogs on and the gearbox inner was completed. See photo 25.19.

I then turned my attention to the kickstart mechanism. I checked that the kickstart pawl wasn't too worn and then gave it a good clean, before reassembling it with a new pawl spring. See photo 25.20. I then inserted the lubricated kickstart shaft

25.11 Gearbox sprocket loosely fitted – with spacer behind it.

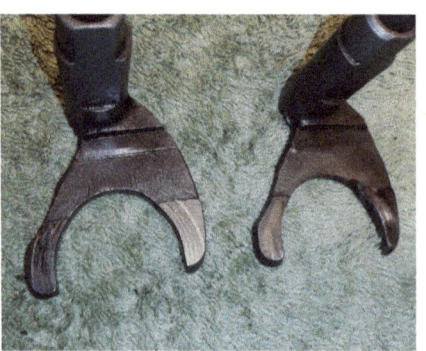

25.12 Selectors, with excessive wear to the one on the left.

25.14 Inner 'top hat' bearing fitted to end of layshaft.

REBUILDING THE GEARBOX

25.15 Mainshaft and layshaft inserted.

25.20 Fitting a new spring to the kickstart pawl.

25.16 Second gears and second selector fitted.

25.18 Screwing the selector shaft in.

25.21 Kickstart shaft inserted in inner cover with pin in line with the layshaft bearing.

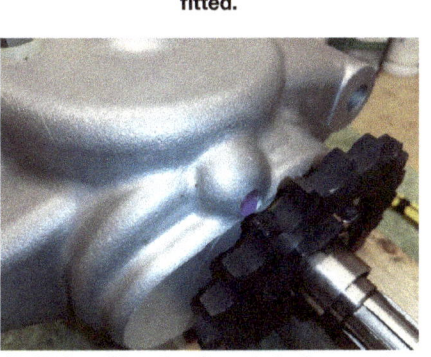

25.17 Loctiting the threads in the gearbox shell to seal the selector shaft.

25.19 All gears inserted and ready to go.

25.22 Kickstart spring attached.

into the inner cover, ensuring that the pin for the pawl was directly in line with the bearing, which I'd previously fitted. See photo 25.21. I then fitted the kickstart spring, see photo 25.22, followed by the inner cover to the main casing with Wellseal and the appropriate gasket. Note that as mine is a MkIII (you've probably worked that one out by now!) I didn't need to fit the knuckle into the jaws of the quadrant before fitting the inner cover, which you do need to do on earlier models. I then fitted the gearbox into the engine plates.

At this point, it's worth talking about layshaft end float. There should ideally be around ten thou end float on the layshaft for it to work properly. That means it can slide end-to-end by ten thou. As the outer end of the layshaft sits inside the kickstart shaft, and butts up against it, the way to adjust the endfloat is to add or remove spacers between the kickstart shaft and the layshaft. You can measure layshaft endfloat by simply pushing and pulling the kickstart shaft – even when the gearbox is fully assembled. The amount of play on the kickstart shaft equates to the amount of play on the layshaft. To reduce the end float you should use shims over the end of the layshaft, where it butts up against the kickstart shaft. However, these shims are not manufactured and you will need to make/adapt your own – apparently isolastic shims are easy to modify to fit.

HOW TO RESTORE NORTON COMMANDO

In my case, the play was about 15 thou, which I thought was fine, so I left it as was. How crucial the amount of end float is on the layshaft is a matter of some debate.

As mine is a MkIII it's very easy to fit the gearbox into the engine plates. The engine plates have a large diamond shaped aperture and you simply turn the gearbox to the 11 o'clock position, insert it in the frames, and then turn it back to the 12 o'clock position and bolt it up – simple! See photo 25.23. However, earlier models are somewhat different and, as with gearbox removal, refitting isn't necessarily as straightforward as for the MkIIIs, but the procedure is still much the same. Don't forget to insert the spacer on the top mounting. See photo 25.24.

I then prepared to tighten the mainshaft nut up to its required torque of 50lb/ft by temporarily fitting the rear wheel and rear chain and then locking them with two pieces of wood jammed between the chain and sprockets. See photo 25.25. This enabled me to tighten the gearbox nut with my torque wrench, having first liberally coated it with Loctite. See photo 25.26. I must admit to being a bit surprised that there wasn't any type of locking washer provided – but these gearboxes have withstood the test of time, so maybe I shouldn't be worried.

I then prepared to torque up the gearbox sprocket, but it was only at this point that I realised my folly – with the mainshaft now inserted, it was impossible to get a socket onto the nut! I should have tightened the gearbox sprocket earlier, in the vice, before the mainshaft was fitted. I therefore had to resort to tightening the sprocket as best I could with the aid of a large box spanner. See photo 25.27. This was pretty effective but of course I have no idea if I achieved the required torque. Note that the gearbox sprocket nut is a **left-hand thread**.

I then tried to screw the locking ring to the sprocket, but failed miserably. By chance, the hole in the locking ring would simply not match up with either screw hole in the sprocket. I therefore started to enlarge the hole in the lock ring but didn't do this properly, and I ended

25.23 Gearbox installed.

25.24 Don't forget the spacer on the drive side of the top mounting.

up with a ruined lock ring, a screw with a stripped thread and a stripped hole in the sprocket. Great. I therefore had to resort to using the old lock ring, more carefully cut down, and a short bolt to securely lock the nut. See photos 25.28 and 25.29. Note that I had Loctited the nut and used plastic gasket on the splines of the mainshaft. The plastic gasket was to try and stop oil from seeping down the splines and leaking out. I think that maybe I should have done this on the spacer behind the sprocket to be more effective, but something is better than nothing (I hope).

With the mainshaft nut tightened, I got ready to fit the clutch operating mechanism. See photo 25.30. To begin with, I dry fitted the assembly to test all was well (always a good idea) and discovered a problem. The main body of the mechanism is screwed to the casing with a large locking ring, but when I tightened the locking ring as much as possible, the body was still loose. Hmm. I eventually realised that for some reason, the bearing that the body sits on was too deep in the casing. I'm still not exactly sure why, as it sits on shoulder in the casing, and I can only think that the bearing itself was thinner than the original. I can't say for definite as I didn't compare the new one with the old one before

25.25 Locking the gearbox with the chain.

REBUILDING THE GEARBOX

25.26 Torqueing the gearbox mainshaft nut.

25.30 Clutch operating mechanism and extra washer.

25.27 Tightening the gearbox sprocket nut.

25.31 Extra washer in situ.

25.28 Gearbox sprocket nut tightened and locked – after a fashion.

25.29 Remains of the new locking washer and screw.

25.32 Aligning the clutch operating mechanism.

I fitted it – and I didn't fancy taking it out again to have another look. After some thought and discussion with Commando experts, I took the pragmatic decision to fit a spacer of the correct size under the mechanism body to move it slightly outwards, and enable it to be fully tightened. Okay, in a perfect world I'd have taken the whole thing apart again and found the cause of the problem; but it's not a perfect world. See photo 25.31. (With the bike completed, the clutch works perfectly.)

I then loosely fitted the clutch operating mechanism and the outer cover, in order to line up the clutch actuating mechanism body with the cable hole in the casing, using a piece of stiff wire: an operation that is essential for a smooth clutch action. See photo 25.32. Note that I needed to do this as I had misunderstood where to put the punch marks when dismantling the gearbox, which would have told me where to set the operating body. Also note that you need to remember to fit the large ball bearing (see photo 25.30 again) under the mechanism body before screwing it on. Having set the position of the clutch mechanism body so it aligned with the cable hole in the casing, I removed the outer cover and tightened the mechanism body lock ring with the special tool (highly

131

HOW TO RESTORE NORTON COMMANDO

25.33 Tightening the clutch operating mechanism.

25.35 Inserting the kickstart oil seal (MkIII).

25.37 Preparing to fit the gearchange mechanism in the outer casing.

25.34 Operating mechanism assembled.

25.36 Belatedly fitting the gear change shaft oil seal (MkIII).

25.38 Fitting the ratchet spring with dog-leg to the bottom, and then bending it to just clear either side of the half-moon pawl.

recommended). See photo 25.33. I then assembled the rest of the operating mechanism on the body. See photo 25.34. Note that the large circular washer runs round a small collet on the bolt. This collet is slightly wider than the large circular washer, serves to hold the jaws of the body apart, and allows the large washer to spin freely when the through bolt is tightened.

I then inserted a new kickstart shaft oil seal into the outer cover (see photo 25.35), and prepared to fit the gear shaft oil seal, at which point I discovered my second schoolboy error. On most models of Commando (with right foot gear changes), the gearshaft oil seal fits in the outer cover, where the gearlever exits the casing, but on the MkIII (with the left foot gear change), the seal fits to the rear of the inner cover, as the gear shaft exits inwards, towards the primary chaincase – and I had already fitted the inner gearbox cover. This meant that access to the rear of the inner cover was very limited and I might have to take it back off again to fit the seal. Damn! Luckily, though,

I found that I could actually fit the gearshaft oil seal with the cover in situ, with a bit of fiddling and with the aid of the correct size socket and a long extension bar. See photo 25.36.[1]

I then prepared to fit the gear change mechanism to the inside of the outer cover, complete with two new springs and thorough lubrication. I loosely assembled the pawl carrier mechanism with a new return spring and a new ratchet spring (see photo 25.37), and then slotted the assembly into position and adjusted the ratchet spring. The manual stipulates that the arm of the spring with a dog-leg in it must go to the bottom (I'm not sure why, but apparently the gearbox won't change gear if it's inserted upside down), and that the arms of the spring should be very close to the pawl, but not actually touching it; I bent the arms slightly to achieve this. The arms are therefore slightly bowed around the pawl. See photo 25.38. After this, I bolted the mechanism to the cover and then slid the ratchet plate onto the shaft as well. Note that the curved side of the 'half-moon'

pawl faces the ratchet. See photo 25.39. The outer cover was then ready to be fitted.

I dry fitted the gasket and discovered that one of the bolt holes didn't line up and I needed to trim the gasket slightly before fitting it properly. See the bolt hole on the top right in photo 25.40. Note that I'd also fitted the trunnion in the jaws of the quadrant and held it in place with a couple of blobs of grease. I then fitted the outer cover on the inner cover. The main problem was ensuring that the prong of the ratchet plate engaged cleanly with the trunnion and slid home properly. In order to achieve this I used a screwdriver to poke up in the gap between the covers and line the ratchet up with the trunnion. The cover could now be pushed fully home and tightened up. I temporarily fitted the clutch mechanism inspection cover and it was job done: gearbox fitted! See photo 25.41.

---

[1] I believe that earlier models didn't have proper oil seals fitted to the kickstart shaft or to the gear shaft, but upgrades are readily available in the form of either 'X' rings, which are basically uprated 'O' rings and easy to fit, or conversions to take proper oil seals, which require a bit more work to fit.

REBUILDING THE GEARBOX

25.39 Gearchange mechanism fitted along with the ratchet plate.

25.40 Gasket trimmed to fit.

However, my joy was to be short lived. After completing the gearbox I rebuilt the primary chaincase, and when that was completed (see chapter 26) I checked that the gearbox worked properly and that I could select all gears – but I couldn't. The gear selection felt strange, and no matter how hard I tried, I couldn't select first gear. Something was wrong in the gearbox, and it meant that I had to strip the whole thing down again.

At this point, I should mention Robert M Pirsig and his legendary book, *Zen and the Art of Motorcycle Maintenance*. I'm sure that many of you will have heard of this book, and if you haven't already done so, then I'd definitely recommend reading it (or at least the first half as there's some pretty impenetrable philosophy in the second half!) One of the main things I took from it when I read it, many years ago, and which still holds true today, is his mantra on having to take something apart you've just assembled because it doesn't work properly.

He says that you need to look on these events not as a nuisance but as an opportunity to learn more about how that part works, as by taking it all apart and rebuilding it again, you'll understand it more completely, and you'll complete the work in half the time it took you originally, as you're now familiar with it. I have to tell you, with great certainty, that he is absolutely right on both counts: you learn and understand more, and it takes you a fraction of the time it originally took to dismantle it, sort it, and put it back together again.

I can't tell you the number of times I've found myself feverishly repeating his mantra as I'm just about to take apart something I thought was finished because it doesn't work properly. But the mantra holds true and by muttering it you can see the job through, and indeed gain greater satisfaction, with the job now properly sorted, and the workings more fully understood: enlightenment!

I therefore removed the gearbox outer cover to see that the quadrant looked a bit low when at its highest point, with fourth gear selected. See photo 25.42. I surmised (correctly for once) that the quadrant was incorrectly indexed and needed adjusting. On removing the inner cover I again noted the position of the quadrant relative to the stud next to it. See photo 25.43. I then removed the selector shaft and

25.41 Gearbox fitted!

133

HOW TO RESTORE NORTON COMMANDO

25.42 Quadrant at its highest point as was.

25.44 Quadrant at its new highest point.

25.43 Quadrant at its highest point as was, with the inner cover removed.

25.45 Quadrant at its new highest point with the inner cover fitted.

the gear clusters and loosened the camplate just enough for it to move sideways, far enough for me to move the quadrant round another tooth before tightening it back up again. I was then able to replace all the gears etc (far, far faster than before). I noted that the new position of the quadrant in fourth gear was that little bit higher than before in relation to the gearbox stud next to it. See photo 25.44. I then replaced the inner cover and noted how much nearer the top of its groove the quadrant was than before. See photo 25.45. I then thoroughly checked (unlike the first time!) that the gearbox was working and that I could select all gears. In order to do this I loosened the plunger on the camplate again. If you look at photo 25.46 you can see the position of the quadrant with the bike in first gear – right at the very bottom of the opening. Clearly, the quadrant was previously indexed incorrectly and, as it was lower than it should have been, must have hit the bottom of the opening before first gear was engaged.

I was then able to quickly and easily reassemble the rest of the gearbox (not forgetting to re-Loctite and re-tighten the plunger for the camplate), as I'd already done it once before. This time the gearbox worked perfectly when tested with the gearlever. Finally sorted! Note that I took the opportunity to check why I needed a spacer under the clutch actuating mechanism to get it to tighten – but I couldn't see anything, so I rebuilt it using the spacer again.

LESSONS LEARNT
- Check all parts for wear, especially the bearings, gears and gear dogs, selector forks and shafts (for straightness).
- I would recommend replacing all the bearings in the gearbox as a matter of course, and changing the rear layshaft bearing for an uprated roller type.
- Oil seals are always fitted open side to the oil.
- Always worth changing the gearbox sprocket as they are invariably worn (as they're so hard to change) and are often of an unwanted size. (The Americans are pretty obsessed not with top speed, but acceleration,

REBUILDING THE GEARBOX

25.46 Quadrant at its new lowest point – with first gear engaged!

in the form of the standing quarter mile, and US bikes are almost always geared down as a result.)
• On MkIII models, don't forget to fit the gearshaft oil seal to the inner cover before fitting it to the gearbox.
• Tighten the gearbox sprocket nut before the mainshaft is fitted by wrapping the rear chain round the sprocket and locking it in a bench vice. You can't get a socket on the nut when the mainshaft is in place! (Alternatively, fit the gearbox shell to the bike without the mainshaft inserted, and tighten the gearbox sprocket before rebuilding the rest of the gearbox.) Don't forget that it's a left-hand thread.
• You can easily check that the quadrant is indexed properly before the gearbox is fully rebuilt, or even before the gears are added, by ensuring that the camplate plunger is only half-way in, loosely locating the inner cover and checking that the quadrant moves fully in the slot and that all gears can be engaged by checking that the plunger locates with all the notches in the camplate.
• On earlier gearboxes you need to fit the trunnion in the quadrant before fitting the inner cover.
• Locking the gearbox by jamming a piece of wood between the rear chain and sprockets may be a bit brutal, but it works.
• Don't forget to fit the ball bearing in the clutch operating mechanism before fitting it.
• Fit new springs to the camplate plunger, the kickstart pawl and the gearchange mechanism in the outer cover.
• Fit the ratchet spring in the outer cover with the dog-leg to the bottom.
• Make sure the prong of the ratchet is properly fitted inside the trunnion before pushing the outer cover fully home.
• Put a bit of plastic gasket on the mainshaft splines to stop oil creeping down them.
• I believe that uprated kickstart oil seals are available for earlier models.
• Remember Robert M Pirsig's mantra – you'll need it.

Chapter 26
Primary chaincase reassembly

Time to rebuild the primary chaincase. Having thoroughly cleaned the inner casing and then had it vapour-blasted I gave some of the more exposed surfaces of the inner casing a polish. See photo 26.1. In order to do this, I used some small mops held in my cordless screwdriver in conjunction with Solvol Autosol. This method works well on surfaces that were previously polished and that don't require a total mirror shine.

Having done this, I fitted new oil seals in the gearbox mainshaft and gear shaft holes (MkIII), along with a new grommet in the small hole the alternator (stator) leads exit from. (This long grommet can be seen in photo 26.6, just to the right of the engine sprocket.)

After this I cut open the old rubber sleeve that connects the two halves of the gear shaft in order to retrieve the splined connector inside (MkIII). See photo 26.2. I then tried to insert the connector inside the new rubber sleeve. See photo 26.3. This is one of those jobs where the connector is considerably larger than the rubber it's supposed to slide into. Anyway, after much 'garage language' (far worse than

26.1 Polishing the inner casing with small mops and Solvol.

pit language!), a lot of oil and sheer brute force, the connector was successfully inserted. I then slid one end of the connector onto the gear change shaft exiting the gearbox, in readiness for it to accept the shaft through the inner primary chaincase.

At this point I also bolted the chaincase steady to the engine frames. See photo 26.4. The steady required a basic setting at this point, so that later on, when the chaincase was bolted up, the steady could be tightened with the correct amount

PRIMARY CHAINCASE REASSEMBLY

26.2 Opening the rubber sleeve to remove the gearshaft connector.

26.3 Inserting the connector in the new sleeve.

26.4 Bolting the chaincase steady to the engine frames with appropriate spacers.

26.5 Preparing to fit the inner casing.

26.6 Inner casing loosely in position.

26.7 Centring the gearbox mainshaft.

of thread protruding through the casing to allow the securing nut to be tightened: too little thread and the nut couldn't be properly tightened; too much thread and it may interfere with the chaincase internals. To set it, I loosely offered up the rear casing to the engine to check how many washers (spacers) were required to set the steady at the correct distance from the engine plates to provide the correct length of thread. There had been four washers behind the long nut on the steady when I dismantled it, and four washers were still required this time. There was a small nut and washer left on the threads, and these would be used to position and tighten the inner casing later on.

I temporarily fitted the large Woodruff key to the crankshaft and checked that the engine sprocket slid on without jamming. All was well so I applied Wellseal to the mating faces and prepared to fit the inner casing. See photo 26.5. Note that I left the rear chain hanging over the gearbox sprocket as it's such a pain to fit when the chaincase is fitted – just makes life that little bit easier. I fitted the circular gasket to the crankcase and then slid the casing onto the four studs. See photo 26.6. Note that at this point the casing cannot be bolted up – it just sits loose on the studs for now. (NB: The grommet on the left of the casing in the photo is for the alternator leads.)

The next job was to centre the gearbox mainshaft. Despite the gearbox being able to be bolted up in just one position (MkIII) there is still fractional room for manoeuvre on its mountings. I looked at how central the gearbox mainshaft sat in the oil seal in the casing and indeed, it was slightly off centre. With the gearbox mounting bolts already loose, I therefore tapped the gearbox towards the engine, just a fraction, until it was as central as I could get it, and then fully tightened the gearbox mountings. See photo 26.7 of the now centralised gearbox mainshaft. If the shaft isn't centralised then there is a lot of eccentric pressure on the oil seal and it will almost certainly leak after a while. (Note that the oil seal on the left of the chaincase in the photo is for the gear change shaft – MkIII)

With the inner casing loosely fitted I gave all the components that go inside the primary chaincase a thorough clean with a mixture of White Spirit and WD40. See photo 26.8. If you remember, when I dismantled the casing, everything was covered in a slimy black coating. I think that previous owners had

HOW TO RESTORE NORTON COMMANDO

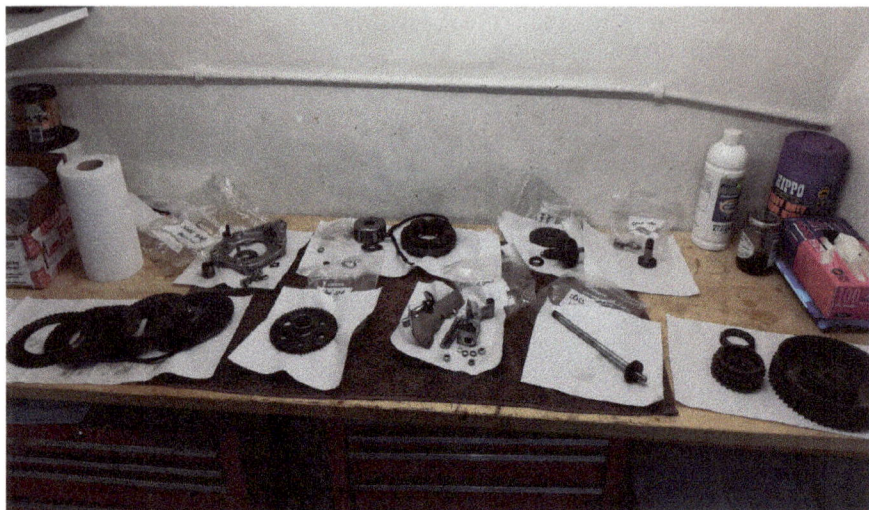

26.8 Cleaning all the internals of the chaincase.

26.10 Spacer and shim fitted to mainshaft.

26.9 Rear of clutch basket with spacer and three shims.

simply neglected to change the oil in the primary chaincase when they changed the engine oil 'as it didn't need it' – not a good idea.

With everything cleaned, I inspected the clutch basket, checking the large bearing in the rear, and the teeth on the splines where the clutch plates sit. The bearing seemed absolutely fine and so I left it as it was, and there was hardly any discernible wear on the splines inside. On clutches that have been abused, the splines can be badly worn by the teeth of the clutch plates, causing ridges to form on the splines. The result of this is that the clutch won't disengage properly as the plates can't slide along the splines properly when the clutch is disengaged, and the clutch drags. In my case all was well, though. I collected the grooved spacer and three shims that were behind the clutch basket on removal – I knew that if they were there on dismantling, they would probably need to be refitted during the reassembly. See photo 26.9. (Note that the first thing I did after cleaning the bearing in the rear of the clutch basket was to liberally oil it – never clean a bearing with solvent and then spin it without oiling it first – you will damage it!)

I then slid the grooved spacer and three shims onto the gearbox mainshaft. See photo 26.10. Note that the groove on the spacer goes towards the gearbox as the groove actually sits over the top of the circlip on the shaft, holding the circlip firmly in position. I then slid the clutch basket into position and, checking that the engine sprocket was pushed fully home, I checked the alignment of the engine sprocket and clutch basket with a steel rule. See photo 26.11. It seemed to be spot on. So, those three shims behind the clutch basket that had been inserted previously, were indeed required. If the sprockets had been out of line, then I'd have needed to add/remove shims behind the clutch basket as necessary. With everything checked out, I fitted a new primary chain (as a matter of course, really) and then slid both sprockets back into position. See photo 26.12.

With the primary chain fitted I was able to fit and torque up the clutch hub nut to its required 70lb/ft with the aid of the clutch locking tool that made the job very easy. See photo 26.13. Note that I locked the nut with a new tab washer and Loctite – just to make sure. Note that there is also a special uprated clutch hub nut available with an oil seal fitted that prevents oil from the gearbox coming into the chaincase through the mainshaft, by sealing around the clutch pushrod. I didn't fit one, but they are recommended by many owners. Some owners also fit a Belleville washer behind the nut to hold it secure.

Next up were the starter motor components that fit on the crankshaft. See photo 26.14 showing the order of assembly. Having first fitted the slotted thrust washer into the engine sprocket, I inserted the sprag bearing. See photo 26.14. Sprag bearings are very clever things that lock solid when turned one way, and release when turned the other. They are often used, as in this case, with starter motors. When the starter motor is used, the crank gear that runs on the sprag bearing turns anti-clockwise, the sprag locks, and the engine is turned. When the engine starts, the crank gear is effectively running clockwise and so the sprag disengages – so the starter motor is disconnected from the engine and therefore sits quietly, until required again. Clever stuff. The sprag should be fitted the right way round, with the odd shaped bearings leaning to the left, as in photo 26.15. Don't worry too much though, because as soon as the crank gear is inserted in the sprag you can check that it locks when turned anti-clockwise and frees when turned clockwise. If not, simply remove and reverse the sprag bearing. See photo 26.16 of the crank gear inserted.

Also at this point, I ensured that the starter motor idler gear that sits behind the primary chain was slotted loosely into position, as otherwise you can't fit it with the primary chain fitted. See photos 26.15 and 26.16 again. Note that I had marked the idler gear when I removed it, to ensure it went back in facing the correct way round.

PRIMARY CHAINCASE REASSEMBLY

26.11 Checking the alignment of the sprockets.

26.13 Locking the clutch to tighten the clutch hub nut.

26.12 Sprockets and primary chain fitted.

26.14 Components of the starter mechanism to go on the crankshaft.

I then turned my attention to the hydraulic chain tensioner. The main thing I knew about this was that apparently it doesn't really work. Bad news. It looks like such a great piece of kit and is just what you need on your primary chain – automatic adjustment; but apparently it's pretty ineffective. I'm afraid I'm unaware of a replacement for this item, or how to make it work properly so I thought I'd give it a go and see what happened. My first job was to prime it with oil by filling the two chambers that hold the pistons. See photo 26.17. With the mechanism full of oil I compressed the pistons and then inserted the unit in the chaincase before letting go of the pistons. See photo 26.18. So far so good. I then fitted the cover plate with its gasket behind it, and tightened the three securing nuts up

26.15 Sprag bearing fitted after the inner washer. Note that sprags lean to the left.

to the required, low torque, using my small torque wrench, which can cope with low torque settings. See photo 26.19.

Fitting the cover plate creates a natural reservoir for oil to then feed the tensioner, and so I decided to fill

26.16 Crank gear fitted to the sprag and checked for correct operation.

the reservoir up with oil, in an attempt to give the tensioner every possible chance of success. See photo 26.20. However, it soon became clear that the reservoir wasn't oil tight and the oil slowly but surely leaked out over the next day or so, until the reservoir was

HOW TO RESTORE NORTON COMMANDO

26.17 Priming the hydraulic tensioner.

empty: the best laid plans of mice and men. I wasn't sure that the tensioner was working, as I was able to squeeze together the pistons, which didn't seem right to me – see chapter 38 for the verdict.

At this point I also refitted the Woodruff key on the crankshaft ready to take the rotor – any later than this and too many other things would be in the way.

My next job was to try and slide the wires from the stator through the grommet in the inner cover. See photo 26.21. After copious use of soap and a lot of fiddling, I finally managed to ease the cable through the grommet, and left the stator hanging loosely on the mounting studs. In retrospect, I should have done this before fitting the hydraulic tensioner, in order to provide more room to work. I hadn't done this earlier as I wanted the stator hanging on the studs for as short a time as possible.

Next up I checked the backfire overload mechanism. See photo 26.22. I decided against dismantling the unit as it's pretty self-contained, and all looked in order. The unit is there to protect the starter motor in the event of a backfire, and the engine moving backwards suddenly and violently. This is apparently why Norton abandoned the idea of fitting the starter to the timing case, as there simply wasn't room for such a device, and without it backfires wreaked havoc in the timing case.

It would appear that the device works by having a series of ball bearings holding together two halves of the unit under spring pressure. If the starter works normally, the unit remains locked together and the engine is turned, but if the engine backfires, the ball bearings become

26.18 Hydraulic tensioner loosely fitted.

26.20 Attempting to fill the tensioner feed reservoir with oil.

26.19 With the cover plate fitted the mounting screws are torqued.

26.21 Threading the stator wire through the grommet in the casing, and then fitting the Woodruff key for the rotor to the crankshaft.

PRIMARY CHAINCASE REASSEMBLY

26.22 The backfire device with three disc springs on the right-hand end.

unseated and allow the two halves to turn independently and so protect the starter by not transmitting the backwards rotation to the starter motor. In order for it to work properly, the mechanism is set at a predetermined torque by fitting the correct number of diaphragm springs to the end of the unit: too loose and the engine won't be turned by the starter; too tight and the motor won't be protected. You can see the edges of the three diaphragm springs to the right-hand end of the unit in photo 26.22. There is also a small locking ring (on the left in photo 26.22), which fits on the shaft with the recess over the circlip. I left it all as was and inserted the backfire mechanism into the idler gear to the rear of the primary chain. If you do wish to service the backfire protection device, there is a good article about this on the 'Old Britts' website.

With the backfire protection device in place I then fitted the alloy stator mounting plate onto the crankcase studs. See photo 26.23. Note that the outer end of the backfire mechanism slots into the mounting plate. With the mounting plate in situ, I was finally able to tighten, torque up and lock with locking tabs, the mounting studs to hold the inner chaincase tight. See photo 26.24. This also enabled me to loosely slot the stator into place on its mounting plate. I could then also finally adjust and torque up the nut on the inner chaincase support shaft. See photo 26.25. To adjust it, I screwed up the nut behind the casing until it was up against the casing and then tightened the outer nut. This ensured that the casing was held securely but without putting stress on it. If the support shaft is incorrectly adjusted it can lead to oil leaks (where the casing is warped), cracked cases, or the casing rubbing on the gearbox sprocket.

I then slid the rotor into position. Note that when I had removed the rotor, I found a thin spacer behind it. Eventually, I decided to refit the spacer behind the rotor as it served to align the front face of the rotor with the front face of the stator – although I could find no mention of such a spacer in either the parts catalog or workshop manual. I locked the clutch again and tightened the rotor nut, which was locked with a crimped washer and Loctite. See photo 26.26. With the rotor fully tightened I then checked the gap between the rotor and the stator with feeler gauges. See photo 26.27. There should be a gap of between eight and ten thou all the way round between the two. If there isn't, the only way to alter the gap is by loosening the stator mounting plate and seeing if there's any play, and, if necessary bending the mounting studs slightly by gently tapping them – obviously the rotor is fixed on the crankshaft and can't be moved! In my case, the gap was fine, and I went on to tighten and torque up the stator mounting nuts. See photo 26.28.

I then fitted the small idler gear to the rear of the starter motor housing by inserting the shaft it ran on into the casing. See photo 26.29. Note that I had also marked this one during disassembly as well. Basically, there is a groove on the inside of each idler gear and that side goes towards the casing.

It was now time to fit the clutch. I had decided to fit Surflex plates to my clutch as they had been recommended. Following my previous acrimonious relationship with a Commando clutch, I was very keen to try an upgrade. See photo 26.30. Note that the plates came with an extra plain plate. This is because the Surflex plates require a plain plate at

26.23 With the backfire mechanism slotted into the idler gear, the stator mounting plate is fitted.

26.24 The stator mounting plate is then torqued up and the nuts locked with tab washers.

26.25 Now that the stator mounting plates have been tightened, the support shaft can be adjusted and torqued up.

HOW TO RESTORE NORTON COMMANDO

26.26 The rotor is then slid into position and the rotor nut fully tightened, after locking the clutch again.

26.28 With the gap checked, the stator nuts are tightened to the correct torque.

the rear of the clutch basket, and a plain plate at the front, up against the thicker outer plate of the clutch. This means that the plates at the back and front of the clutch are metal-to-metal. Also, because there is an extra plate, the clutch should be lighter, as there is less spring pressure (the flatter the conical spring is, the less pressure it puts on the plates). (I can now confirm that the clutch works really well – it's quite light, it doesn't drag and it doesn't slip – result!) It's also worth noting at this point that Commando clutches are designed to run dry. The oil's only in there to lubricate the primary chain. Most problems associated with slipping clutches are due to excess oil in the chaincase/on the clutch plates. This also explains why you can fit a belt drive and run the chaincase dry.

I cleaned the plates, which had a lot of dust on them from the manufacturing process, and then slid them into the clutch basket, followed by the thicker outer plate. I then screwed the special tool into the clutch spring and inserted that, ready to fit the large spiral circlip. See photo 26.31. However, when I tried to fit the circlip,

26.27 Checking the clearance between the rotor and stator.

it wouldn't go in. At first I thought that the problem was that the clutch plates were too thick and came out too far, but I eventually realised that I hadn't done the special tool up tight enough – you need to screw it in until the spring goes past flat and is slightly concave rather than convex. As soon as I did this, the circlip slotted in without a problem. I double checked that the circlip was correctly seated (you really, really don't want that spring to break loose!) and then carefully released the special tool. All was well. I loosely fitted the clutch adjuster screw and the primary chaincase was finished! See photo 26.32. Note that I had also fitted the gear change shaft, as for left-hand gear change bikes. This simply slid through the oil seal in the inner casing and then located in the connector and rubber sleeve on the gearbox shaft (see photo 26.2 again).

After this, all I had to do was fit a new gear change shaft oil seal into the outer casing and insert the short gear change shaft that the gearlever sits on, through it. I was then able to fit my highly polished outer cover (polished by the chrome plating company) with a new gasket and Wellseal, and it was a job done! See photo 26.33. Note that this being a MkIII model, it has set screws round the outside to clamp it to the inner casing, rather than the single, central bolt and rubber seal used on earlier models, which is hard (impossible?) to get to seal completely – whatever the case, set screws round the outside will always be tighter than a single, central bolt.

I believe that the best way to achieve an oil-tight seal on earlier models is by proper adjustment and a good rubber seal. Adjust the length of the central mounting bolt as per the manual – too big a gap and the casing will be bowed, or even crack, too small a gap and the casing won't be tight on the seal. Also regularly fit new rubber seals as they can go hard and won't seal that well. However, the rear seal around the gearbox mainshaft on earlier models will always be prone to leak, due to its nature.

Referring back to the MkIII, note that you don't need to index the gear change shaft when you fit the outer cover – as long as the gear change sprockets engage with each other, that's fine. This is unlike the Triumph Trident T160, which doesn't use two toothed sprockets to get its left-hand gear change to work, but rather two strange looking affairs that look like (and are known as) feet, and these need indexing (like the gearbox) if they are going to work – an added complication.

LESSONS LEARNT

• On a MkIII model, the gearbox is fixed but there is just a little 'wiggle room' to allow the gearbox mainshaft to be centralised in the oil seal in the inner casing.

26.29 Fitting the small idler gear and its spindle inside the starter motor drive housing.

PRIMARY CHAINCASE REASSEMBLY

26.30 New Surflex clutch plates waiting to be fitted.

26.31 With the special tool fitted and fully tightened, the spring plate is inserted ready for the large circlip.

26.32 Chaincase and clutch fully fitted. Note the gear change shaft in the middle, which just slots in.

- Check the clutch basket splines for wear to ensure good clutch action.
- Any shims that were behind the clutch should be replaced and then the alignment of the primary chain checked.
- Sprag bearings – a clever mechanism made by clever people.
- A clutch hub locking tool – makes the job so much easier.
- Hydraulic chain tensioner – great idea, but does it work?
- Check for a small gap all the way round between the rotor and the stator.
- Backfire protection device – another clever piece of kit.
- I would advise uprating the clutch on a Commando – Surflex plates are one such item.
- Use a proper clutch release tool – you know it makes sense.
- Polished alloy – don't you just love it! (Well, I do.)

EARLIER MODELS

Note that on earlier models, the primary chain is tensioned by moving the gearbox position. This means that there is a gearbox adjuster and a sliding seal in the back of the chaincase to allow the gearbox mainshaft to be slid forwards or backwards, as necessary.

The adjuster for the gearbox is on the right-hand side of the engine plates. See photo 26.34. There are also upgrades available so that there is a second adjuster fitted to the left side as well, to prevent the gearbox from sliding or twisting – but I think that this is probably only necessary if you are intending on racing or running the bike hard.

The oil seal on the gearbox mainshaft, where it enters the back of the inner primary chaincase, comprises two metal plates that are tack-welded together, either side of the chaincase housing, with a felt seal in the middle. These plates can then slide in relation to the chaincase and allow the gearbox to be adjusted whilst providing (adequate) oil sealing. See photo 26.35 of new sealing plates – old ones can be replaced by drilling out the tack welds, if necessary. The problem is that it's almost impossible to make this seal completely oil tight.

One way of ensuring that the primary chaincase doesn't leak, especially on earlier models, is by fitting a belt drive conversion, and running the chaincase dry. The clutch plates are designed to run dry, rather than in oil, so that's not a problem. (After completing the bike, I accidentally over-filled the primary chaincase with oil, and the clutch immediately began to slip but stopped slipping after I'd drained the excess oil out.) I have a belt drive on my T160 and it works well without any problems to date, you just need to check it for signs of wear, and preferably replace the belt every few years as they can begin to disintegrate with age.

26.33 Outer chaincase fitted – and looking good!

26.34 Adjuster for primary chain tension on earlier models.

26.35 Metal sealing plates for the rear of the primary chaincase on earlier models.

Chapter 27
Carburettors

So to the carburettors. There are five main rules about carburettors (carbs) as far as I'm concerned:
- The main reason a bike won't run properly is usually down to the carburettors (as opposed to mechanical or electrical faults).
- There's an awful lot of mystique around carburettors due mainly to the fact they work (or not!) largely unseen.
- If the bike won't run properly then it's probably a problem with the **carbs**, not the **tuning**.
- Carburettors only really need tuning when first put on the bike or if the bike's been modified (different/no air filters, sports exhaust, big bore conversion, etc).
- Just about every bike I've ever bought, the vendor told me: "The carbs just need tuning." (Vendors' code for: "I've been trying to get this bike to run right for ever and I can't, so I'm selling the bloody thing.")

The beauty of Amal Concentric carburettors is that they are pretty simple to work on and all parts are readily available. The downside is that they are prone to blockages (especially in the small passages of the pilot circuit), and they can wear out very quickly. Amal now makes Premier carbs that are built to much closer tolerances, are easier to clean out if they get blocked, have easily replaceable pilot jets, and are made of different materials that don't wear anywhere near as badly as the originals. For this reason, I'm going to take you through rebuilding and setting the carbs up correctly, but as a matter of course, I bought a new pair of Premier carbs from Amal and put those on the bike rather than trying to recondition my old ones – so much simpler and easier.

Over the years I've spent ages rebuilding carbs and having them re-lined and buying all new internals, which has cost about as much as brand new carbs; and they've still not

27.1 Old carbs and new Premier carbs.

CARBURETTORS

been right! Nowadays, I just buy new Premier Concentrics and have done with it (but I always take the new ones apart and check them before fitting anyway, just to make sure – I'm afraid that quality control on new Amal carbs isn't what it should be). If you want to rebuild your existing carbs, then all the parts mentioned below should be renewed; they are normally available as rebuild/refurbishment kits.

If you look at photo 27.1 you can see the old and new (Premier) carbs side-by-side. From this angle, the carbs look much the same and you can see the two (and only) tuning screws on the side – one to adjust the slow running, and one to adjust the pilot jet. Also note the tickle pins that are used to flood the carbs on starting. Both the old and the new carbs are fitted with the later extended tickle pins, which help avoid getting fuel over your gloves. The original carbs would have originally been fitted with the usual short tickle pins, but mine had clearly been replaced at some point – highly recommended if keeping your old carbs. Looking at photo 27.2 you can see the other side of the carbs and a major difference between the two – the new carb has a brass screw on the side. This screw, a unique feature of the Premier carbs, is the pilot jet, which is removable on Premier carbs and both enables the pilot jet circuit to be thoroughly cleaned, as well as allowing you to change the size of the pilot jets with ease.

Up to about January 2019, Amal fitted size 17 pilot jets to their Premier carbs on Commando carbs, but since then they have changed to size 19 pilot jets, which makes for much easier starting. Since finishing my bike, fitted with 19 pilot jets, starting the bike has been very easy, without any need to tickle the carbs except when starting from stone cold.

By removing the float bowl (sometimes known as the float chamber), the float, float needle and hinge pin are revealed. See photo 27.3. The purpose of the float is to rise as the bowl fills full of fuel and then close the valve (float needle) to stop the carburettor flooding. You might be able to see that the modern float needles are neoprene tipped to aid sealing. Also, modern floats are 'stay-up' floats, so they can't leak and stop working, unlike the originals.

Removing the float bowls reveals the main jets, screwed into the bodies of the carburettor. See photo 27.4. Also note the air passageways which, if the carbs are to be reused, need to be thoroughly cleaned out. Unscrewing the main jet assembly from the carb body reveals the needle jets above the main jets. See photo 27.5. It is very important to have the correct size main jets and needle jets,

27.3 Float, float needle and hinge pin.

27.4 Old and new main jets. Note the air passages in the carburettor body.

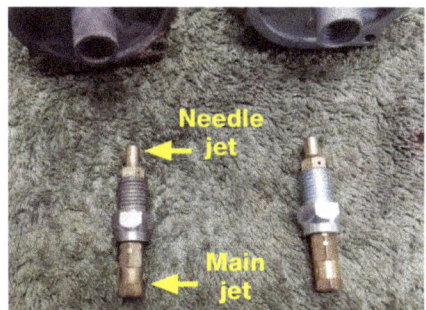

27.5 Main jets and needle jets.

but when I checked to see what sizes my bike should have, there was some confusion.

The Haynes manual says that the main jet should be 260, the Norton workshop manual says 230, and the parts catalog 220! Just to complicate matters further, Amal use smaller 210 main jets in its Premier carbs due to tighter tolerances – and, of course, I wanted to run the bike with open bellmouths, which set the basic settings askew anyway! After much head scratching and talking with Amal, I settled on fitting 230 main jets – 20 higher than Amal would have fitted, in order to cope with the open bellmouths. Luckily, everyone agreed that I should use 106 needle jets. Note that, as

27.2 Old and new carbs.

145

mentioned above, I used size 19 pilot jets. Job done.

If you're intent on reusing your old carbs then the next job is to thoroughly (and I mean thoroughly!), clean out the pilot jet circuit. This means using carb cleaner or such as an ultrasonic cleaner on all the airways in the carbs, paying specific attention to the pilot circuit, especially the very small pilot airway that exits into the main venturi. See photo 27.6. If you spray carb cleaner into one of the other airways, and it doesn't come out of the pilot airway in the main venturi, then it's blocked. Note that increased access to the pilot jet circuit is enabled on Premier carbs by removing the pilot jet. Some owners drill out the factory sealed pilot jet hole on non-Premier carbs to facilitate this, and tap the hole to take a screw plug. That's too much effort in my book, but it can be done.

Next up were the throttle slides. If you look at photo 27.7 you can see how worn the old ones were. The throttle slides wear badly and leak air around them causing erratic running[1]. If the slides are worn, then so are the carb bodies, and the only cure is to have the bodies bored out and re-lined, and new throttle slides purchased. This is the main reason why I buy new carbs these days, as there's not much difference in price, and you now have brand new uprated carburettors. Also note that the new Premier carbs come with new throttle slides made of a different material that doesn't wear as badly as the originals.

After this, I looked at the old throttle needles and discovered that the clips were in different notches on each needle. See photo 27.8. I also discovered that the new needles on the Premier carbs had the clip in the bottom (richest) position whilst the manual states they should be in the top (leanest) position. However, I checked with Amal and it confirmed that they should be in the bottom position for the new Premier carbs. It is worth noting that the tolerances on Premier carbs are apparently closer, and this means that different jet sizes/needle positions are often stipulated than previously recommended. If in

27.6 The pilot jet circuit.

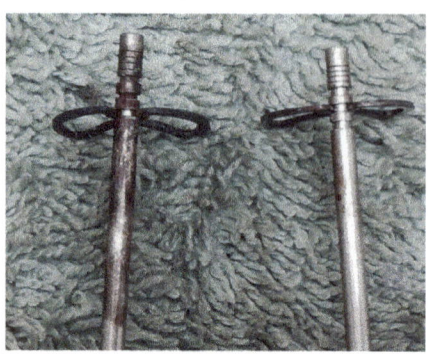

27.8 Needles with clips in different grooves.

27.7 Worn throttle slides.

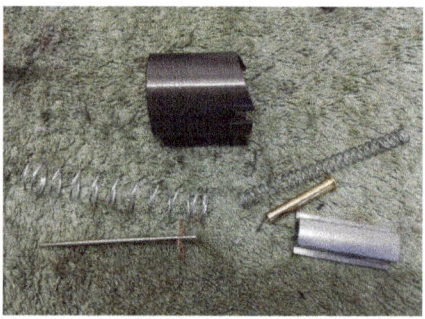

27.9 New throttle slide and choke assembly awaiting cables.

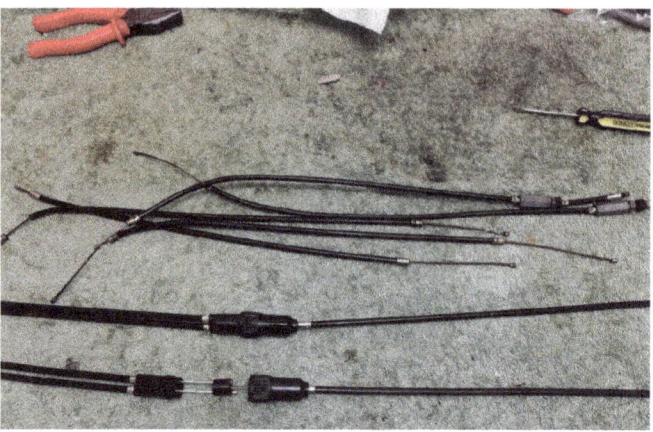

27.10 Assembling the throttle cables.

any doubt I would suggest ringing the technical help line at Amal (Burlen Fuel Systems) and have a chat with someone – the staff are very knowledgeable and helpful.

Turning to my own Premier carbs, I began to assemble the throttle and choke assemblies with the appropriate cables. See photo 27.9 of the new throttle slides and choke mechanisms. Before inserting the cables in the carbs, I assembled the cables and cable junction boxes as it can be very difficult to assemble them afterwards. See photo 27.10. I then inserted the choke cables in the choke sliders. Photo 27.11 shows how the choke cables are inserted into the sliders before sliding the cable to the bottom, where the nipple will secure it in position. Don't forget to insert the cable through the carb tops first! Photo 27.12 shows how to insert the throttle needle in the throttle slides. Basically, run the cable through the throttle top and the large

---

[1] Here's half the problem – they cause erratic running, as air sometimes leaks past the worn slides, and sometimes doesn't, so you end up with a bike that sometimes runs okay, sometimes like a dog; sometimes idles fast and sometimes slow – so it can be very confusing.

CARBURETTORS

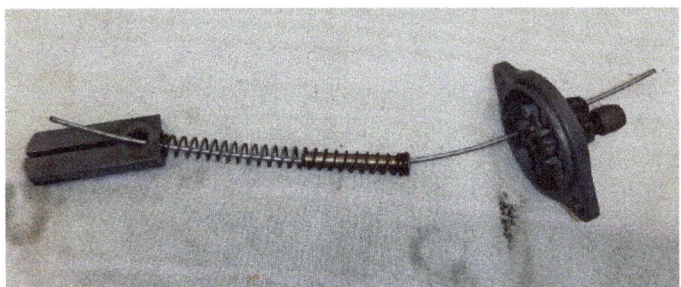

27.11 Assembling the choke mechanism.

27.12 Inserting the throttle needle into the throttle slide.

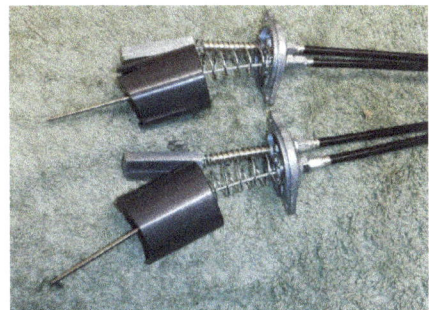

27.13 Chokes and throttle slides assembled.

spring and insert it in the throttle slide. You then need to pull the spring back up, out of the way (not easy – I use a pair of pliers under the spring), and drop the needle down inside the throttle slide, ensuring it seats properly. Looking at photo 27.13, you can see the cables inserted in the choke and throttle assembly. Note that the choke slider will later be inserted in the throttle slide.

It's also advisable to check float heights – the height at which the floats cut off the fuel supply: too low and the bike will run lean; too high and the carb will flood and run rich. To be honest, I'm not obsessed with float height (as some are) but it's worth checking that the floats close the float needle when the edge of the float is just below the rim of the float bowl. I use a small screwdriver to press on the middle of the float hinge to check the float heights. See photo 27.14. If the float heights are incorrect then adjust them by simply bending the tangs on the float as necessary.

I have also heard reports of some new Premier carb floats sticking, and not working properly. This can be either due to flashing left on the side of the floats during manufacture, or improperly formed hinges to the rear of the float that are loose on the spindle. Worth checking.

My last job was to synchronise the carbs. This isn't as fancy as it sounds, it just means ensuring that both throttle slides are set at the same height and so power each cylinder equally. If you look at photo 27.15 you can see that the old carbs were way out of sync and that the carb on the right would have been powering its cylinder considerably more than the other one, as the throttle slide is set much higher. You need to use the tickover screws to set the slides so they are the same. See photo 27.16. You should do this before fitting the carbs, as you need to look at the throttle slides from the cylinder side to be able to adjust them properly. Also note in this photo the rubber 'O' rings used to get an air tight seal on the manifolds.

My manifolds had previously been painted silver, so I took them to be vapour-blasted – with some trepidation as I could tell that they were made of a much lighter alloy than engine cases etc. I was right to worry, as when they came back they looked pretty bad. See photo 27.17. I therefore set to with a small wire brush on the Dremmel, followed by a good polish with Solvol Autosol and they came up really well. See photo 27.18. I mounted the manifolds onto the carbs, ready to fit them to

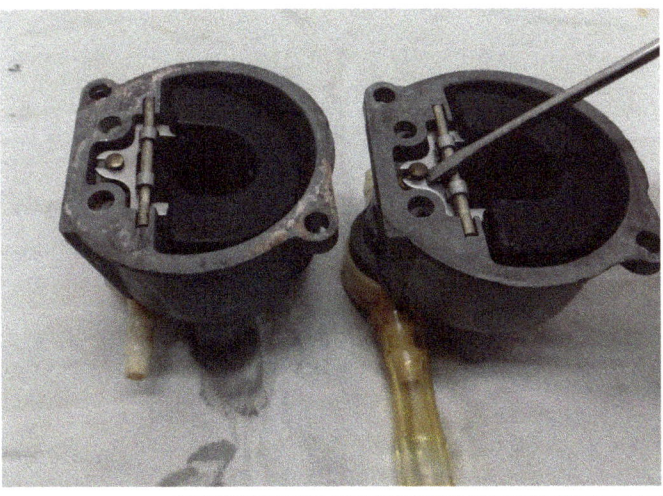

27.14 Checking float heights.

27.15 Old carbs were incorrectly synchronised.

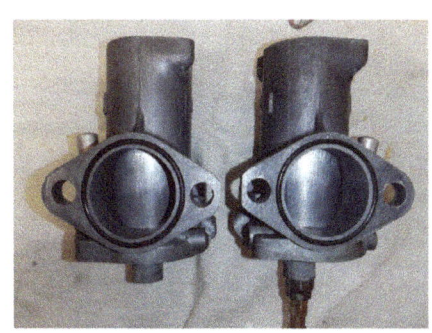

27.16 Carbs synchronised.

147

HOW TO RESTORE NORTON COMMANDO

27.17 Carb manifolds back from vapour blasting – not great.

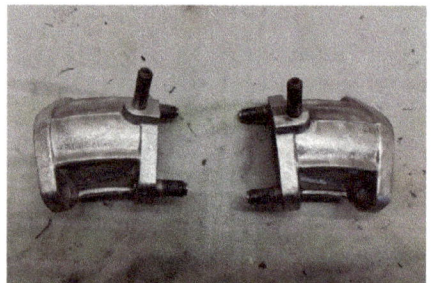

27.18 Looking better after polishing.

27.19 Carbs ready to be fitted, but hold on a minute – they're different!

the head (see photo 27.19), when I suddenly realised a major problem – the carburettors were different to each other!

Up until this point I had worked on each carb separately so hadn't really noticed, but now that they were side-by-side it was clear that they were very different – one had a smooth finish and the other a slightly rougher finish. Bugger. I rang Amal who were very apologetic and explained that the one with the smoother finish was an older carb, the one with the rougher finish, a newer one. So much for the 'matched pair' that I had supposedly bought. Anyway, they agreed to replace them, which they duly did, without fuss.

However, I then had to take the carbs all apart again as I'd replaced the standard screws holding the carbs together with stainless ones of my own, and I had to remove the cables from the throttle slides and choke assemblies. As I say, quality control at Amal isn't all it should be.

I was repeating Robert's Zen mantra furiously as I took the new carbs apart, ready to replace them – with new carbs! A few days later, the replacements arrived, and they were a matched pair – both with the slightly rougher finish. The replacements came together in one big box whereas my original carbs had come in separate boxes, and so I was more assured that the replacements were actually a matched pair. Always check and strip parts such as carbs, even if brand new to check that all is well – from my experience it often isn't.

I quickly stripped the new carbs and fitted the cables, new screws and larger main jet and manifolds, and was just about to fit them to the head … when I had a sudden change of heart regarding the air filter! Up to this point I had always intended not to use the original filter, but go to open bellmouths on the carbs instead. However, when I offered the carbs up to the head, I changed my mind. I still wasn't going to use the original filter, though! No, I suddenly decided to fit a 'U' shaped air filter from an earlier model rather than open bellmouths. "So," you're thinking, "he's finally seen the light and thought it wouldn't be good for his engine to use open bellmouths." Not a bit of it. I decided to use the earlier air filter purely for looks!

When I presented the carbs to the head I realised that there was a large empty space behind the cylinders – where the big original filter had been – that just didn't look quite right. But I really didn't want to reuse the original air filter (and anyway it was a bit late to fit it!) and so I thought I'd fit an earlier style air filter, as I think they look so much better. I therefore ordered a new 'U' shaped air filter assembly plus a new (expensive) battery tray, which was required to fit the earlier type filter (not to mention that I'd already fitted the original battery tray and oil tank at this point so it all had to come off again!). Anyway, I'm glad I made this decision at this point as it meant that I was just in time to take the float bowls back off the new carbs and put the original size 210 main jets back in, as required with air filtered carbs. It also meant that it wasn't too much trouble changing the battery trays over at this point.

Anyway, I could now finally fit the carbs to the head. I fitted the thin insulation board between the head and the manifolds in lieu of gaskets and tried to screw the Allen screws that hold the manifolds on. However, this turned out to be one of those simple jobs that was an absolute bugger to do. See photo 27.20. Despite having cut down one of my Allen keys especially (I hate damaging tools!), to be able to get to the screws, it was still a complete nightmare getting the Allen screws to engage at all in the first place; trying to tighten them was even worse. Eventually, however, they were on. See photo 27.21. The main problem had been that the holes in the insulation board weren't in exactly the right place, and so prevented the manifold screws from engaging in their threads. Slightly enlarging the holes in the insulation board sorted the problem.

After this, I slid the throttle slides into the carbs and fitted the carb tops, as well as temporarily fitting the fuel lines just to check they fitted okay. See photo 27.22. I also fitted a couple of rubber bungs to the

CARBURETTORS

27.20 Fitting the carbs to the cylinder head.

27.22 Throttle slides inserted into the carburettors and fuel lines loosely attached.

27.21 Carbs on the head – eventually!

take-offs on the manifolds that had been used as part of the old engine breather system. See photo 27.22 again. I then spent quite a long time sorting out the best routing for the choke and throttle cables. This wasn't as easy as it sounds, as the frame and head steady are right in the way. Eventually, though, I was happy with it, after I'd resorted to running some of the cables through the head steady rather than around it (you can quite easily remove one of the side plates without disturbing the whole head steady). In this photo you can also see that I'd removed the original battery tray in readiness for fitting an earlier one to take the new air filter.

When the filter arrived, I fitted the battery tray that went with it and then tried to fit the filter assembly. However, it immediately became clear that the filter badly fouled the live connection on the starter motor (Note that I'd already fitted the starter motor, and this is covered in a later chapter). Just my luck. See photo 27.23. I removed the starter motor to see if I could change the position of the live terminal, but I discovered that the only other position it could possibly go in was 180 degrees round, when the live terminal was virtually touching the crankcases! Typical – only two positions the terminal can go in, and both the worst two possible locations! See photo 27.24.

After a bit of head scratching, I thought I'd have a go at cutting down the air filter to make it thinner, in an effort to get it to clear the starter motor terminal. I therefore reached for the Dremmel and cut about ⅜in off the metal gauze. See photo 27.25. I then cut a similar amount out of the centre of the air filter element (there's a rubber seal on either end, so better to cut the filter down in the middle).

HOW TO RESTORE NORTON COMMANDO

See photo 27.26. I then refitted the cut down air filter and I must say that I was very happy with the result. See photos 27.27 and 27.28. I think that the slightly cut-down version looks even better than the original, mainly because it clears the starter motor more (which obviously isn't there on earlier models), and you can actually insert it past the starter motor! Having done all of this, I subsequently discovered that RGM sells a thinner, stainless steel filter assembly, specifically for this purpose! Ah, well.

However, I also realised that even though the filter now cleared the live terminal, it only did so by a very small amount – too small for safety. The engine can apparently move by up to ½in on the isolastics and so it could quite easily make contact during start-up, and maybe cause a spark – not good when you think that it's sitting directly beneath the carburettors; carburettors you probably just tickled!

So, in the end, I realised that if I ground a little off the end of the live terminal and left it facing the crankcase then I should be able to get away with it. The theory being that, with the cut-down terminal, there was now a good ¼in gap between the terminal and the crankcase, and, as the two are bolted together there shouldn't be any movement between them, unlike between the starter motor and the air filter. I also planned to fit a thick rubber boot over the terminal and hopefully all would be well.

I fitted the twist grip to the throttle cable and right-hand handlebar switch (see photo 27.29), which wasn't too difficult, but it's worth noting that the new throttle cable had a metal tube at the end which screws into the handlebar

27.23 Earlier air filter fouls on the starter motor live terminal.

27.24 Starter motor terminal turned 180 degrees just clears the crankcases.

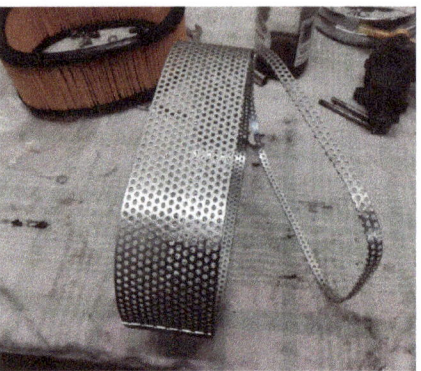
27.25 Cutting down the air filter housing ...

27.26 ... and the air filter itself.

27.27 Cut down air filter fitted 1.

27.28 Cut down air filter fitted 2.

CARBURETTORS

27.29 Fitting the throttle cable to the throttle.

27.31 Throttle in position.

27.32 Adjusting the throttle and choke cables.

switch, and you need to screw the cable tube into the switch housing before fitting the switch to the handlebars. The new cable with the shaped tube is a big improvement over the original though (which had caused my original switch to break and needed to be replaced at great cost. See Chapter 31). I then sorted out the handlebar grips. Note that these are actually handed with the one with the larger internal diameter going on the throttle. See photo 27.30. I was then able to fit the throttle on the handlebars and then slip the grip on, which I achieved with the aid of soap. See photo 27.31.

My final job at this point was to adjust the choke and throttle cables. This is a really important job; there's no point having perfectly synchronised carbs if you then have misadjusted cables that lift the throttle slides unevenly. I therefore spent considerable time adjusting the cables by means of the little adjusters on the top of the carbs. See photo 27.32. I started by ensuring that both throttle cables were just tight on the cable junction box and then fine-tuned them by removing the front of the air filter so I could reach in and touch both throttle slides, which told me if they were both moving at the same time. I then repeated the operation with the choke cable, to ensure that both chokes disappeared up into the carb body when they were in the off position and weren't protruding into the venturi at all, which would have prevented the carbs from giving full power with the throttle fully open.

So the carbs were done for now. When the bike was finished and running I finally set them up by adjusting the air screws using a pair of vacuum gauges fitted to the manifold take-offs, to try and achieve perfect synchronisation between the carbs. See chapter 38.

LESSONS LEARNT
• For my money, it's worth replacing old Amal carbs with new ones, especially Premier ones: they're not that expensive, don't wear out as quickly, and you now have brand new carbs that mean the bike should run beautifully from the off. The pilot circuit can also be cleaned out easily.
• You can refurbish Amal carbs, but by the time you've bought all the new jets and needles and had them re-sleeved with new throttle slides fitted, you might just as well have bought new ones, which are far superior anyway.
• The new Premier carbs seem to run better (and especially start better) with size 19 pilot jets, rather than the 17s, as fitted to some earlier Premier carbs.
• Another alternative is to fit completely different carbs (or carb), such as Mikunis or SUs or MkII Amals. See photo 27.33 of a pair of later Amal MkII carburettors fitted to a Commando. Not for me, though (I love Amal Concentrics – they're not the best, but for me they're an intrinsic part of the bike/engine).
• A lot of faff is talked about tuning

27.30 Different size grips for each side of the handlebars.

151

HOW TO RESTORE NORTON COMMANDO

27.33 Later MkII Amal carbs fitted to a Commando.

carbs. The only tuning adjustment on standard Amal carbs is the air screw. Apart from synchronising the carbs initially, and setting the pilot/air screw, there is no other tuning.

• If you modify your bike with different exhausts, different air filters, high-lift cams, a big bore conversion, larger valves, etc *then* you need to retune the carbs to suit. The problem here is that it's very easy to get lost in a nightmare of carb changes that don't work and only make the bike run worse than it did before it was modified. Do you change the main jet, or the needle jet, or the pilot jet, or the needle clip position, or the needle itself, or the throttle slide for one with a different cutaway, or a combination of any of the above? I once spent 18 months trying to cure a low/mid-range misfire on my Trident after I simply replaced the air filter with open bellmouths. Eventually, having changed just about everything else, I discovered that I simply needed to change the throttle slides from a four to a more restrictive three and a half cutaway, which allowed less air to pass through – but that was after 18 months of frustration!

• If the bike won't run properly, and it's a standard bike, then the chances are that it's the carbs that are the problem. It's almost certainly not the tuning, but a problem with the carbs themselves: a blocked pilot jet, a damaged jet needle, incorrectly assembled parts (remember the clips on my throttle needles were in different grooves on both carbs), misadjusted throttle cable, air leaks from the manifold (or round the throttle slide in worn carbs), etc.

• If the bike won't run properly and it's a modified bike then the chances are that it will still be the carbs that are the problem; this time, not only could it be any of the above, it could also be that the carbs haven't been re-tuned to suit the medication(s) properly and now you've got to try a lot of different permutations to sort it. Good luck! In this case I would recommend a rolling road tune: expensive, but well worth it.

• Always worth taking new carbs (or indeed, anything new) apart, to check that they've been set correctly.

• Keep muttering Robert M Pirsig's mantra.

• If you're going to change your mind about how you want the finished bike to look, but it means taking stuff off again, then go for it. Now's the time to do it and get it right. You won't have the time or the impetus to change it when the bike's finished (and if you still have the money by then, you must be loaded!).

• Where there's a will there's a way.

• RGM makes thinner stainless steel airbox assemblies.

• Adjusting the throttle cables correctly is just as important as setting the carbs up correctly.

• Don't forget, it's always the seemingly simple jobs that are the hardest: "I'll just bolt the carbs to the head." Ha!

• One of the very few parts that remains unobtainable for Commandos is the MkIII airbox. If you have one, hang onto it! (Unless at some point in the future they're re-manufactured, with the advent of 3D printing etc – in which case you might wish you had sold it!)

• It's worth remembering the following information regarding which section of the rev range each part of the carburettor is responsible for – this can make diagnosing problems a bit easier: Up to ⅛ throttle, the pilot jet circuit. From ⅛ to ¼ throttle, the throttle slide cutaway. From ¼ to ¾ throttle, the size and position of the jet needle. From ¾ to full throttle, the size of the main jet.

Chapter 28
Fitting the head steady

Time to fit the head steady. On MkIIIs the head steady is a bit different (along with most other parts of the bike!) as it has the usual rubber-mounted head steady bracket, but this time combined with a tensioning spring. One slight bugbear of Commandos over the years was the tendency for the engine to vibrate alarmingly in the frame at tickover. No real harm done, but it never did much for the street cred of owners trying to show off their bikes in the café car park. Not only this, but most of the weight of the engine on earlier bikes is taken by the isolastics, and this can cause them to wear prematurely. There are several aftermarket upgrades to the standard head steady available (including one by Dave Taylor), and upgrading to the MkIII type by adding the tensioning spring, is a straightforward option. For earlier models, one of these should be a definite consideration.

One simple upgrade, especially for the MkIII, is to replace the standard bracket with a much thicker and more robust one. This upgrade can also be carried out on earlier models, generally in conjunction with adding the tensioning spring. I therefore bought a thicker bracket, as can be seen in photo 28.1. My original, standard bracket is on the left. However, I soon realised that I had been supplied with a head steady for an earlier model, which didn't have the facility to bolt the tensioning spring to it (note that ordinary head steady brackets can be drilled to take the tensioning spring – but not this aftermarket stainless steel one). I was going to exchange it for the correct uprated part, but in the end I decided to just stick with my original. Why? Well, in the end I thought that as mine was already a factory uprated system, with the extra spring, then I didn't really need to change the head steady bracket, especially as I wasn't planning on thrashing the nuts off the bike when it was finished. Why wasn't I going to thrash it? Because I have far too much respect and love of machinery, and I'm not the mad, teenage, go-as-fast-as-you-possibly-can-at-every-opportunity rider I once was.

So I persevered with the original system, as fitted to MkIIIs, and changed/plated parts as necessary. Two parts I replaced were the rubber cotton reel mountings that screw into the frame and the top of the triangular side plates. If you look at photo 28.2 you can see how distorted one of the mountings had become; was clearly in need of replacement. After this, I fitted the mounting plate for the tensioning spring to the frame centre rail. See photo 28.3. From this, you

28.1 Original head steady bracket, and thicker, uprated one – for an earlier model.

28.2 Original distorted rubber mounting.

HOW TO RESTORE NORTON COMMANDO

28.3 Spring mounting bracket being fitted, together with the ignition coil mounting bracket.

28.4 Original head steady bracket bolted to the engine and rubber mountings screwed to frame.

28.5 Fitting the studs in the head steady bracket, together with spacers on the inside of the bracket.

can see that I had it nickel plated, and that it mounts in the same holes as the ignition coil bracket and so I fitted this at the same time. Also note that there are two possible mounting positions for the spring, and which one is used to achieve the correct spring tension will vary from bike-to-bike. In my case, I noted that on dismantling the spring had been in the forward of the two positions, so I set it in that position. See photo 28.4.

At this point, I also bolted the head steady bracket to the cylinder head, using three Allen screws. See photo 28.4 again. This is another of those simple sounding jobs that turned out to be anything but. The main problem was trying to fit the central Allen screw, as it fits down inside the middle of the bracket and it's very difficult to get it in its thread without dropping it; as my screws were stainless steel (of course), I couldn't fish them back out with a magnet. What I did eventually was to use a socket Allen key and 'glued' it into the Allen screw with Blu-Tack so I could then hold the socket and insert the Allen screw that way. Also note that I had bolted the spring tensioner bracket to the front of the head steady bracket before fitting the head steady bracket to the engine.

I then slid the two mounting studs through the head steady bracket, not forgetting to insert the two long spacers on the studs that fit inside the sides of the bracket and prevent it from being crushed. See photo 28.5. I then mounted the two triangular plates that go between the head steady bracket and the rubber mountings. I also loosely hooked the spring tensioner round the trunnion, ready to tension it. See photo 28.6.

Before I could tension the spring properly, I had to take the weight of the bike off the main stand to ensure that the head steady was properly tensioned. I therefore employed my trolley jack and a lump of wood again, and lifted the bike under the frame until the main stand was off the ground. See photo 28.7. Note that I only lifted the bike just enough to get the main stand off the ground, as the bike didn't feel that secure on the jack (I'd had to loosen the straps to enable me to jack the bike up).

I then started to tension the spring as per the manual. The manual says that the correct tension is achieved when the spring is stretched to about 1½in, and there is between ¼in and ½in of thread showing below the trunnion. However, by the time the tensioner was almost at the limit of its adjustment, the spring

FITTING THE HEAD STEADY

28.6 Head steady and spring assembly loosely fitted.

28.7 Supporting the frame on a trolley jack to take the weight off the stand.

28.8 Spring length being measured – but it's not right as the spring is accidentally in the rearmost position on the frame bracket.

28.9 Spring moved to the front position and tensioned to the set length.

was still only just over one inch in length – nearly ½in short of what it should be. See photo 28.8. After a bit of thought, I suddenly realised that the spring had moved whilst being fitted, and was now in the rearward mounting position on the frame, which accounted for why the springs wouldn't adjust properly. I therefore loosened everything off again, moved the spring to the forward mounting position, and tried again. This time I managed to tighten the spring sufficiently to stretch it to 1½in. See photo 28.9.

However, I was uneasy at having the spring at 1½in as it appeared to me that the spring was under way too much tension. So I slackened it off a little and thought that I would leave it there and see how the bike went and what the vibration was like when the bike was running. Note that there is no 'bench setting' for the spring tension; it is fine-tuned when the bike's finished and adjusted according to how well it works when riding.

LESSONS LEARNT

- MkIIIs have an uprated head steady in the form of two added springs, and these apparently work well – various head steady upgrades are available for earlier models.
- As well as preventing excess engine movement and vibration, improved head steadies take some of the stress off the isolastics.
- As with the isolastics, only ever set the head steady tension when the weight of the bike is off the engine plates.
- On a MkIII, the final setting of the spring tension is achieved by trial and error.
- If you need to hold a nut tight in a socket, use a bit of tissue paper round the nut, and that should be enough to hold it in the socket without falling out. Also use this method to torque up nuts you don't want damaged, as the tissue paper protects them.

You can also use Blu-Tack (as above) and superglue to hold bolts and screws on the end of a tool whilst it is located in its thread.

Chapter 29
The starter motor

Time to sort out the starter motor and get it to work properly. It's a pretty well established fact that the original Commando starter motors weren't really up to the job. Even Norton themselves referred to it as being 'starter assist' rather than proper electric start. The starter motor itself wasn't helped by batteries that weren't that powerful and wiring that was too thin to help pass maximum current. However, the good news is that all this can now be easily rectified! There are a number of aftermarket upgrades and replacements available – as well as full conversions to electric start for earlier models.

After some consideration, I decided to go for an uprated starter motor conversion, as supplied by Ray Wild, which would enable my original starter to work properly – and look a whole lot better too! This meant replacing my original two brush motor with a new, more powerful four brush motor, plus there was an option in chrome too – which I, of course, opted for! But, needless to say, it wasn't quite as simple as it sounds! The new starter motors aren't a direct replacement for the original motors and so you have to 'mix and match' the motors, using some parts from the new motor, and some from your original motor, to create a more powerful and better looking starter motor. Anyway, the new starter motor arrived, and looked good. See photo 29.1. Straight away you can see that the main shaft (on the end of the armature) is different to the original, as is the end plate – both these needed to be swapped and reused in the new motor.

The first thing I had to check was the direction of rotation on the new motor compared to my original. I therefore hooked them up to my battery using a pair of jump leads.

29.1 New and old starter motors.

See photo 29.2. As I had feared, the rotation of the new motor was opposite to that of the original (I think the original one went clockwise and the new one anti-clockwise – but to be quite honest, I can't remember exactly – all I know is that they both ran in opposite directions!). This wasn't as bad as it sounds though, as all that was required to reverse the direction of rotation was to move the four brushes round one position in the brush plate. Now, don't ask me why, but by some kind of electrical trickery, if you move the brushes round one position, it reverses the direction of travel. Unfortunately, I don't really understand it – all I know is that's what happens. Note that on some conversions, you have to solder the new brushes on – luckily this wasn't the case here.

I began to dismantle the original starter motor by removing the two long bolts holding it together, allowing the end cap to come away. I was surprised at just how dirty it was inside. See photo 29.3. The starter motor is so easy to remove on a Commando (compared to a Trident!) and yet clearly it had not been cleaned for a while, probably not ever. The cap was full of dust, mainly from

THE STARTER MOTOR

29.2 Checking the direction of rotation on both motors.

29.3 Original starter motor was very dirty inside – mainly brush dust.

the brushes which were worn down almost to the ends. See photo 29.4. Lifting the brush plate away revealed just how bad the wiring inside was, with the insulation to the brushes having virtually disintegrated. See photo 29.5. No matter though, as all these parts would be discarded. I then carefully cleaned the commutator on the original armature because this would be reused. You have to be careful cleaning commutators as they can easily be damaged: don't use abrasives like sand paper etc, but gently clean them with a cloth and something like white spirit.

I then dismantled the new motor and withdrew the armature (which would be replaced by the original), and the four new brushes were revealed. See photo 29.6. Why a motor works better with four brushes rather than two, again, I'm uncertain. It just does, okay?! (I mean, obviously four is better than two, innit?) I then removed the brushes from their housings and moved them all round one position (I could only move them in one direction due to the length of their wires). At the time it seemed unlikely that this would actually work, but later on I was to discover that indeed the motor was now running in the opposite direction. Magical electrickery!

However, I knew I had to overcome a major problem if I was to succeed in replacing the armature: how to hold back four strongly sprung brushes at the same time, in order to insert the commutator between them? No problem, as I had a cunning plan. I used four very small cable ties to hold the brushes fully back in their housings. I could then slide the original armature into the body of the new motor, with the commutator in-between the brushes, before removing the cable ties. Sorted! See photo 29.7. Crikey, I'm amazed at my own brilliance, sometimes! I then put the original plate on the drive end, and the new brush cover plate on the other, and replaced the long mounting bolts.

29.5 Wiring is very threadbare.

After this, I slid a new rubber 'O' ring over the drive plate, and the motor was ready to be mounted. See photo 29.8.

I loosely mounted the motor in place, using the two mounting screws on the inner primary chaincase. See photo 29.9. All seemed well. Note that there is also a third long mounting screw that goes through from the outer primary chaincase. For this reason, I was unable to check that the motor was running fine on the engine until the outer primary chaincase was fitted, as I didn't want to risk damaging anything due to the motor only being secured by two bolts, instead of three. Later on, when the outer casing was fitted, and the starter motor more firmly secured, I once again hooked up the motor to a battery and checked it worked okay, turning the engine over as it should. Thankfully, it did. See photo 29.10.

I replaced the original, thin power cables with much thicker ones. The starter motor takes a huge current and if the cables are too thin then they will serve to create high

29.4 Armature removed revealing two worn brushes.

29.6 Armature removed from new motor, revealing four new brushes.

HOW TO RESTORE NORTON COMMANDO

29.7 Brushes moved round one position, and held in place with small cable ties enabling armature to be inserted.

29.9 Motor loosely in situ.

resistance and reduce the power going to the motor, as is the case with the original starter motor wiring on a MkIII Commando. Thin cables will also get hot, and, in extreme cases, I have even seen earth wires fried. You can see how much thicker the new cables were, compared to the originals, in photo 29.11. Also, again because of the very high current the motor uses, the motor is switched on by a very large switch, capable of handling the current: a solenoid. See photo 29.12. So the current to the starter button on the handlebars is minimal, but when this is pressed, it operates the solenoid, and it is this, in turn, that sends the huge current to the motor, via the thick cables, direct from the battery. If the starter motor current went straight through the starter button on the handlebars, it would burn it out immediately. (For similar reasons, horns and other accessories that take a lot of current are often connected through relays, which perform the same function as the solenoid – but I think that solenoids can cope with a much higher current.)

I began to wire the solenoid up: one thick live wire to the battery live, and another one to the motor. I then connected the small wire from the starter button to one of the small spade connectors, but the other small wire was no longer required. This was the wire that went from the solenoid to the ballast resistor, and would temporarily allow the coils to run normally during start-up when any current is necessarily reduced by the huge amount taken by the starter motor. As I was fitting electronic ignition, the ballast resistor was no longer required, and so neither was the wire. See photo 29.13. I then fitted the solenoid to the frame in its upside down position. See photo 29.14. (NB Some electronic ignitions apparently do still recommend using the ballast resistor, so check the requirements of any system you fit.)

After this, I attached the new earth lead for the starter motor. I wanted to get the earth lead directly onto the engine to provide as best a contact as possible. I looked at various possible locations, but in the end I settled for mounting it onto the head steady bracket, where it bolted directly onto the cylinder head. See photo 29.15. This seemed to be the best place both in terms of a good earth and routing of the cable.

All seemed well until I came to fit the new air filter from an earlier model. The new air filter fouled directly on the live terminal of the starter motor. See photo 29.16. I therefore cut the air filter down so that it fully cleared the starter motor (see chapter on carburettors). I also tried to move the live terminal to a more suitable position. I dismantled the starter motor again, only to discover that there were only two possible positions the live terminal could be in – where it was originally, and 180 degrees round, facing (and very close to) the crankcases. I eventually

29.8 Motor reassembled with new outer cover and end cover, and original armature and end plate on the drive side.

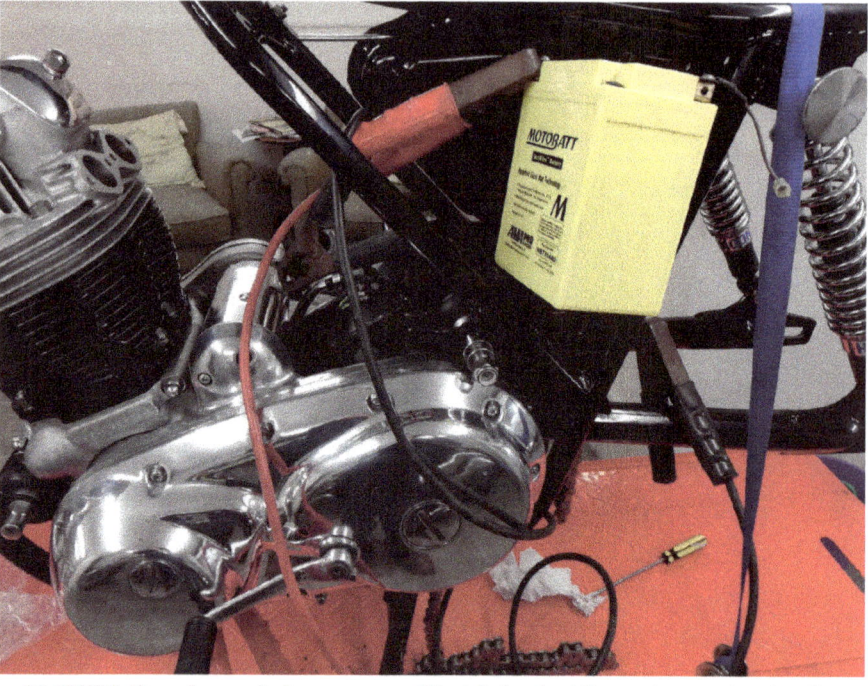

29.10 With the primary chaincase cover fitted, I checked the motor was turning the engine.

THE STARTER MOTOR

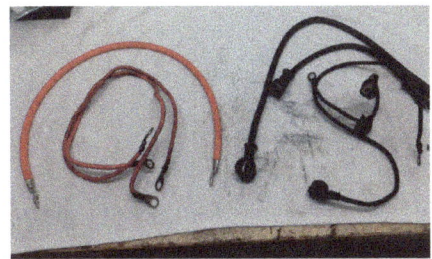

29.11 The thin old cables compared to the much thicker new ones.

29.12 The starter motor solenoid and its mounting bracket.

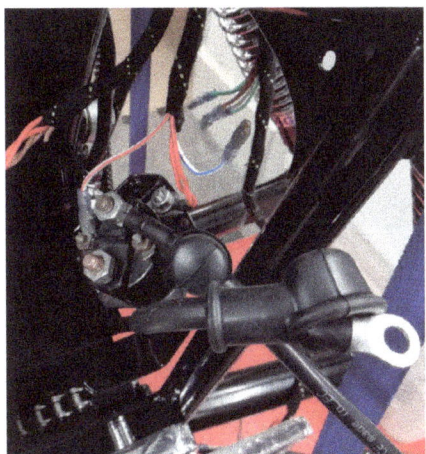

29.13 Wiring the solenoid.

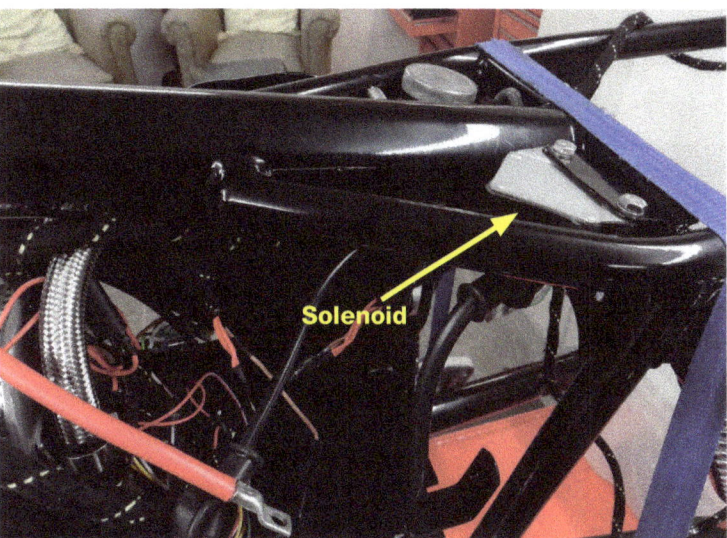

29.14 Solenoid mounted in its upside down position on the frame.

29.15 Earth lead bolted directly to the engine to ensure a good connection.

29.17 Starter motor live terminal moved round 180 degrees, cut down, and insulated with a rubber boot.

29.16 Starter motor live terminal fouling on the air filter.

decided to leave the terminal facing the crankcases, as even with the air filter cut down I was worried that it might still foul on the terminal when the engine vibrated on start-up. I therefore cut the terminal post down as low as I dared and insulated it with the rubber boot supplied with the lead. See photo 29.17.

Having now connected and fully tested the motor, I'm really happy with the way it works – it turns the engine over really quickly and all seems well. Hopefully, the motor will continue to work well and the live terminal will remain isolated from the crankcase – if not, then it could mean that one day I'll tickle the carbs, press the starter and then … Great Balls of Fire!

LESSONS LEARNT

- There are several alternative solutions available to upgrade the starter motor, as well as conversions to electric start for earlier models.
- I went for a four-brush conversion as it looks much like the original (and there's a chrome option!) – but you need to use your original armature and end plate.
- The Commando starter motor is very easy to remove, take apart and clean – but not many owners do.
- Solenoids and relays are there for a reason – to prevent excess current travelling through the wiring loom.
- In order to change the rotational direction of the motor (any motor?) move the brushes round one position.
- You can hold the brushes in their holders with cable ties to allow you to insert the commutator.
- There are only two possible positions the live terminal can go in.
- The starter motor will also work better with thicker live and earth leads and a modern battery.

Chapter 30
Horn & oil feed system

Time to fit the horn and the oil feed system (hoses, filter, tank and breather). As most Commando owners will tell you, just about the first part to be fitted to a Commando in the factory was the horn. Whilst this isn't exactly true, you certainly do need to get the horn in early on in the restoration, together with the battery tray that it mounts under. Once the bike is assembled, the only way to access the horn is by removing the rear mudguard, which it sits behind.

To begin with, I had the horn vapour-blasted to remove old, flaking paint, and then sprayed it black with an aerosol. See photo 30.1. After this, I temporarily wired it up to the battery to check that it was working okay. (You don't want to discover that it's not working when the bike's back together!) At the same time, I adjusted it to get maximum volume. There's a small screw on the back of the horn (see photo 30.2) and this adjusts the horn. Oftentimes the horn will just click or make a feeble noise, rather than blaring out, and this is all down to adjusting that little screw.

When I was happy that the horn was working and that it was adjusted to its loudest volume, I mounted the horn to the rear of the battery tray.

30.1 The horn cleaned and sprayed black.

30.2 Horn painted, showing adjustment screw.

See photo 30.3. Later on, I found that I needed to mount the horn facing in the other direction as otherwise it fouled on the rear chain. (I also changed the battery tray when I made the late decision to use an air filter from an earlier model.) I then slotted the tray into position with the horn – and the wires going to the horn – don't forget to fit them! See photos 30.4 and 30.5.

However, much later in the rebuild, I discovered that the horn is bolted to the battery tray with long bolts that fit the other way round, and these bolts mount both the horn and the rear mudguard. I therefore had to remove the horn from the battery tray and refit it with the longer bolts. See chapter 34.

Also in photo 30.5 you can see the hole in the battery tray for the bottom mount of the oil tank. Later on, this hole will have a rubber grommet and metal spacer inside it, in which the oil tank mounting fits. Note that getting to this mounting is about as hard as getting to the horn, so ensure that the oil tank is fitted at the same time as the hoses. The tank is bolted on with the bottom mounting and two rubber mountings at the top. Rubber mounting the tank helps to prevent fractures, but it can still happen, especially round the bottom mounting, and this should be checked before fitting the tank.

Earlier models also had a chain

HORN & OIL FEED SYSTEM

30.3 Horn mounted onto battery tray – with the incorrect bolts, as it turned out.

30.4 Horn and battery tray fitted.

30.5 Battery tray in situ.

oiler fitted, running from the top of the oil tank, which, in theory, was a good, practical idea. In practice, I find them a pain in the arse, serving only to cover the rear of the bike in oil (apart from the chain itself!), and my recommendation, especially if the bike is for occasional use only, is that they are best sealed off and forgotten. Sorted.

I then turned my attention to the oil feed system. To begin with, I decided to use braided stainless steel hoses throughout. This was simply for appearance, as they are not really required, but I think they always make a rebuild look that bit more professional (and I'm just a poser). Having bought these on eBay, I fitted them to the oil filter housing and the main feed banjo from the oil tank. See photo 30.6 showing the new hoses ready to go on the bike, together with the old hoses, which I used as a pattern for the new ones. Another feature of most Commandos is that they boast a remote spin-on oil filter in the return oil feed, mounted on the engine frames under the swinging arm.

I mounted the oil filter housing in the engine frames below the swinging arm, and screwed on a new oil filter. See photo 30.7. After this I fitted the supply and return hoses to the oil pipe manifold, and loosely bolted it to the crankcases. See photo 30.8. Note that the outer oil pipe is the oil feed pipe that comes from the rear of the oil tank; the inner pipe is the return pipe and that goes to the oil filter first, before continuing to the oil tank. I believe that the external oil filter was fitted to all but the early Commandos and is a great improvement. Early models can be

30.6 New stainless hoses to replace old ones.

161

HOW TO RESTORE NORTON COMMANDO

30.7 Oil filter mounted.

30.8 New feed and return pipes fitted.

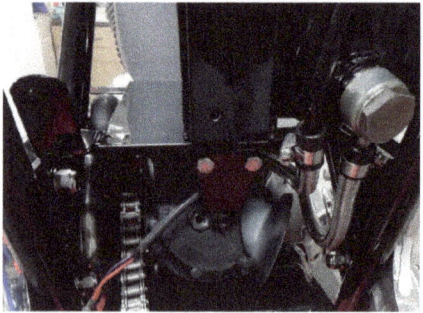

30.9 Oil feed and return pipes connected to the oil tank.

30.10 Non-return valve ready to be fitted to the engine breather hose.

altered to accept an oil filter, I believe, and this modification might be worth considering as part of a complete rebuild.

The oil feed pipe is mounted to the tank via another filter that sits in the oil tank (that makes three!) and is sealed with two alloy washers, whilst the return feed, from the oil filter, slides onto an external pipe. See photo 30.9. It was at this point that I realised I had to change the position of the horn to clear the rear chain and the oil pipes.

With the oil feed and return pipes sorted, I looked at the engine breather pipe. On MkIIIs, the engine breather exits from the rear of the timing case and goes up into the oil tank. I decided to add a one-way valve in the pipe so the engine could breathe, but not suck(!). One problem that Commandos suffer from is pressurising of the crankcases. Both pistons rise and fall at the same time, so when the pistons come down, they naturally pressurise the crankcases, and this can cause oil leaks as the air tries to escape wherever it can. Apparently, the best place for a breather to try and avoid this, is the rear of the timing case, which is where the breather is attached on MkIIIs. By fitting the non-return valve, this should help further by ensuring there is less air in the cases to be pushed out when the pistons come down as a partial vacuum is created in the cases. This also helps to increase bhp as there is less air for the pistons to push – but not so much that you'd notice! See photo 30.10 showing the non-return valve ready to be fitted.

I decided to fit the non-return valve in the hose just behind and to the breather side of the air filter. See photo 30.11. I hoped that this would be okay, as I was slightly concerned that it might foul on the side panel, when fitted. Unfortunately, the side panels were away being painted, with the tank, so I couldn't find out if the valve fouled the side panel until I got the panels back. I later discovered that the valve wasn't in the way when I came to fit the side panel – all good (but the bottom of the valve is visible).

I think that some earlier models suffered more from engine breather problems, and different specialists have different solutions, so it may well be worth speaking to them about how best to tackle this problem.

After this I fitted my new rocker box oil feed pipes. I loosely bolted the banjo bolt to the crankcases, next to the oil feed manifold, and experimented with how best to route the pipe up to the cylinder head. In the end, I ran it up in front of the air filter and up in-between the carburettors. See photo 30.12. I then looped it over to the right side of the head where I mounted it on a double banjo. See photo 30.13. I then fitted the short feed pipe to the other side of the head, routing it round the front of the head. See photo 30.14. Note that the connections on the rocker feed pipes were all left loose at this point, as I knew that when other parts of the bike were added, it might be necessary to re-route the pipes.

Finally, I fitted the vent hose from the oil tank to the rear of the air filter. See photo 30.15. On MkIIIs there is a quite complicated (sophisticated?) vent system, which is designed to burn as many fumes from the oil tank as possible so as to meet increasingly stringent emissions limits. That system vents back into the

HORN & OIL FEED SYSTEM

30.11 Non-return valve and oil tank fitted.

30.13 Oil feed pipes on the cylinder head.

30.12 Breather pipe fitted along with rocker feed pipe.

30.14 Oil feed to the other side of the head.

combustion chambers, both through the air filter, and through small intake pipes on the carb manifolds. Earlier models only vent into the air filter with (most) fumes being sucked back into the engine to be burnt and, as I had an earlier air filter fitted, that is what I did.

LESSONS LEARNT
• Fit the horn early!
• Adjust the horn for maximum volume before fitting.
• Use the correct long bolts, facing outwards, to mount the horn, so that the rear mudguard can be bolted onto them later on.
• If you're a poser you can use braided stainless hoses!
• The inner oil pipe is the return feed, and the outer pipe is the supply. So, remember: Inner is out, and outer is in.
• Fit the oil tank at the same time as the spin-on oil filter.
• Most Commandos have a spin-on oil filter – very worthwhile.
• Fitting a non-return valve in the engine breather pipe is a recommended upgrade.
• Upgraded rocker feed pipes are available – along with most other Commando parts!
• Only loosely fit parts such as cables, wires and pipes, etc to begin with, as they made need re-routing later when other parts are fitted.
• Chain oilers – who needs them? (Seriously though, if you're planning on doing some serious riding, then chain oilers are a good idea, but for occasional Sunday jaunts out, then probably not.)
• MkIIIs have a more complicated/ sophisticated engine breather system.

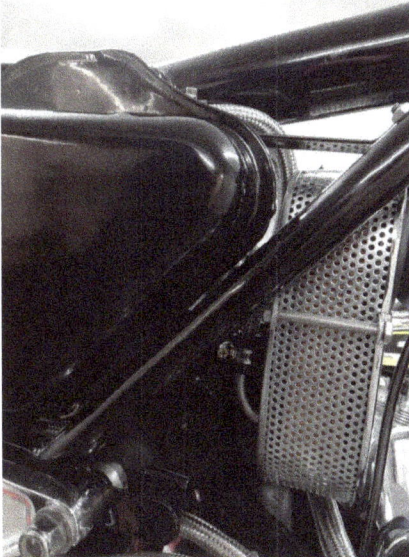
30.15 Oil tank vent pipe runs to the rear of the air filter.

Chapter 31

Handlebar switches

Time to sort out the handlebar switches. The handlebar switches, although working, were all looking very tired and in need of refurbishment. Not only that, but as I tried to remove the brass ferule the throttle cable screws into, the casing around the thread gave way and was basically irreparable. See photo 31.1. Now, at this point, I didn't realise that repro switchgear was in fact available for the MkIII. I knew that replacement switchgear was available for the earlier models, but not for the singular MkIII models. I therefore set about reconditioning my originals, and it was only after I'd completed them that I discovered brand new repro ones were in fact available and would have saved me a whole lot of bother – and not cost that much more money! Ah, well, at least I had the satisfaction of having done them myself (though I'm still trying to convince myself of that!).

I began by dismantling the broken lower right-hand side switch, by first removing the switch lever, held down by three small screws. See photo 31.2. I then removed the wiring and the switch itself from the housing. The right-hand lower switch and left-hand lower switch both work in the same way, with a small spring-loaded contact being slid across three contacts on a Bakelite board by the switch lever. If you look at photo 31.3 you can see the spring-loaded contact and its white plastic housing to the top left, the Bakelite board to the lower left, and the switch lever to the right. Note that there is also a push button switch which is self-contained and not designed to be taken apart.

I then dismantled the left-hand upper switch, which is a slide switch. See photo 31.4. This works in a similar way to the lower switch – in that a small metal contact, held in the white plastic, is slid along a Bakelite board with different contacts on it – except that it also has a small spring and ball bearing on the side of the plastic housing to ensure positive switch action. The right-hand upper switch is identical to the left-hand one. I finally dismantled the left-hand lower switch, which was also the same as the right-hand one. See photo 31.5.

I had been 'lucky' enough to find a secondhand replacement lower right-hand switch on eBay, to replace the one that was fractured, but as originals aren't available any more, it

31.1 Lower right-hand switch casting broken.

31.2 Dismantling the right-hand lower switch.

HANDLEBAR SWITCHES

31.3 Right-hand lower switch dismantled.

31.4 Left-hand upper switch dismantled – with spring and small (dirty) ball bearing.

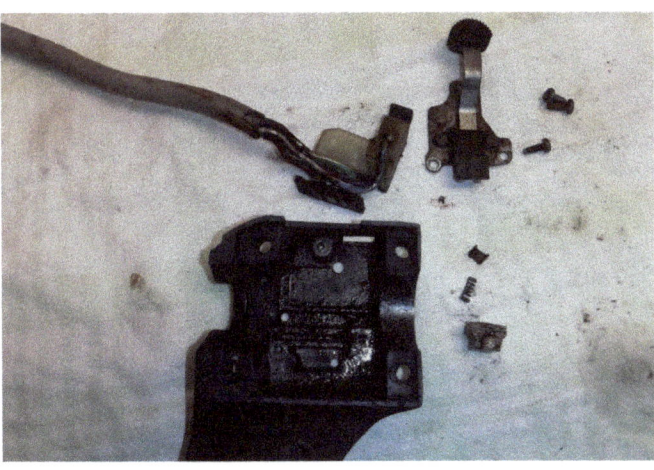

31.5 Left-hand lower switch dismantled.

31.6 Sheared screw in the top left mounting.

31.7 Sheared screw drilled out, ready for the easy-out.

31.8 Easy-out sheared off in the screw.

cost me over £80 (£10 more than a complete new repro switch, as I later discovered!) and needed refurbishing when it came, but at least I had one. However, I also discovered that one of the screws in the top left switch had sheared off and was left flush with the casting. I therefore cut it down to leave a tang with which I tried to unscrew it, to no avail. See photo 31.6. I therefore drilled a hole down through the remains of the screw (see photo 31.7) in order to insert an Easy-Out thread removal tool. This is basically a left-hand threaded tap that goes into the hole and, as it tightens, unscrews the broken stud – supposedly. I duly screwed the Easy-Out into the hole and, as it tightened, it sheared off. See photo 31.8. I was now in a far worse pickle than I had been when I started. I now had a sheared off screw seized inside an irreplaceable casting with the tip of a very hard and very brittle Easy-Out tool jammed down inside it. Not good. In the end I took it to the engineers who managed to remove it but only by drilling the whole lot out and replacing it with a larger size thread – 6mm rather than 5mm (note that the threads in the MkIII switches are all metric). I should have taken it to the engineers in the first place – lesson taught for about the fifth time, but still not learnt!

Whilst this was all going on, the three halves of the switches I did have were ready to be refurbished (at this point I was still waiting for the secondhand lower right switch

HOW TO RESTORE NORTON COMMANDO

31.9 Switch castings ready for refurbishment.

31.10 Painting the lettering white.

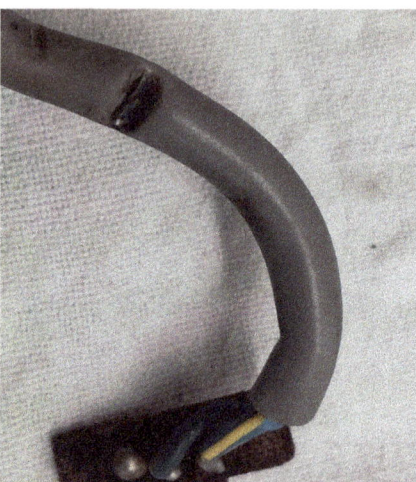

31.11 Cable cut by being trapped under the switch casting.

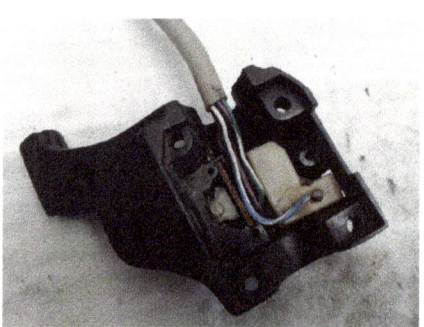

31.12 Left-hand lower switch being reassembled.

31.13 Left-hand lower switch assembled.

31.14 Right-hand upper switch assembled – with spring and ball bearing.

to be delivered). See photo 31.9. I gave them a very thorough clean and then sprayed them Satin black with an aerosol. After this I used a small tin of white Humbrol paint on the writing. See photo 31.10. Basically I carefully applied the paint onto the lettering by dabbing it on with a small screwdriver, and then quickly wiped the excess off the casing with a mixture of dry rag and rag dipped in white spirit. This left the lettering painted, but not the rest of the casing. This simple method seemed to work well.

Another issue to address was the cables themselves, which, over the years, had been cut and trapped and generally abused. If you look at photo 31.11 you can see an example of a typical cut in one of the cables caused by trapping it between the switch and the handlebars when tightening the switch casing up. In this case, as the wires inside were exposed but not shorting out, I simply mended the cable by adding a small amount of superglue and ensuring that it was properly routed when fitted. If I'd have bought new repro ones, they would have been supplied with brand new cables. Ho-hum.

I then reassembled the left lower switch, with the little contact and spring inside the white plastic moulding. See photo 31.12. This was followed by the switch lever itself which acts on the white moulding and moves it across the contacts on the Bakelite strip. See photo 31.13. I then reassembled both upper switches, this time with their little springs and ball bearings. If you look at photo 31.14 you can see the ball bearing on the left, sitting in one of two recesses that gives the switch a positive feel.

With the replacement right-hand lower switch now delivered and also refurbished like the other three, the switches were ready to go back on the

31.15 Switches reassembled.

166

HANDLEBAR SWITCHES

31.16 Left-hand switchgear in place.

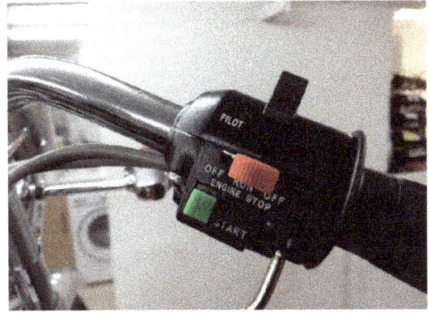

31.17 Right-hand switchgear in place – with new throttle cable.

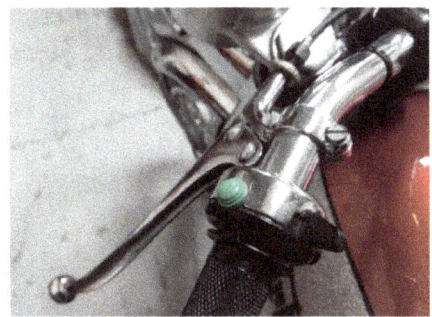

31.18 Very early Commando switchgear.

LESSONS LEARNT

- Just because one company says that switchgear is unavailable, doesn't mean that it's not available from another company! (Parts suppliers tend to see each other as rivals, rather than as part of a global brotherhood!)
- Where the throttle cable screws into the lower right switch casting is a weak point.
- The MkIII switches aren't too difficult to restore – no springs disappearing off into the corner of the garage – just a bit fiddly, and usually totally gummed up.
- I know that I shouldn't try to remove a broken stud myself as it'll only make things worse – but I still do it, every time. Some lessons just can't be learnt.
- MkIII switchgear threads are all metric.
- You can repaint the lettering on the switches relatively easily.
- Original wiring has often been cut by being trapped in the switchgear when tightened.
- It is quite satisfying to do things like this yourself rather than buying repro parts – it's another bit of the bike that you now understand and have no fear of – there's no unknown mystery anymore.
- New throttle cables with an angled tube on the end are so much better than the originals.

handlebars. See photo 31.15. Photo 31.16 shows the left-hand switch assembly in place, and photo 31.17 shows the right-hand switch in place, together with the throttle. Note the angled tubed section on the throttle cable where it screws into the switch housing – far superior to the original.

Just for information, if you look at photo 31.18 you can see the switchgear from very early Commandos, and photo 31.19 shows the later, chunky Lucas switchgear. (Note that there's some confusion about the continuing supply of the replacement Sparx units for the chunky Lucas switchgear – there is apparently the possibility that they may become unavailable as a result of a recent company take-over. However, spares to refurbish the originals are still available.)

31.19 Later chunky Lucas switchgear.

167

Chapter 32

Wiring & electrics

Time to sort the electrics. Always a moment of slight dread for many home mechanics (myself included), as our knowledge of the 'dark arts' of electricity and how it all works tends to be somewhat limited. Meaning: we know bugger all about it. However, even with my own limited knowledge in this area, I have learnt, over the years, that electrics on a classic motorcycle aren't that daunting or complicated, and that if you approach the whole thing calmly, you slowly discover that electrics are very rational, and there is a logical way they work that can be understood and mastered – or at least sufficiently understood to wire up a bike.

Do I know anything about ohms or amps or current or joules or impedance or square loop rectifiers? No. But I do have an idea of what a rectifier does, what Zener diodes do, how to properly crimp a terminal, how to make a good earth, and what colour code the main wiring on a British (Lucas) bike tends to be. That's enough to get things working. But please be aware that I'm really not that knowledgeable about electrics, so if in doubt consult someone who does know about these things.

Anyway, for what it's worth, here is my idiots' guide for Commando electrics (and most British bikes of the era):
- All Commandos are positive earth, so the + connection on the battery goes to earth.
- There are three basic parts to bike electrics: the *charging system*, the *ignition system*, and the *lighting system*. These will be dealt with one at a time – see below.
- The colour codes on a wiring loom are not random! There is actually a basic logic to it that can be very helpful! Some coloured wires are always the same:
  - Red: Earth
  - Brown/blue (or sometimes plain brown or black): Permanently live wires
  - White: Switched live (so these wires are only live when the ignition is switched on)
  - Blue/white: Headlight main beam
  - Blue/red: Headlight dipped beam
  - Green/white: Right-hand indicator
  - Green/red: Left-hand indicator
  - Brown: Stop light
  - Brown/green: Rear light/sidelight

Just knowing this is a big help, as for instance, you know that every red wire you come across is an earth wire. Also, if say you discover you need an extra switched live, if you find the nearest white wire, you can connect to that. Makes life a bit easier.
- The alternator (also known as a generator) has two parts to it – a rotor and a stator, is housed in the primary chaincase, and generates electricity to charge the battery (hopefully!). The alternators on Commandos are generally single-phase 150watt items, but the ones fitted to the MkIII are more powerful 180watt items. If you wish to, you can either fit the more powerful single-phase alternator, or a three-phase alternator, which are even better, as they produce more power at lower revs.
- The alternator produces AC (alternating current).
- The bike runs on DC (direct current).
- You therefore have a rectifier (see photo 32.1) which turns the AC from the alternator into DC for the rest of the bike.
- The alternator keeps on generating current even when the battery is fully charged, and it would damage the battery to overcharge it. You therefore need some kind of regulator

WIRING & ELECTRICS

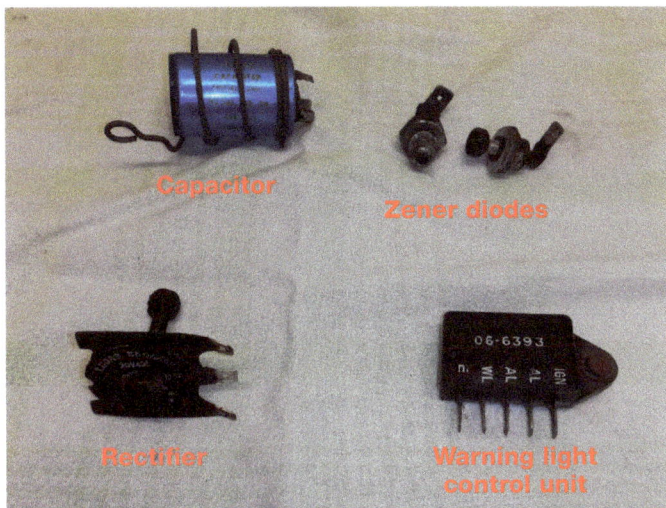

32.1 Some of the stranger electrical components on a Commando.

that allows full charge to go to the battery when it needs it, but cuts it off when it doesn't. In the case of Commandos, you have a Zener diode (or in the case of the MkIII you have two Zener diodes!) and these control the current from the alternator by turning any unwanted current into heat, which is then dissipated away. See photo 32.1. This is why you have the Zener diode(s) on a Commando mounted on the footrest supports, as they do a very good job of dissipating the heat (Triumphs and BSAs have that strange finned thing under the headlamps to cool their Zener diodes). The Zener diode is a fairly rudimentary form of regulator.

• On a MkIII, there is also a means of being able to start your bike, even if the battery is flat. This is achieved thanks to the capacitor. See photo 32.1. The capacitor retains electricity inside it (like a small battery) and can provide just enough current to fire the ignition (sparkplugs) and get the bike started in the event of a flat battery – allegedly.

• There is also a slightly weird thing on Commandos called a warning light control unit, or assimilator. This has the job of controlling the ignition warning light in the instrument panel/headlight so that it's on when there's no power from the alternator, and off when there is.

• You can fit something like a power box from Boyer, which takes the place of the rectifier, and Zener diodes, and capacitor, and warning light control unit and is much more efficient than the original components.

• Fitting LED headlamp and tail bulbs is pretty straightforward, and massively reduces strain on the charging system.

• Wiring diagrams are a godsend, especially coloured ones – use as many as you can as there are always discrepancies and anomalies.

• Always ensure you have a really good earth to all components – bad earths are a major cause of electrical problems.

Buy a proper crimping tool to make really good connections on bullet connectors etc. Another of the main causes of electrical problems on bikes is down to poor connections. See photo 32.2 of a pair of proper crimpers on the left and some wire strippers on the right. I bought my crimpers at one of the Stafford shows. Wonderful – and not to be confused with cheap, inferior ones that look similar, but are rubbish. I find soldering connections very difficult and even if a good connection is achieved, the solder makes the wires more brittle and therefore more prone to snapping. I also have a few boxes of assorted connectors, and almost literally hundreds of crimped bullet connectors – you can see them in-between the crimping and stripping tools in the photo. I also have a selection of spare wiring for that extra connection that's required somewhere. I use thicker 0.78mm diameter wire.

If you look at photo 32.3 you can see that a proper crimping tool makes a really good, professional looking crimp that ensures excellent connectivity, and that won't come apart in normal usage. A good test of a crimp is to see if you can pull a bullet out of a bullet connector by the wire, without the bullet sliding off the end.

32.2 Crimping and stripping tools plus assorted connectors.

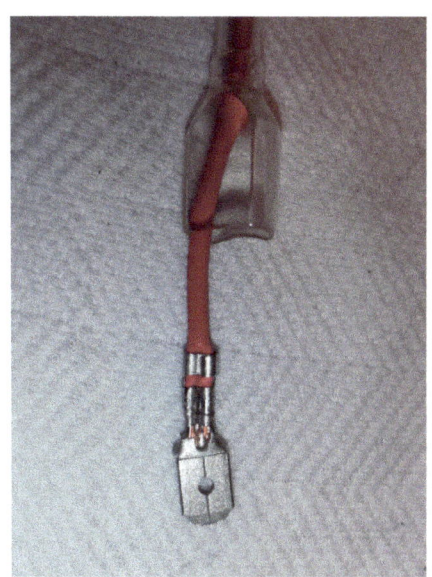

32.3 Creating a good crimp on connectors – very important.

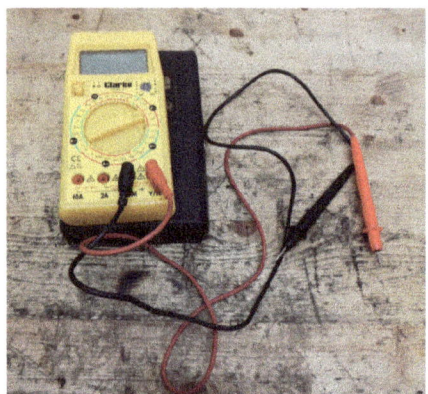

32.4 Circuit tester and voltmeter.

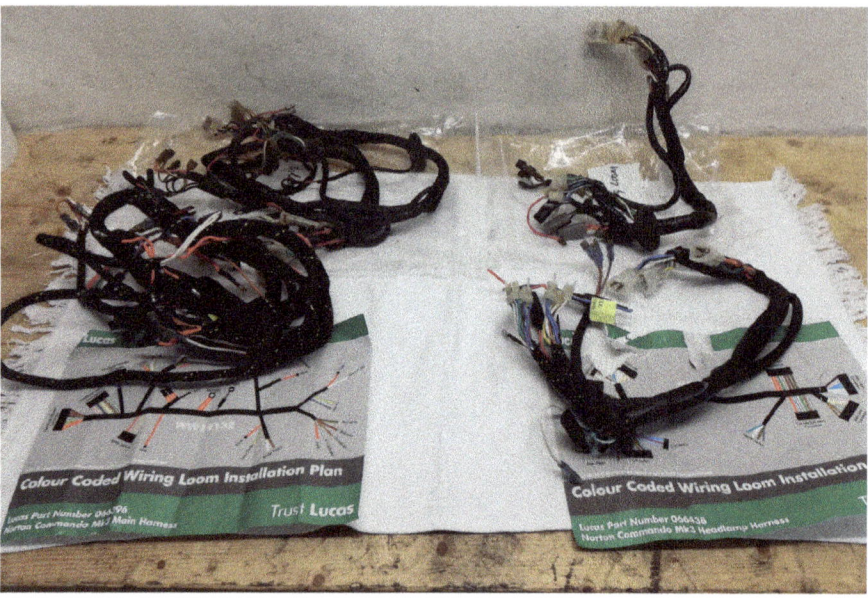

32.6 Old and new wiring looms – and clear wiring diagram.

- A very basic circuit tester and voltmeter is a pretty essential tool. See photo 32.4. I use the circuit tester to find out what wire is connected to where and to check connections etc. The voltmeter is good for checking the battery condition and the charging system.

THE CHARGING SYSTEM

I began the wiring by looking at the charging system on the bike. I decided to replace a lot of the charging electrics with a Boyer power box system. See photo 32.5. This basically does away with a lot of the original parts and replaces them with one box. The power box is an integrated unit that takes the place of the rectifier, Zener diodes, Capacitor and Warning light assimilator. It has several advantages over the original system, the main one being that it is far more efficient, and makes full use of the current provided by the alternator. It is also less prone to failure (I hope) and it is compact and very easy to wire up.

The downsides are that it's not original (I love my Zener diodes!), and it means that you have an awful lot of wiring left over from the main wiring loom, which used to go to all the above components but is no longer required, and is now generally in the way. Anyway, I went with it as it's very practical – but to be honest, with my style of riding (Sunday morning jaunts around the Peak District in the summer, and with LED bulbs fitted), I didn't really need it, as there would be little strain on the charging system – but there you go.

I'd chosen to install it to the rear of the air filter, attached to the battery box with self-tapping screws. See photo 32.7. This was because, now that the huge MkIII air filter was no more, there was a suitable space just there for it to go. Ideally, the unit should be mounted in a place that gets a lot of airflow, to cool it down (as it does get warm in use), but unless you are riding the bike hard and long in high temperatures, it'll be fine fitted under the seat, as in my case.

Having fitted the power box in position, I looked at my new wiring looms (wiring harnesses). Photo 32.6 shows the new and old looms. I opted for the expensive braided ones, as I think they look so much better – but you actually get to see so little of them when the bike's back together,

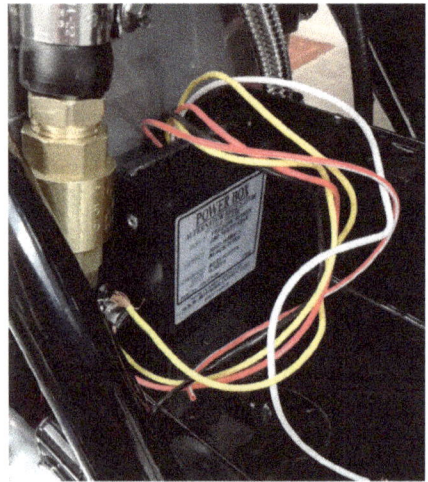

32.5 Boyer power box.

I'm not sure it was worth it. Anyway, the new looms arrived, complete with original multi-pin connectors and, in particular, two colour diagrams of the basic wiring layout of the looms. If you look again at photo 32.6 you can see these diagrams at the front. I can't tell you how useful these basic colour diagrams were. The problem is that you have two looms (main and headlamp sub-loom) that resemble a load of twisted spaghetti and no idea as to which strand of spaghetti goes where. The colour diagrams clearly showed what each strand of wire was for and therefore where it physically went on the bike. Gold dust. You can look at a schematic wiring diagram all day long, but it doesn't show where the wiring physically goes on the bike; and having that knowledge made life so much easier. Needless to say this was augmented and verified by looking at the photos I'd taken of the original wiring looms before removing them. One bonus of the MkIII is the use of multi-pin connectors at the main junctions – fiddly to connect, but so much less of a faff than the earlier types with countless bullet connectors.

There were a couple of quality control issues with some of the connections on the new looms (see photo 32.7), and I had to check all the wiring for such flaws as they could easily have shorted out against the frame etc if left as they were. Having

WIRING & ELECTRICS

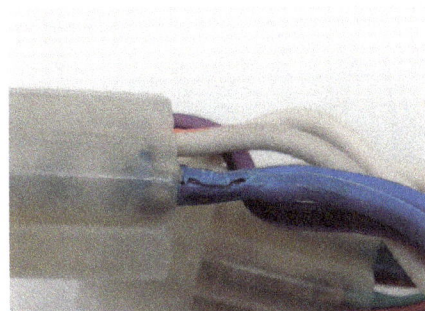

32.7 Some quality control issues.

completed this, I fitted the new looms onto the frame of the bike, and began to clip the big multi-pin connectors, which join the two looms, together under the fuel tank. See photo 32.8. With the main wiring loom in place, I was confronted with a mass of wiring in and around the battery box that required sorting. See photo 32.9. The strange thing was, I soon realised that the majority of this wiring was now redundant, thanks to the new power box.

I think I went from 18 wires and connections in and around the battery box down to five, thanks to the power box. To begin with, I left the redundant wiring hanging, just in case it wasn't actually redundant. Later on, when I'd established that they were definitely not required, I cut the wires down and sealed the ends. Note that I had also decided not to refit the original power socket, which was supplied with MkIIIs just above the support bracket on the right-hand side. It was very useful in its day, but is now rather dated, and I thought that I could easily add a power outlet to the battery if I required it at any point. (I later did this to power my mobile phone/Google maps, but it can be transferred easily between bikes.)

After a little while, I slowly started to tame the wiring and wire up the power box, which was very straightforward – full, simple instructions were supplied. See photo 32.10. Note that the ignition warning light is now connected directly to the power box, without the need to go through an assimilator first. The only problem that I had, which came to light after the bike was finished, was with the live wire to the power box. When I started the engine all was well, but when I turned off the ignition, the engine continued to run! Very disconcerting! I turned off the engine with the kill switch and investigated.

I soon realised that what I'd done had been to wire the power box to switched live (white wire) rather than permanent live (brown/blue wire). The result of this was that when the ignition was turned off, the engine was still turning and therefore the alternator was still producing current. This current was enough to keep the ignition going, and hence the engine continued to run! I simply connected

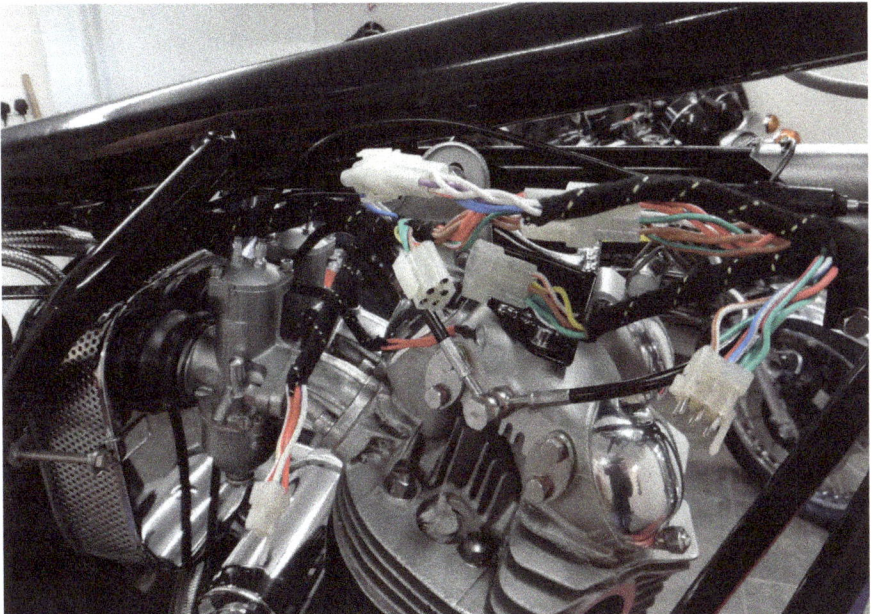

32.8 Beginning to lay out the two main looms and connect them together.

32.9 Wiring chaos in the battery compartment.

32.10 Slowly taming the wiring.

HOW TO RESTORE NORTON COMMANDO

the power box to permanent live rather than switched live, and all was well. I also checked that the alternator was charging properly with my voltmeter – full details on this in the chapter on fettling the engine. The charging system was now wired up.

THE IGNITION SYSTEM

I had decided from the outset to fit electronic ignition. There are several different makes of electronic ignition to choose from, including Pazon, Rita and Boyer-Bransden, but my personal favourite is Tri-spark, especially the newer versions that are fully contained under the points cover. It's not the cheapest, but I rate it as one of the best. However, like oil and tyres etc, everyone has their own opinion, and the choice is very much up to the individual owner, according to their preferences.

To begin with, I set the engine at the fully advanced position using the timing marks in the primary chaincase, by aligning the mark in the rotor with the 28 degree mark on the indicator. See photo 32.11. As the indicator in the primary chaincase can be adjusted slightly, I confirmed the timing by removing the timing plug in the right-hand side of the engine to reveal a groove in the crankshaft which, when central with the hole, sets the timing at 28 degrees exactly. See photo 32.12. I have a small special tool for this that screws into the hole and locates with the groove in the crankshaft. (Note that oil dribbled out of the hole as I had previously pre-filled the crankcases with oil, ready for initial starting.)

With the ignition timing set to full advance, I inserted the ignition module into position, with the screw holes exactly in the middle of the adjustment grooves, and put a mark on the timing case exactly in line with the 'B' marking on the module. See photo 32.13. (The 'B' marking is for engines, like the Commando, where the camshaft runs anti-clockwise, and the 'A' marking is for engines running clockwise – modules are set for one or the other and are not interchangeable.)

Having done this, I removed the module and screwed the backplate/rotor loosely onto the camshaft with an Allen screw (supplied). I turned it until the two small magnets on the rotor aligned with the mark I'd made on the casing. See photo 32.14. I then tightened the Allen screw. After this, I checked that the rotor was recessed at least 2mm below the level of the casing, using the small guide tool provided. If it's not recessed enough, the system won't work properly – a small air gap is required between the two components. See photo 32.15. After this I connected the old wires, that used to go to the points, to the new module, and loosely fitted it in position using the original pillar bolts. See photo 32.16.

Next up were the ignition coils. It is worth remembering that the old

32.13 Marking the 'B' position with the electronic ignition module centralised.

32.11 Timing set at fully advanced.

32.14 Backplate fitted to the end of the camshaft with magnets lined up to the mark made previously.

32.15 Checking the backplate is recessed sufficiently to clear the outer plate.

32.12 Ignition timing confirmed by crankcase timing plug.

WIRING & ELECTRICS

ones looked rather complicated, with a ballast resistor and condensers fitted between the coils. See photos 32.17 & 32.18. Condensers help prevent the points from arcing, and ballast resistors help to maintain current to the coils when an electric start is being used, taking most of the power from the battery with it. Now that the electronic ignition was fitted, both these components, and the associated rats' nest of wiring, were no longer required. Instead, the wiring couldn't be more simple: the black/white wire coming out of the new electronic ignition module went to the negative on one coil, a link then went from the positive to the negative on the second coil, and then an earth wire from that positive to earth. See photo 32.19. Note that I had also fitted new HT leads and plug caps.

The only other wiring that was required was a switched live feed to the ignition module, to replace the multi-pin connector from the original setup. I therefore found the switched live in the multi-pin connector, that came from the kill switch, and connected that to the black/yellow on the module. See photo 32.20. The ignition was now wired up.

Later on, when the battery was connected, I set the ignition timing statically, with the aid of the little built-in LED on the module. I once again set the engine to fully advanced 28 degrees BTDC (before top dead centre), switched the ignition on, and

32.16 Ignition connected up and loosely tightened.

32.19 New coils in situ without the ballast resistor, condensers, or associated wiring.

32.17 Original ignition coils and wiring.

32.20 One wire required to provide power.

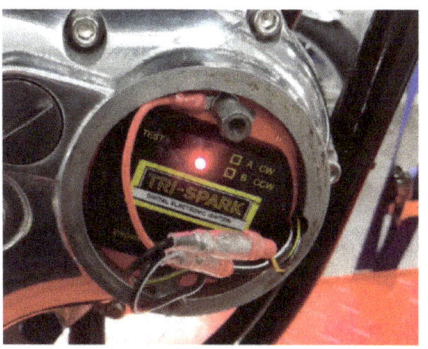
32.21 Statically timing the ignition with the built-in LED.

32.18 Ballast resistor and condensers.

32.22 Electronic ignition completed, and hidden behind the points cover.

HOW TO RESTORE NORTON COMMANDO

then turned the ignition module until the LED just illuminated. See photo 32.21. This meant that the ignition was now roughly set and I semi-tightened the pillar bolts. It would be checked with a strobe when the bike was started to set the timing exactly (see chapter 38). I then temporarily fitted the points cover and the ignition system was sorted. See photo 32.22.

THE LIGHTING SYSTEM (AND INSTRUMENTS)

Before I go any further, let me just say that I think that one of the most effective and easy ways to upgrade the electrics on any classic motorcycle is to change the battery to an absorbed glass mat (AGM) battery, often referred to as a gel battery, but gel batteries are actually slightly different. They are more reliable, maintenance free, have no liquid acid in them to spill (and therefore don't require topping-up either), hardly lose any charge when left standing (and are not damaged if they do discharge), and they are far more powerful than the originals. I have them in all of my bikes and I fitted an MBTX14AU AGM battery by Motobatt to the Commando and it's great. Highly recommended. Note that different AGM batteries may be recommended for different models. Check the 'amp hour' rating to give an idea of how powerful the battery is.

The lighting (and horn) system is probably the most straightforward on the bike – there's just a lot of wiring to sort out and lots of awkward fiddly bits to try and get to work and look tidy at the same time. To begin with, I reconditioned some of the electrical components, starting with the headlamp reflector and rim. See

32.23 Fitting the headlamp reflector into the new rim.

32.24 Instrument binnacle looking tired.

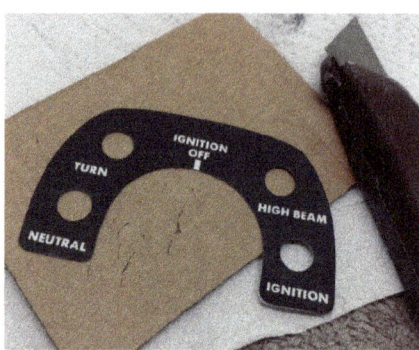
32.25 Preparing to fit a new legend on the binnacle.

32.26 Fitting the idiot lights to the binnacle with new clips from Andover Norton.

photo 32.23. The reflector is held in position in the rim with 'W' clips, and these love nothing better than pinging off at high velocity to distant corners of the workshop at every opportunity when attempting to refit them. One solution is to assemble the reflector and rim inside a large, clear freezer bag, so you can see what you're doing, but the 'W' clips can't escape! Note that there is a lug on the reflector that aligns with two prongs on the rim, to ensure that the reflector is mounted in the correct position. This is visible in the 11 o'clock position in the photo.

I fitted an LED bulb to the headlight as they take so much less power than a normal bulb and I ride with my headlight on at all times (my reasoning is that even if it only makes you 5 per cent more visible to car drivers, that's a bonus, and I think it maybe makes you about 20 per cent more visible – but each to his own). Also, these days I don't ride at night, so I wasn't worried about how effective it was as a proper headlight. The bulb is a straightforward swap with the original.

I then looked at the instrument binnacle (MkIII) which had seen better days (see photo 32.24). After thoroughly cleaning it, I prepared to fit a new legend to the fascia. See photo 32.25. It took me absolutely ages to peel the backing off the self-adhesive sticker, as it's so thin! At one point I wasn't even sure that the backing came off, but eventually I managed it, and the legend was duly stuck in place. I then thoroughly cleaned and refitted the idiot lights to the binnacle, using special clips from Andover Norton. See photo 32.26. These clips were different to the 'spire' clips that were originally fitted, but seemed to work better, giving a good, secure fit to the lights. There's absolutely nothing worse than a warning light pushing up, out of the binnacle or headlamp, usually at a jaunty angle, and it can't be pushed back down. Infuriating! Now's the time to ensure they're really secure. The binnacle looked good. See photo 32.27.

After this, I cleaned the ignition switch and re-wired it. I'd taken copious photos of the wiring before disconnecting it during dismantling, and these helped a lot in ensuring that it was reconnected correctly. However, I also discovered that each connector was numbered, and these corresponded with the numbers in the wiring diagram in the workshop manual – just in case you haven't any photos to help you. See photo 32.28.

I then began to sort the wiring in the headlight by joining as many multi-pin connectors together as possible, to get them out of the way. This is where all the wiring from the handlebars and the main harness join, so it's pretty busy in there – but everything's colour coded so it just takes a little time and patience. See

WIRING & ELECTRICS

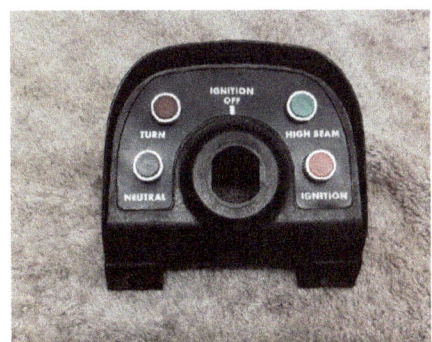

32.27 Refurbished binnacle.

32.28 Ignition switch has numbered contacts.

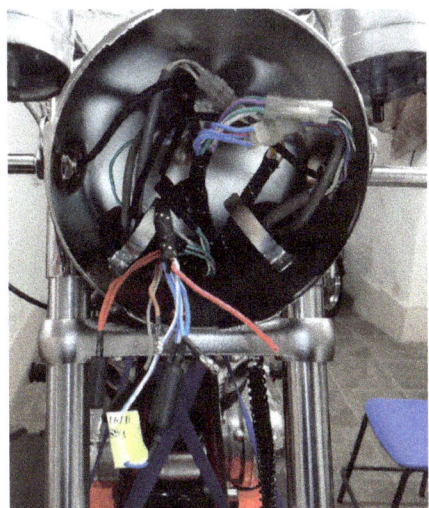

32.29 Beginning to sort out the headlamp wiring.

32.30 Indicator flasher unit sits loose in the headlamp shell.

32.31 Refitting the original instruments as the new ones won't go in.

photo 32.29. I also connected the indicator flasher unit which simply sits loose in the headlamp shell. See photo 32.30.

I then tried to fit my new, minimalist tacho and speedo in the extended alloy housings as fitted to MkIIIs. There was nothing wrong with the original French Veglia instruments on my bike, but I'd decided to change them for two reasons: firstly, I don't like the look of the Veglias, and secondly, it is virtually impossible to recondition Veglia instruments – there is no stock of spares anywhere, and no-one has the licence to remanufacture them. You can't even change the chrome bezels or clock faces. I had therefore bought a new, plain tacho and speedo with more 'classic' styling and planned to fit them instead. However, I soon realised that my new speedo had the trip adjuster on the side, rather than on the bottom, and so wouldn't slide into the alloy housing I had spent considerable time stripping from the original black and polishing up. I therefore simply decided to re-install the originals, at least temporarily, until I either found new brackets to take the new instruments, or new instruments to fit the original brackets. See photo 32.31.

I then looked at the rear light. As with the headlamp, I had decided to change it to an LED – it's much brighter and takes far less current. The problem with the rear light, though, is that the bulb points downwards, not rearwards, and so you have to replace the bulb and reflector with a little board of small LEDs. Photo 32.32 shows the original bulb and reflector, which are then removed from the alloy holder and replaced with a small board of LED lights, screwed to the alloy holder. See photo 32.33. (There are a couple of LEDs on the bottom edge that shine down onto the rear number plate). It may look small, but it's much, much brighter.

I mounted the rear indicators into the rear light bracket, adding an earth lead to each one just to be sure they were both properly earthed – the brackets had all been powder-coated. See photo 32.34. I then mounted the new rear 7½in x 8½in black and silver pressed alloy number plate. See photo 32.35. Black and silver plates can now be fitted to any vehicle over 40 years old in the UK. The smallest permissible plate is 6½in x 8½in, but they look a bit dinky, so I went with the slightly larger one; still much smaller than the original black and yellow ones, which I hate with a vengeance. Again, each to his own. Note that I used large penny washers to the rear of the plate to hide the mess of holes drilled by previous owners in the mounting plate.

My final job, as with the front indicators, was to fully tighten the nut inside the head of the indicator, to prevent them from turning when in use. After protruding/loose warning lights, indicators that droop in use are my second most hated irritant. (Don't forget that I'm a bit OCD!) See photo 32.36. I then loosely attached the rear light assembly to the rear mudguard to test it before final fitting. See photo 32.37.

With everything temporarily wired up, I gingerly connected the battery – no sparks! No smoke! And then tested all the lights and indicators etc (and the horn) and everything worked as it should. See photo 32.38. One point of interest was that when trying to wire up the warning lights on the instrument binnacle I was confused by having two green/white wires instead of one green/white and one green/red wire. It was only when I pulled back the sheathing on the wire that I realised that over the years one wire had been bleached in the sun,

HOW TO RESTORE NORTON COMMANDO

and was in fact a green/red wire! See photo 32.39.

I wired up the instrument binnacle and inserted the ignition switch, only to discover that there was an unholy mess of exposed wires protruding from underneath it. See photo 32.40. I therefore set about trying to tidy it. I applied some heat shrink sheathing to the exposed wires on the warning lights (see photo 32.41) and then discovered that I was also missing a rubber boot for the underneath of the ignition switch, which I duly purchased and fitted. See photo 32.42. Needless to say this now made fitting the spade connectors into position very fiddly and awkward, but eventually I triumphed. The result isn't perfect, but is a lot neater than how it was before. See photo 32.43.

The instrument binnacle, ignition switch and instruments were now fitted! See photo 32.44. Note that I had not fitted the small lighting bulbs in the speedo and tacho. (Naughty, naughty!) I have no intention of riding in the dark and I always find these little lights awkward and troublesome at the best of times. I therefore simply left them out, together with the rubber boots on the bottom of the instrument brackets, as I think it makes the whole finish a lot cleaner/neater.

I then finished fitting the rear brakelight assembly to the rear mudguard, together with its slightly strange fibreglass cover. See photo 32.45. I had toyed with the idea of fitting an alloy rear light assembly from a Triumph instead of the original, as I think they look so much better, and I know that other owners have done this modification. In the end though, I left it as was, for reasons of time, money, worry that the Triumph item wouldn't fit the mudguard, and a desire to grow to like the flimsy, black, weirdly sculpted, fibreglass Norton unit. (I'm still working on it!)

All that remained to be done was go round the bike adding cable ties where appropriate. Note that not until the wiring was completely finished did I start tying anything up – you can guarantee that you'll only have to cut the cable ties off again. I also ensured that I didn't stretch any wires or trap anything that needed to move, such as the wires round the headstock. Note that apart from a couple of very necessary cable ties on the speedo cable, to keep it away from the rear chain, no cables were tied down, as they need to move freely if they are to work properly.

I also used small, white cable ties on the handlebar wires to give a neat, crisp finish (do I sound like a wine waiter?). Job done.

The electrics were now finished! Hurrah!

32.32 Original rear light bulb and reflector.

32.33 Original bulb replaced with an LED.

32.35 Rear light assembly completed.

32.36 Removing the indicator bulb to tighten the stem.

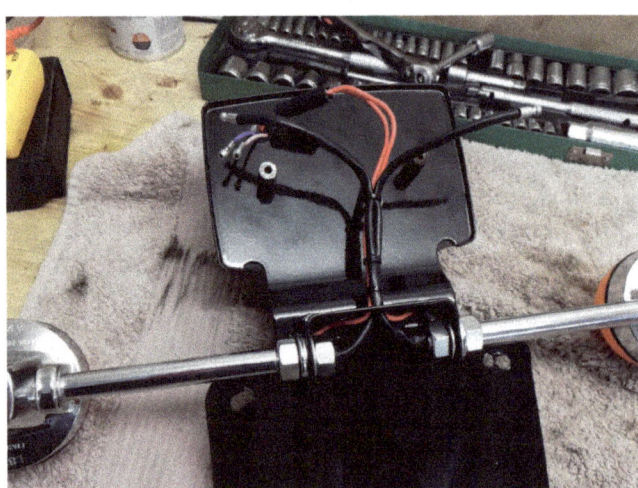

32.34 Rear light screwed to mounting and indicators fitted with extra earth wires.

32.37 Rear light assembly in situ.

WIRING & ELECTRICS

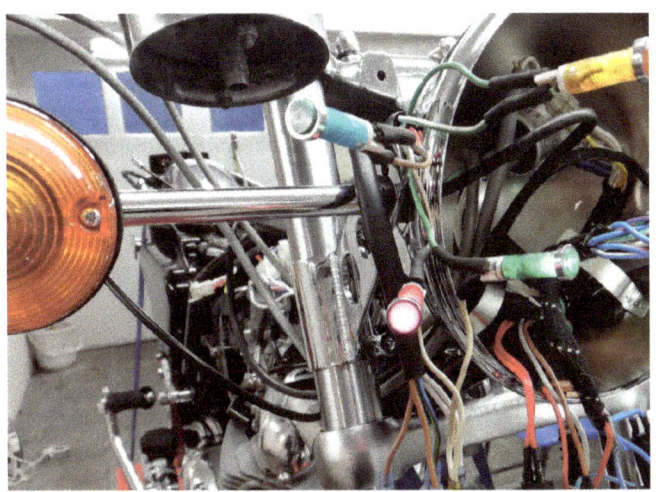

32.38 Testing the electrics are working before fitting.

32.45 Rear light assembly fully fitted with fibreglass cover.

32.39 Showing how the green and red wire became a green and white wire in the sun!

32.42 Fitting rubber boot to ignition switch wiring.

32.40 Wiring to the instrument binnacle in place, but very messy.

32.43 Wiring a lot tidier under the binnacle now.

32.41 Fitting heat shrink to the idiot light wiring.

32.44 Instrument binnacle and instruments fitted.

LESSONS LEARNT

- You don't need to have great electrical knowledge to wire a bike back up; as long as everything's plugged into the right place, you're good.
- Bad earths and poor connections are often the main causes of electrical problems.
- There are several upgrades available for the electrics to bring them up to more modern standards – worth considering depending on how you intend to use the bike.
- AGM batteries: the answer. Now, what's the question?
- There are three main electrical systems on a bike: charging, ignition and lighting – tackle them one at a time and it's much easier.
- Electronic ignition – highly recommended. Which make you choose is up to you. (There are more opinions on this than on which oil to use!)
- LED bulbs – I use them and love them, but again, not everyone's cup of tea.
- If you try and fit even the simplest of upgrades (like changing the speedo and tacho) then you can just about guarantee that the last thing they'll turn out to be is a simple upgrade.
- Don't start putting cable ties on until everything is finished and checked.
- Two things to really annoy any classic biker: protruding warning lights and drooping indicators! Ugh!

Chapter 33
Fitting the support plates

Time to fit the iconic support plates. Again, I think that the support plates were a bit of a compromise from designers under an incredibly tight time schedule. They needed to find a way to fit the footrests and pedals to their new frame, and bolting on a couple of extra plates on either side of the bike was a quick and easy solution, although maybe an act of slight desperation. But, as with the rest of the Commando story, not only did they work, but they served to enhance the look of the bike and make it into something greater than the sum of its parts. I mean, they enhance the look of the bike and they are an iconic part of any Commando, rather than looking like a hasty add-on by desperate designers under pressure. Just one of those times when all the various odd bits came together to create a great bike – when on paper they shouldn't have!

I'd had the alloy plates highly polished, and they looked great! Each side is held on by three bolts: the long bolt going through the rear isolastics and two smaller bolts into the frame side plates – and they bolt on easily and quickly with three spacers behind them. Both the left-hand and right-hand support plates were quickly fitted. See photos 33.1 and 33.2.

I quickly added the footrest bracket to the left-hand plate (see photo 33.3) followed by the footrest rubber, which I slid on with just a hint of soap, as I wanted the soap to evaporate as soon as possible to leave the rubber tight on the shaft. See photo 33.4.

33.1 Right-hand support plate being fitted.

33.2 Left-hand support plate in place.

FITTING THE SUPPORT PLATES

33.3 Left-hand footrest fitted.

33.5 Master cylinder, brake pedal and footrest in place.

33.4 Left-hand footrest and rubber fitted.

33.6 Footrest, brake and kickstart lever fitted.

On the right-hand side, I fitted the refurbished master cylinder (see chapter 35), the footrest and the brake pedal. See photo 33.5. Note that I'd had to have the brake pedal straightened before re-chroming as it was bent towards the timing case, probably caused by the bike having fallen over at some point. My local garage obliged with this, making use of its oxy-acetelene torch to apply high localised heat to the pedal, and they successfully bent it back to its correct shape. On the MkIII, the brake pedal is held away from the support plate by a large triangular spacer to accommodate the master cylinder. Lastly, I fitted the kickstart lever and the support plate was sorted. See photo 33.6.

LESSONS LEARNT
• The support plates were a compromise to try and get a bike into production quickly – but rather than look like a belated add-on, they really enhance the look of the bike and helped turn the Commando into a classic.
• The support plates are alloy, and they polish up really well.

Chapter 34
Refitting the rear wheel & mudguard

Time to rebuild and refit the rear wheel. Before going any further, I think it's important to remember that while the exploded diagrams in the *Parts Catalog* can give an idea of how parts are assembled, they should never be relied upon to be accurate, and the rear wheel assembly on a MkIII is very much a case in point. Note that even some of the exploded diagrams in the *Norton Workshop Manual* aren't always quite correct, and so you do have to be a bit wary.

To begin with, I looked at the exploded diagram in the *Parts Catalog*, only to find a catalogue of errors (geddit?). If you look at photo 34.1 you can see that the main axle spindle is depicted as a stud, not a bolt, the nut on the left-hand side short axle is shown on the right-hand side, the oil seal that should go in the back of the sprocket is shown as being in the middle of the speedo

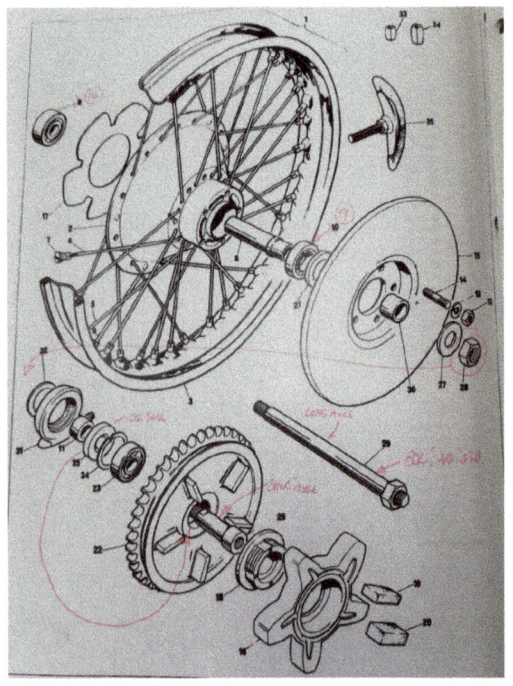
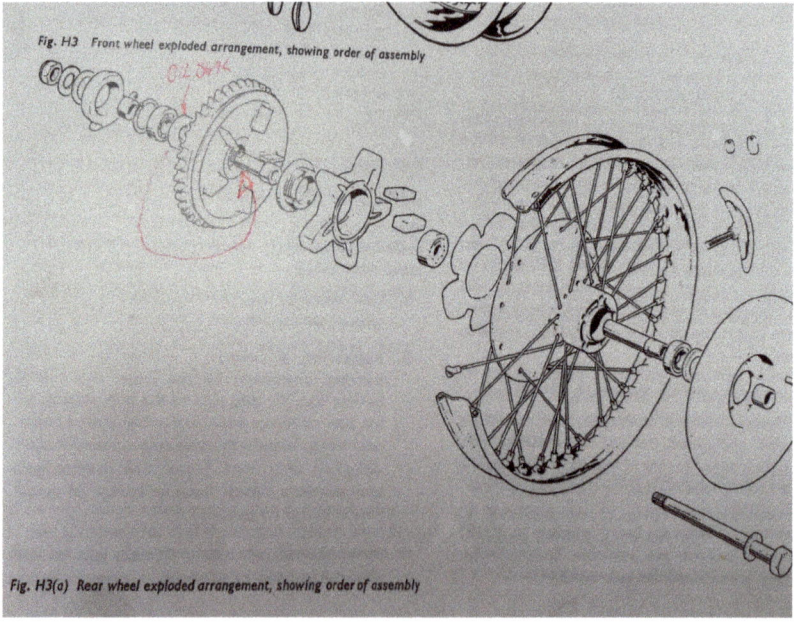

34.1 (Left) Errors in the *Parts Catalog*. 34.1a (Above) Error in the *Norton Workshop Manual*.

180

REFITTING THE REAR WHEEL & MUDGUARD

34.2 Driving in the right-hand bearing, but not too far.

34.3 Sleeve or spacer tube inserted.

34.4 Left-hand bearing fitted.

34.5 Fitting the wide sprocket bearing, after it was found! Circlip holds it in place.

34.6 Beginning to insert the shock absorber rubbers between the hub and the drive centre.

drive, and the part numbers for the two rear hub bearings are reversed – apart from that, all okay! The *Norton Workshop Manual* makes a better fist of it, see photo 34.1a, but still shows the sprocket oil seal on the wrong side of the sprocket. It took me a lot of head scratching, reference to my dismantling photos and the odd phone call to the wonderful technical helpline at Andover Norton to sort all this out – just something to be aware of.

Anyway, with the order of assembly finally clear in my head, I began rebuilding the rear wheel by inserting the larger hub bearing in the right-hand side of the hub. See photo 34.2. As ever, I heated the hub, and cooled the bearing in the freezer before trying to insert it. Note that it is not driven all the way home, but to a depth of about 5/16in below the rim of the hub. Also note that I used the hub sleeve/spacer as a drift to knock the bearing home. This isn't a recommended method of bearing insertion as you are knocking on the inner bearing race, not the outer, and therefore risking damaging the bearing itself. I did this as I couldn't find a socket of the correct size to sit on the outer race, and because the bearing wasn't too tight a fit in the hub.

With the first bearing in situ I removed the sleeve/spacer and inserted it into the hub from the other side. See photo 34.3. I then inserted the smaller left-hand bearing in the hub (having heated the hub, cooled the bearing, and used a socket as a drift). See photo 34.4. Note that there are three bearings in the rear wheel assembly on most Commandos– two in the hub and one in the rear sprocket.

For more information on the earlier models with different rear sprockets, refer to Chapter 6.

At this point, I thought that I may as well fit the wide bearing in the rear sprocket as well, but when I came to fit the bearing, I couldn't find it. I knew I'd bought it, but I looked everywhere and it was nowhere to be seen. In the end there was nothing for it but to order a new one. When the new one arrived I prepared to fit it and opened the freezer ready to cool the bearing before fitting. Needless to say, there was the original bearing sitting on the top shelf smiling at me! Damn! I'd put the bloody thing in the freezer at the same time as the hub bearings, and immediately forgot that I had. Please give generously to the Alzheimer's society. Anyway, I finally fitted the bearing (well, one of the two that I now had!) using the normal method, and then held it in position with its circlip. See photo 34.5.

Turning back to the rear wheel I began to insert the rubbers in the hub, between it and the drive centre. See photo 34.6. These form the engine shock absorber, or cush drive. The rubbers are there to help soften, or cushion any sudden surge of power from the engine to the back wheel. Without them, there can be a lot of stress placed on the primary and rear chain under sudden acceleration. Some bikes have them in the primary chaincase, and others in the rear wheel, as the Commando generally does. Most notably though, there is no cush drive or other form of engine shock absorber fitted to the very early Commandos and so I wouldn't recommend trying to pull a wheelie on one of these.[1]

On MkIII cush drives, there are five longer rubbers and five shorter ones. My original ones looked almost

---

[1] At this point I have to make reference to the legendary cult biker film *Stone*. It's a great film, and if you've not seen it, then I recommend that you do. Although the bikes featured are mainly Kawasaki Z1s (it's an Ozzie film) there is one brilliant scene where a Z1 and a Commando (Combat?) race head-to-head around the streets of Sydney – wheelies galore! Type 'Bikes drag race 1974 from great Oz movie, Stone' into YouTube and the scene should come up. I wish I could ride like those stunt riders! PS The whole film is on there, somewhere, too.

34.7 Inserting all the shock absorber rubbers using soap.

34.8 Tightening the lock ring over the drive centre.

34.10 When assembled there will be a slight gap between the sprocket and the hub.

new so I reused them. The longer rubber goes in the longer gap and the shorter ones in the shorter gaps – so the longer ones take most of the shock of the engine power. I used soap to help them slide in, and although it was a bit fiddly, it wasn't a nightmare job as some cush drives can be, with the rubbers sliding in without too much fuss. See photo 34.7.

Needless to say, it was only at this point that I realised I had failed to fit the backplate behind the rubbers first. If you look again at photo 34.7 you can see the plate at the bottom of the photo. Bugger! Two things here: Firstly, I should have known that there was a problem as the shock absorber went together so smoothly – if everything goes together very smoothly, it usually means that it's lulling you into a false sense of security, knowing full well that you've left a bit out and are going to have to take it all apart again – they're damn clever these bikes! Secondly, it was time to once again repeatedly mutter Robert M Pirsig's mantra, with a scowl on my face!

With the cush drive dismantled and reassembled again with the backplate in position, I screwed the locking ring into the hub. See photo 34.8. However, the locking ring wouldn't seat on the drive centre and I thought this was due to my having fitted the right side bearing too deep in the hub. I therefore gently heated the hub and, using an appropriate socket, I knocked the left-hand bearing in slightly, which, due to the sleeve/spacer tube, moved the right hand bearing out slightly. See photo 34.9. I was then able to fully tighten the lock ring.

I then trial fitted the sprocket

34.9 Moving the bearings slightly.

on the hub. See photo 34.10. The sprocket has three veins that slot into grooves in the cush drive. Note that there is a slight gap between the hub and the cush drive. This is supposed to be there – due to the rubbers, the sprocket and hub moving relative to each other under hard acceleration, they need that gap for the hub and the cush drive to move independently, without grinding against each other.

I then turned my attention to the speedo drive, and after thoroughly cleaning and polishing it, I pumped new grease into it, expelling any old grease at the same time. See photo 34.11. I was then ready to fit the sprocket assembly on its short axle and laid the parts out in the correct order. See photo 34.12. Note that I had also fitted the oil (grease) seal to the inside of the sprocket, behind the bearing. The rear sprocket was then loosely fitted to check that all was okay. See photo 34.13.

Before I could fit the rear wheel, I needed to fit the rear mudguard. The first thing I needed to do was to remove the horn – again! I suddenly realised that the mudguard bolted onto the same bolts that the horn mounting bracket was on. The bolts for mounting are very long,

34.11 After cleaning the speedo drive, it is filled with fresh grease.

34.12 Order of assembly of the rear sprocket and speedo drive on the short axle stub.

so mounting both the horn and the mudguard at the same time. I therefore replaced the short bolts I'd originally used to mount the horn bracket with much longer ones. After this, I bolted the upper mudguard mounting plate in position on the frame and the mudguard was ready to be fitted. See photo 34.14.

I loosely fitted the new mudguard only to find that it wouldn't fit – it fouled on the return pipe to the oil tank. I compared the new mudguard with the old one, and, sure enough they were different; the new mudguard wasn't shaped as thinly as the original at the bottom,

REFITTING THE REAR WHEEL & MUDGUARD

and that was why it wouldn't fit. See photo 34.15. I therefore used my rudimentary metalwork skills to reshape the mudguard and make it thinner so it cleared the inlet pipe – thank God you can't see where I 'reshaped' it when it's on the bike! I then loosely mounted the mudguard on its three mounting bolts. See photo 34.16.

After this, I connected the rear chain to the rear sprocket and fitted the rear chainguard. See photo 34.17. Note that I had left the chain sitting on the gearbox sprocket since rebuilding the primary chaincase, as it's such a bugger to try and feed the chain onto the gearbox sprocket. As it was, the job was very easy. I fitted a standard chain to my bike. You can fit 'O' ring chains to Commandos, but in order to do so you need to fit a special gearbox sprocket, that is slightly thinner, and machine down the rear sprocket, as thinner ones are not available. For my occasional use this was all rather unnecessary, so I just used the standard chain and sprockets.

Also note that on MkIIIs there's a very practical but very ugly plastic extension on the rear of the chainguard, held on by a spring clip, which is no doubt very effective at stopping grease etc being flung about, but looks hideous, so I left it off.

The rear mudguard, chain, chainguard and rear sprocket were all now loosely fitted and ready to accept the rear wheel. See photo 34.18.

Turning back to the rear wheel, I prepared to refit the disc by inserting a new bearing oil seal and the spacer that goes through it. See photo 34.19. I then cleaned and painted the original rear disc. See photo 34.20. I would like to have fitted a drilled disc, rather than the original solid ones, simply because I think they look better, and I think that they are available, but funds were running low by this time, so I reused the original.

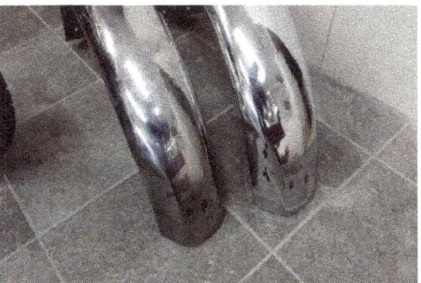
34.15 New mudguard was wider than the original.

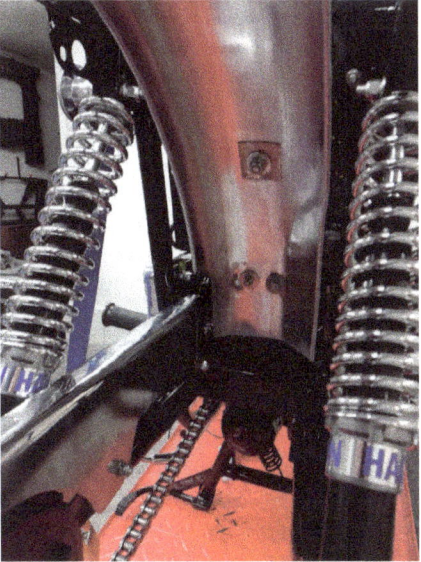
34.16 Mudguard loosely bolted onto its three front mountings.

34.13 Rear sprocket loosely fitted.

34.14 Having taken off the horn for the umpteenth time, I fitted the proper long bolts to fit the mudguard, together with the square mounting plate, higher up.

34.17 Rear chain fitted on the sprocket and chainguard in place, minus end piece.

HOW TO RESTORE NORTON COMMANDO

34.18 Rear mudguard, chainguard and sprocket fitted.

34.21 Rear disc fitted.

34.19 Oil seal and spacer fitted to the right-hand side of the wheel.

34.20 Giving the rear disc a quick make-over.

After painting it, I bolted the disc to the rear hub. See photo 34.21.

It was time to fit the rear wheel in the swinging arm. However, despite having the wonderful new 'quick release' rear wheel, it was anything but – as I discovered when removing it. The problem is that the mudguard is just in the way and the manual recommends 'leaning the bike over slightly' to get the wheel in. With just me, and the bike on the lift, that was never an option. However, I did have a bike lift with a removable rear section and that allowed me to lower the wheel down into the hole, and then pull it back up into position. See photo 34.22. (Although even that was a lot harder than it sounds). I then loosely fitted the rear calliper bracket onto the rear of the lower shock absorber mounting and juggled the wheel in position, having replaced the removable section on the bike lift. The rear wheel was now in! See photo 34.23. (Note that at this point I still had the old central plug in the rear calliper in place, which I went on to replace. See chapter 35.)

PS One slight modification I made before fitting the rear wheel was to put alignment marks on the tops of the swinging arm where the wheel spindles fit, so I could more easily align the rear wheel when adjusting the chain etc. You can probably see them the clearest in photo 34.17. A simple mod. But very worthwhile!

34.22 Fitting the rear wheel is still a faff despite the 'quick release' design!

REFITTING THE REAR WHEEL & MUDGUARD

LESSONS LEARNT
- The exploded diagrams in the *Parts Catalog* and the *Norton Workshop Manual* are often very helpful – but they can't always be relied upon for accuracy.
- Who put that bloody bearing in the freezer?!
- Engine shock absorber/cush drive – saving chains the world over.
- If something goes together easily and smoothly, it's lulling you into a false sense of security.
- Remember the mantra: If you have to do it all again, then the second time it's so much easier and quicker – and you understand it more. It does help mitigate the pain!
- How many times did I fit that bloody horn?!
- The rear mudguard sits on long bolts that mount the horn as well.
- 'O' ring chains are difficult to fit to a Commando.
- The chainguard bolts on one lower shock absorber mounting, the rear calliper bracket to the other.
- Quick release rear wheels – Hmmm!

34.23 Rear wheel loosely in position with rear brake calliper bracket in place.

Chapter 35
Refurbishing the brakes

Time to fit the front and rear disc brake systems. (See the end of this chapter for some info on the earlier drum brake models.) To start with I had a dilemma: I wanted the best brakes I could get, but I also wanted to keep the beautiful, unique, original Norton-Lockheed 'clamshell' brake callipers (MkIIIs have two). Eventually, I decided to change the front master cylinder, calliper and brake disc for upgraded versions, but keep the original rear calliper and master cylinder.

I began by reconditioning the rear master cylinder. The master cylinder is basically in three parts: a fluid reservoir, an alloy housing, and the master cylinder itself. First of all, I removed the fluid reservoir by unscrewing the nut in the bottom of the reservoir. See photo 35.1. After this I separated the master cylinder from its alloy housing. The two are screwed together and then locked with a small grub screw underneath. I loosened the small grub screw before unscrewing the master cylinder. See photo 35.2. After this I removed the clevis arm and its locking nuts from the end of the shaft on the master cylinder, and unscrewed the master cylinder from the alloy housing. See photo 35.3. Whoops!

I discovered after this that the two locking nuts on the pushrod are set at the factory and should never be removed, or else the master cylinder won't work properly. Oh, dear. I can vouch for the fact that this is the case, as mine didn't initially work after reassembly, but after a bit of trial and error I'm glad to say that I got it working really well. See chapter 38.

With the master cylinder removed from its housing I was able to dismantle and inspect the internal components. In order to dismantle the master cylinder I removed the circlip at the end, which holds everything together. My first check was of the internal bore of the master cylinder itself – if the bore is rusted or worn then it's basically scrap and not worth

35.1 Removing the reservoir from the master cylinder.

35.2 Removing the grub screw holding the master cylinder and its housing together.

REFURBISHING THE BRAKES

35.3 Master cylinder separated from its housing.

35.5 Compressing the spring to allow the refitting of the circlip.

35.4 The master cylinder stripped and new seals fitted.

35.6 Ready to fit a new 'O' ring to the reservoir.

repairing and the whole cylinder should be replaced. In my case all was well and all that was required (as a matter of course) was to replace the rubber seals inside, after having thoroughly cleaned the internals. If you look at photo 35.4 you can see the internals of the master cylinder with all new seals fitted and the old seals below them. Note that the open end of the seals face away from the open end of the master cylinder, as in the photo.

I think it's also worth noting at this point that my bike had clearly had some renovation work done to it before being laid up, including a new exhaust system and new tyres. It became clear that the bike had also had the braking system thoroughly overhauled with new stainless steel master cylinders and new stainless steel pistons fitted in the callipers. But I wanted to recondition them anyway just for peace of mind. If you are reconditioning the braking system, I would always recommend fitting a stainless steel master cylinder and stainless pistons in the callipers.

When all was ready, I slid the internals back into the master cylinder, smearing them with the special red grease that came with the seals, and compressed them with the end of a screwdriver whilst I re-inserted the circlip holding them all together. See photo 35.5. I then re-inserted the pushrod assembly into the alloy housing, and screwed the master cylinder back into the housing. On Lockheed master cylinders, you screw it back in until there is no play between it and the pushrod, then screw it in one more complete turn. Finally, screw the master cylinder in a part turn until the long groove on the cylinder lines up with the grub screw in the alloy housing (the groove is just visible in photo 35.5). This could be up to nearly a whole extra turn, which doesn't matter. Whatever the case, never screw it back out to line things up – always screw it inwards. Then tighten the grub screw, which should tighten into the groove on the master cylinder.

With the master cylinder back in its alloy housing, I thoroughly cleaned the fluid reservoir, replaced the 'O' ring to the bottom of it (see photo 35.6) and mounted it back onto the master cylinder. See photo 35.7. Note that I had taken the opportunity to polish the alloy housing whilst the unit was apart. I also loosely fitted the adjusting nuts and clevis arm to the operating rod.

With the master cylinder rebuilt, I could then fit it to the bike via two Allen screws through the footrest arm (see photo 35.8) but I had to remove

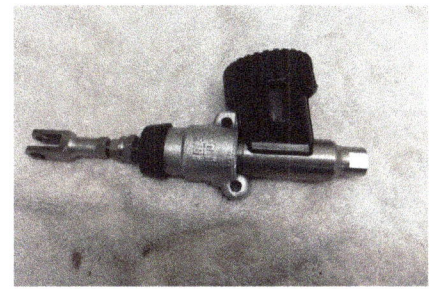

35.7 Master cylinder reassembled with polished housing.

HOW TO RESTORE NORTON COMMANDO

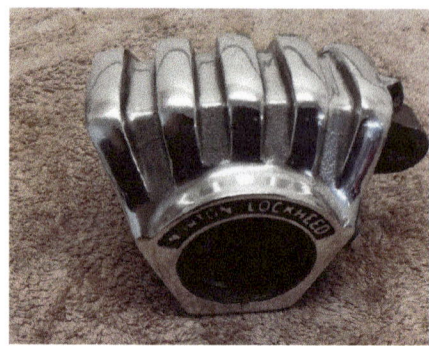
35.8 Master cylinder assembly fitted to the support plate.

35.11 Iconic rear 'clamshell' calliper dismantled and polished.

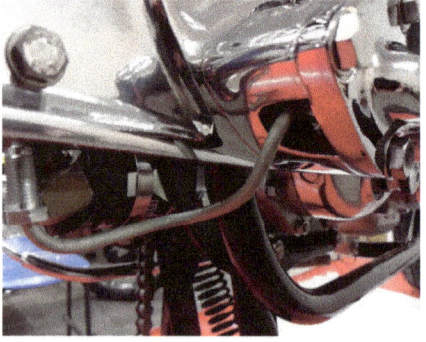
35.9 Brake pipe exits through the spacer.

35.10 Brake pipe attaches to the brake switch on the support plate and in turn to the flexible hose.

it again to screw the short brake pipe into the rear of it, which goes from the master cylinder to the rear brakelight switch. See photo 35.9. I subsequently connected the flexible brake hose to the other side of the brake switch, ready to connect it to the calliper mounting bracket. See photo 35.10.

Next up was the iconic 'clamshell' brake calliper. Aren't they just the most beautiful looking calliper ever?! I must say that I had been in two minds about upgrading the front calliper as it meant losing the wonderful original. In the end, however, I decided to change it as I really wanted a good front brake (when you've got used to a really good front brake, it's difficult to ride a bike without one) and I knew that I would still have the original on the rear.

My first job was to overcome a problem all of my own making. Having failed to properly read the manual during dismantling (ahem!) I hadn't removed the pistons from inside the callipers when the brakes were still on the bike and I could have used the hydraulic pressure to push them out (especially the rearmost piston).

After removing the calliper and unscrewing the end plug with a special tool made for the job (highly recommended as otherwise you have to use a hammer and punch to remove/tighten the end plug and that damages the holes in the plug), I immediately realised that there was no easy way to push the rear piston out as the calliper is made in one piece and there's no way to get behind the rear piston and push it out. Oh, dear. I could have used compressed air from my compressor to blow it out, but this can be a bit hairy as the pistons tend to eject from the calliper at very high speed, and the front piston would just have kept coming out, not the rear one. In the end, I decided to take it to the engineers and they were able to screw a very large tap into the cup of the rear piston and pull it out. Lesson learnt. I then prised out the old piston seals and the calliper was ready to be refurbished.

I gave the calliper a really good polish and it came up looking great. See photo 35.11. I then assembled all the parts I required to refurbish the calliper – bar one. See photo 35.12. In this photo you can see the pistons, new seals, bleed nipple and 'green stuff' brake pads and brake fluid (I always use these green stuff pads to eliminate brake squeal – always worked for me so far). However, you can also see my original, and very damaged, end plug for the calliper, just below the brake fluid. I have to report that I bought a brand new stainless steel replacement for the original, but when I came to fit it, it only went in a couple of turns and then locked solid – something was clearly wrong with the threads. I duly sent it back and waited over a month for it to be returned, during which time I was told it had been returned to the manufacturer.

However, when the stainless plug was finally returned, it was exactly the same as it had been before, and I was told that I wasn't fitting it correctly. I was told to heat the calliper, lubricate it, and screw the plug in hard. I

35.12 All parts ready to assemble the calliper – apart from a new end plug.

REFURBISHING THE BRAKES

35.13 Cylinder bore ready to accept calliper pistons and seals.

35.14 New seals inserted in the grooves.

was nothing wrong with the part. Not happy. Rant over. (And I eventually got my money refunded.)

Anyway, onwards and upwards. I gently but thoroughly cleaned the internal bore of the calliper (see photo 35.13) before liberally lubricating everything with brake fluid and inserting new piston seals into the grooves. See photo 35.14. After this I prepared to slide the first piston into place. However, I realised that I'd inserted both calliper seals and it meant I'd have to slide the furthest piston over the first seal, which wasn't ideal, so I carefully removed the first seal so that the piston could easily slide down the bore and into position without any danger of damaging the first seal.

Having lubricated the sides of the pistons, I used the wooden shaft of a hammer to gently push the first piston down into position, open side uppermost. Until it was almost fully down. See photo 35.15. I then re-inserted the second seal and refitted the second piston, open side facing inwards, in the end of the calliper, but not too far in. I ensured that the edge of both pistons aligned with the edge of the calliper, providing maximum gap to allow the brake pads to be fitted. See photo 35.16. I then screwed in my old end plug (grrrr!) and lightly greased the rear of each brake pad with Copperslip before inserting them, to further reduce the chance of brake squeal. See photo 35.17. In this photo you can also see the special 'peg' tool used for loosening and tightening the end plugs without damage. (It also tightens other similar items and locking rings). Well worth the expense.

Having inserted the brake pads, I slid the calliper over the brake disc and bolted it to its bracket. I then attached the flexible brake hose to

should mention that I had previously tried the new plug in both my callipers and it jammed solid in both. I also compared it with both my old end plugs, and they screwed in easily and smoothly, all the way home, in both callipers. Just to be certain, however, I heated the calliper, greased the threads and used the special tightening tool to try and screw the new plug in again. It was no surprise to me that two turns in, it locked completely solid. I then applied what I estimate to be at least 50lb/ft of pressure on the tool, but the plug just wouldn't screw in. I emphasise that I wasn't trying to tighten the plug, just screw the bloody thing in. The part was still clearly wrong. I wasn't happy. I therefore sent the offending item back asking for a refund (but I was only given credit) and ordered a new standard plug from another supplier. During all this, I had to use my original, damaged end plug and therefore I couldn't fill the brake with fluid as I knew I'd have to swap the plugs over when one finally arrived that fitted. I was very annoyed as the whole episode had taken over a month and yet at the end of it I was told that it was my fault and that there

35.15 Inserting the lubricated pistons down the bores.

35.16 Pistons inserted, but with maximum gap left for the brake pads.

35.17 Pistons inserted and old end plug temporarily inserted. Brake pad backs smeared with grease.

HOW TO RESTORE NORTON COMMANDO

the calliper bracket and finally fitted the short brake pipe from the flexible hose to the calliper. With a new bleed nipple in place the calliper was sorted. See photo 35.18. Unfortunately, though, at this point, I was still waiting for the stainless item to be returned (that didn't fit even when it did come back), so I was unable to bleed the brake at this point. I had to wait for the new, new end plug to arrive before I could do so.

Eventually, after what seemed like an eternity, a new calliper end plug arrived from a different supplier! Hurrah! Without further ado I used my special plug tool to remove the original plug and screw the new one into place – which, of course, screwed in perfectly. See photo 35.19. The new plug was now fitted!

See photo 35.20. I filled the master cylinder reservoir with fluid and attached my bleed tube to the calliper bleed nipple and began to bleed the rear brake. See photo 35.21. However, there was a massive air lock in the master cylinder, and it took an awful lot of pumping and tapping the cylinder with a mallet, before fluid finally began to flow through the system.

During this process, I realised that the adjusting nut on the operating rod wasn't fitted correctly. The round groove on one side of the nut should engage with the rubber boot on the end of the cylinder, and I had fitted it with the groove facing the other way. See photo 35.22. I therefore turned the nut round and adjusted the locknuts to where I thought they should be to make the brake work properly. See photo 35.23. (However, the brake didn't work properly on the road, and the rod nuts had to be readjusted – see Chapter 38.) I also provisionally set the height of the brake pedal by screwing the clevis arm along the operating rod. See photo 35.23 again. This would be adjusted once again when the bike was on the road to set the pedal at my favoured height.

With the rear brake finally sorted, I could turn my attention to the front brake. I had already fitted the upgraded front disc and calliper,

35.20 New calliper end plug screwed into place.

35.19 Fitting the new calliper end plug at last!

35.21 Bleeding the rear brake.

35.18 Calliper mounted in position and pipes connected.

35.22 Master cylinder operating rod incorrectly assembled.

REFURBISHING THE BRAKES

35.23 Operating rod correctly assembled and pedal height adjusted by moving the clevis.

35.24 New master cylinder with stainless brake hose and Kawasaki brake switch rubber!

35.25 New master cylinder.

and all I needed to do was to fit the master cylinder and new brake hoses and pipes, and bleed the system. I had decided to fit an uprated master cylinder which was of a slightly smaller internal diameter, moving less fluid than the original, but at higher pressure. (I know it sounds like a master cylinder with a bigger bore would be better, but whilst that would move more fluid, it would do so at a lower pressure – trust me!) The only real problem being that with the smaller master cylinder, more lever travel is required to move the same amount of fluid.

Anyway, I therefore didn't need to refurbish the original item, just simply screw the new master cylinder onto the back of the right-hand switchgear. See photos 35.24 and 35.25 of the new master cylinder and brake lever in situ. Note that I also fitted a small rubber boot (from a Kawasaki Z1) over the brakelight switch, as I really, really don't like those huge cumbersome rubber boots covering the switch and hose outlet, as fitted originally. I think it looks so much cleaner and less clunky now.

Should you wish to refurbish your original unit, this is much the same as for the rear master cylinder: clean everything thoroughly and replace all the seals with new. On reassembly, screw the cylinder into the bracket until all play between the brake lever and pushrod is gone. Then screw the cylinder in one more full turn, and then another part turn in order to line up the grub screw with the groove in the cylinder. As with the rear cylinder, only ever screw it inwards to line up everything, not outwards.

I also decided (as with the rear) to fit the original brake hoses and pipes. When I bought the bike it had been fitted with replacement stainless steel braided hoses, front and rear, but although this sounds good, they were very long items that replaced all the original hoses and pipes and went straight from the master cylinders to the callipers. I found these unwieldy and messy – especially the really long ones on the front. I therefore replaced the replacements (!) with the originals. One exception to this was the flexible hose from the front master cylinder to the first join on the top yoke, which I had made up in stainless steel, just for looks. See photo 35.24 again. I would have also had the other two flexible hoses copied in braided stainless, but they aren't cheap, and by this time the piggy bank was empty.

I also realised that the final original pipe from the hose bracket to the calliper on the front wouldn't fit as I was using such a different calliper setup. I therefore made up my own short copper brake pipe to go from the final flexible hose into the calliper. See photo 35.26. Although I say it myself, it doesn't look too bad.

With everything connected, I then tried to bleed the front brake – to no avail. The front brake just wouldn't bleed, at all. I had feared that this might be the case, due to the position of the calliper bleed nipple, a good couple of inches below the highest point of the calliper – the air simply sat in a pocket above it. If you look at photo 35.26 again, you can just see the position of the bleed nipple, on the extreme left of the calliper. After

35.26 Flexible hose goes to bespoke brake pipe into calliper.

HOW TO RESTORE NORTON COMMANDO

a few hours of futile bleeding, and much wasted brake fluid, I realised I had to try something else.

I therefore removed the brake calliper and, using the flexible hose, swung it up so the calliper was upside down on the front mudguard with the bleed nipple now at the top. See photo 35.27. With the calliper in this position, the brake bled straight away. Note that I jammed a screwdriver in-between the pads to stop them closing up whilst bleeding (Note the use of passata rather than brake fluid in this case! – Joke!)

The brakes were now sorted.

35.27 Bleeding the front calliper off the disc.

LESSONS LEARNT

• The Norton-Lockheed 'clamshell' brake callipers are the most beautiful ever made – fact!
• Remove the pistons from the callipers before taking them off the bike.
• Thank heavens for engineering shops.
• If taking apart the master cylinder, don't forget the little grub screw underneath.
• Don't disturb the two locknuts on the pushrod on the rear master cylinder if at all possible.
• If refurbishing the braking system I would recommend using stainless steel master cylinders and pistons.
• As I get older I tend to hate poor service more than I hate poor parts – and I really don't like poor parts!
• I prefer the original brake hoses and pipes rather than one great long hose – preferably stainless and copper though!
• Unless the bleed nipple is at the top, it won't bleed!
• My Commando is now 99 per cent Norton and one per cent Kawasaki!

EARLIER MODELS WITH DRUM BRAKES

I'm just going to add a few notes on how to fettle the front and rear drum brakes, but you should refer to the relevant *Norton Workshop Manual* for your bike for full guidance.

The front brakes are twin leading shoe (TLS). This means that there are two cams in the hub, one on the end of each brake shoe and they operate together, pushing both brake shoes against the drum at the same time. In order to do this effectively, the link arm between the two cams must be properly adjusted, otherwise only one shoe will be fully operative. To adjust the link arm, remove it at one end and, with the cable removed, ensure that both cams are fully applied, and then re-set the link arm. This operation is much easier with the help of someone else. It's also essential on early models, and probably advisable on later models, to then centralise the brake drum. Loosen the wheel spindle, apply the brake fully, and then re-tighten the wheel spindle with the brake still on. See photo 35.28 of a twin leading shoe front brake.

The rear brake is single leading shoe which means that there is only one operating cam that operates on the end of both shoes. To centralise the rear brake, loosen the rear wheel spindles, apply the brake and then re-tighten the spindles with the rear brake still applied. See photo 35.29 of a rear drum brake.

NB: In the case of drum brakes my general advice is to always change the brake shoes when rebuilding. I've found that brake shoes tend to glaze and harden with age and just stop working, even though there's still a lot of meat left on them. Modern brake shoes also often use a slightly softer compound which is more effective than the originals. In my experience, changing the shoes can transform the brakes.

35.28 A twin leading shoe front brake.

35.29 Single leading shoe rear brake.

Chapter 36
Painting the tank & side panels

Time to sort out the fuel tank and side panels. I discovered on dismantling, that my tank had originally been red (Candy Apple Red), which was nice as I'd already made the decision to repaint it red. It had been resprayed black at some point, but only with an aerosol over the original paint, and the finish was uneven, with many pinholes in it. However, I wasn't sure who I could get to paint the tank for me (having no skill or equipment for this myself) and after making a few enquiries I decided to entrust the work to Nick, my local car body restorer and painter. In the past he'd sprayed my E-Type and made a wonderful job of it and it was nice to keep the work local and completed by someone I knew and trusted. For his part, Nick wasn't that keen on doing the job for me as there was little money in it, and it's a pain of a job – especially the pin-striping – but he eventually agreed to paint it for me on condition that I stripped the tank and side panels first. I agreed and he gave me a can of professional paint stripper and told me to get on with it.

Before stripping the paint off the tank I needed to thoroughly clean it inside as it was rusty and very gooey in there, from years of standing idle.

A few years ago I found this method of cleaning the inside of a tank in one of the classic motorcycle magazines, and I've used it ever since. Rather than shake nuts and bolts around inside the tank you let chemicals do the work for you – much easier! My only caveat would be that I have always then gone on to repaint the tank, but if you're not planning on doing that, you might want to think again, as I always end up staining the existing paintwork with the rather strong chemicals involved.

First of all, I donned thick rubber gloves – these chemicals can easily burn skin! Leaving the fuel cap in place with the vent hole taped over, I then filled the tank three-quarters full of water, having found two bolts to screw into the bottom of the tank, in place of the fuel taps, to seal the holes. I then poured the entire contents of a 500g bottle of caustic soda into the tank – the water immediately got hot with the chemical reaction! See photo 36.1. Never pour the caustic soda crystals in first and then add the water, as the chemical reaction will be too

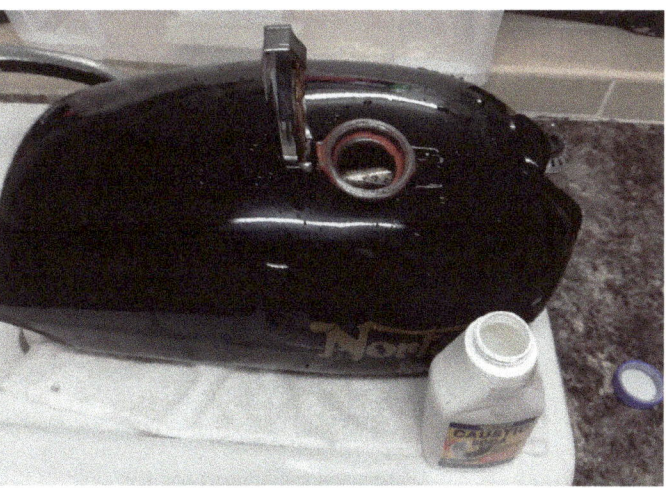

36.1 First cleaning with caustic soda.

HOW TO RESTORE NORTON COMMANDO

36.2 Second cleaning with spirits of salts.

36.3 Stopping the chemical reaction with bleach.

36.4 Drying out the tank.

environmentally, I think it's okay. After this, I gave it a thorough rinse out and then poured about a pint of water into the tank and added about a third of a 500g bottle of spirits of salts (hydrochloric acid) to the water, closed the cap and swilled it round, once again removing the cap to release the pressure. See photo 36.2. I left it 30 minutes and then added some more spirits of salts, repeating the swilling and followed 30 minutes later by the remaining third of the bottle. I left the mixture overnight and then emptied the contents down the sink – again spirits of salts are a drain cleaner. I now had a very shiny tank, where once there was rust and crud.

I then added a small amount of bleach (see photo 36.3) to stop the chemical process created by the spirit of salts as it can continue etching the paintwork otherwise. The bleach neutralises the acid. After this, I dried the tank as quickly as possible, using a heat gun set on low, as it's amazing how quickly the tank will start to rust if left wet. See photo 36.4.

I like to seal the inside of my fuel tanks with sealant, but this is controversial and many owners will tell you not to, and give you the usual horror stories about someone who used tank sealant and it caused all sorts of problems. Personally, I believe that it helps keep the tank from deteriorating further and the only reason for the horror stories is where owners have used sealant without having cleaned and prepared the tank beforehand. Sealant will not stick to rust and gunge, only clean metal. For my money, I use POR 15 sealant available from Frost Auto Restorations amongst others, as it's always worked for me. There are also other sealants available that other owners recommend.

When the tank was completely dry (at least 24 hours with intermittent heating), I thoroughly stirred the POR 15 (it really does need very vigorous mixing) poured it into the tank, closed the cap, swilled it around several times, and then drained the excess off. Job done. See photo 36.5 of the POR 15 before being added to the tank. I left the tank to dry for a couple of days, and then removed the fuel cap (which I was going to replace anyway) by drifting out the split in the

36.5 Preparing to add the POR 15 sealant.

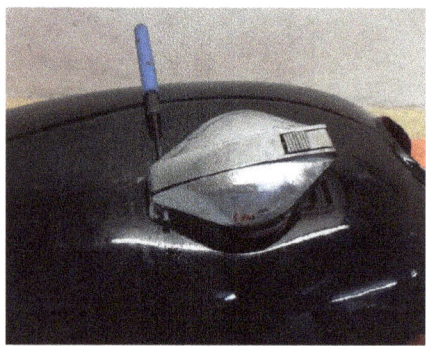

36.6 Removing the fuel cap.

hinge (see photo 36.6), then taped over the hole and the tank was ready for stripping.

To begin with, I scored the existing paint with a Stanley knife to help the stripper get underneath it. See photo 36.7 of the tank resembling something from the horror film *Hellraiser*. I then liberally coated the tank with paint stripper and it went to work immediately. See photo 36.8. Note that I was using strong paint stripper, rather than the emasculated stuff that's on general sale these days, and that made the job a lot easier – but even then it was a hard job. After about half an hour, half the tank was stripped (see photo 36.9), and eventually it was down to bare metal. See photo 36.10 revealing filler that was previously used to cover a dent. It's not unusual to find such things under paintwork.

I then set to on the side panels, stripping them in the same way. See photo 36.11. Note that after I'd stripped them I also found a considerable amount of filler on the right-hand panel, covering a host of small dents and scratches from where the panel had clearly been hammered back to shape after some serious damage.

I finished cleaning both the tank

great; always water first and then the caustic soda. I then filled the tank to the top with water, shut the cap and swilled it around a bit to disperse the chemicals in the water. I undid the fuel cap briefly to release the slight pressure build up in the tank from the chemical process. After this I just left it for two days to do its work, swilling the tank round every now and then – you can leave it longer, up to a week for maximum cleaning.

After a couple of days I decided to move onto the next process, so I simply poured the foul, dark brown thick liquid that the water had become, down the sink – caustic soda is a drain cleaner, so

PAINTING THE TANK & SIDE PANELS

36.7 Scoring the tank – looks like something from the horror film *Hellraiser*.

36.8 Applying the paint remover.

36.11 Stripping the side panels.

36.9 Tank half-stripped.

36.12 Tank fully stripped and ready for the painters.

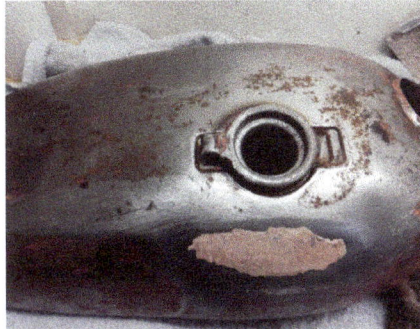

36.10 Tank stripped with filler covering a large dent.

36.13 Side panels fully stripped – but you can still just read 'Norton Commando'!

With the tank and panels now as clean as I could get them, I took them down to Nick to weave his magic. All I could do then was wait.

With the tanks and panels at Nick's, he began the long and painstaking job of prepping and finishing them. Step one was to blast clean them so that any residual paint and rust was completely removed. Note that you need to strip the tank etc first and then gently blast clean them – both processes are necessary.

After a mild blast cleaning, he gave them a very thin coat of etch primer to stop them rusting – as bare metal they will begin rusting immediately if left unprotected. He removed the worst of the large dent from the tank, before using several coats of filler to finish both the tank and the panels (especially where the right one had been damaged). Note that he applied several thin skims of filler, in place of the single large blob that had been there before, carefully sanding down between each coat, to ensure the best possible finish, beginning with an 80 grit paper and finishing off with 180 grit.

Eventually, the tank and panels were ready for their undercoat and he painted them in the spray booth with two-pack grey high-build primer. The 'high-build' nature of the primer is obtained by having a high chalk content in the paint which makes it thicker. Also note that this primer, being two-pack, contains isocyanates (poisonous) and can only be used by professional sprayers. Nick gave the parts five coats of primer before baking them to dry the paint. See photo 36.14 of the tank and panels after five coats of primer.

After this the panels were 'blocked,' which means that they were rubbed down with a shaping block using 400 grit paper to remove any high spots. They were then put back in the paint booth and given another three coats of primer, followed by another bake. The parts were then finished with a soft pad (as opposed to the hard block) using 800 grit paper.

The real painting hadn't even started yet, and they already had nine coats of paint!

The panels were then finally ready to be painted with their finishing colour:

and side panels with soft wire brushes and abrasive wheels attached to my cordless drill. This helped to get the last vestiges of paint off. See photos 36.12 and 36.13. (If you look closely at the panel on the left, you can still make out the lettering for 'Norton Commando' from the transfer that was on top of the paint, somehow etched into the metal – weird.)

HOW TO RESTORE NORTON COMMANDO

36.14 Tank after high-build primer.

Candy Apple Red (also two-pack). One problem with painting Commandos is that no record of the actual original colours used in the factory still exists, so you have to choose a colour that you either like, or one that is as close to the original finish as possible. The actual colour we chose was *Honda (!) Red Mica 'Pantheon' 163D*, and this had a triple coat finish: base coat followed by several coats of Candy, followed by a coat of lacquer. The first base coat was applied, and this was a copper colour. See photo 36.15. The colour of the base coat dictates what the final colour will be, as the remaining coats are either transparent or semi-transparent.

After this, the Candy paint was applied in five coats. Candy paint is semi-transparent (a bit like a sweet wrapper, from where it possibly gets its name) and, like a sweet wrapper, the more coats you put on, the darker it gets – but it's these coats that give the paint its depth and makes it ultimately look so good. Nick applied five coats of Candy paint to the tank and panels in all. If you look at photos 36.16 to 36.20, you can see the colour of the tank change as the five coats of Candy were applied. The parts were then left for a week to dry thoroughly.

When the Candy paint was deemed to have dried properly, Nick applied the transfers. There are two colours of transfer available: silver and gold. In the end I plumped for the gold as I thought that there was already so much silver (polished alloy and chrome) on the bike that it might be too much – but on the other hand maybe the sudden introduction of the gold would clash with the silver on the rest of the bike? (I needn't have worried)

To begin with Nick applied the 'Norton' logo to the tank, having spent an age working out the position that best suited both sides of the tank (as the logo is effectively reversed on either side of the tank, it needs to be in a position that suits either side). See photo 36.21. Next up were the pinstripes. Now, the pinstripes were originally hand painted on by someone with an awful lot of training and an awful lot of skill in this area, but as Nick wasn't used to

36.15 First copper-coloured base coat.

36.16 First Candy Red coat.

36.17 Second Candy Red coat.

36.18 Third Candy Red coat.

36.19 Fourth Candy Red coat.

36.20 Fifth and final Candy Red coat.

PAINTING THE TANK & SIDE PANELS

36.21 Norton transfer applied.

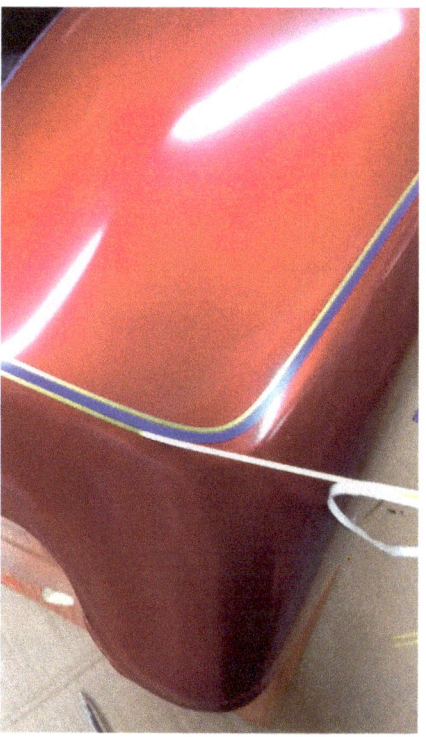
36.22 Second pinstripe being applied with a blue one used as a guide.

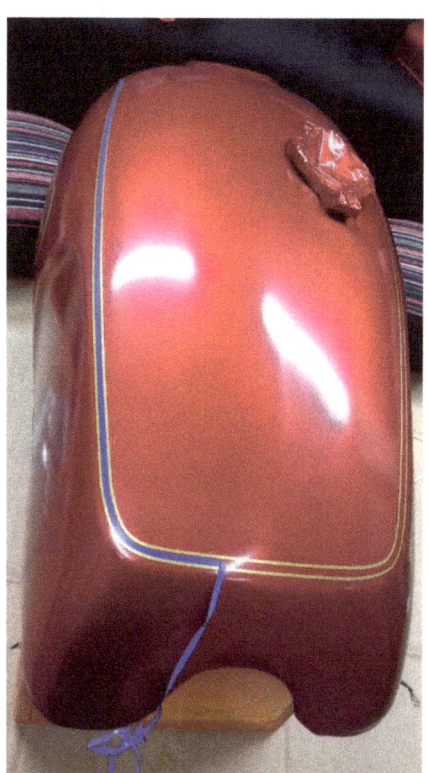
36.23 Blue guide pinstripe being removed.

painting pinstripes, we agreed that it would be best to use transfers. Note that the requirement for hand painted pinstripes means that many owners don't have them put back on following a respray (as had been the case with my tank when I bought it). Also note that 750 Commandos have a single pinstripe and 850s have two – now you know!

The problem with using transfers for the pinstripes is that they don't like going round corners; they wrinkle. The way round this was to use thin, individual pinstripes that weren't thick enough to deform, rather than one double pinstripe that couldn't have coped with the curves. Nick therefore applied the first pinstripe, having spent a long, long time working out where they went. Following this, he applied a blue stripe next to the first, which was used as a guide for the second stripe, to ensure it was exactly parallel to the first one, all the way round. See photo 36.22 of the second stripe being applied next to the blue guide stripe. After this Nick removed the blue guide stripe, leaving the two gold ones. See photo 36.23. He then worked his magic on the side panels in a similar vein. I decided to include the transfers declaring 'Electric Start' on the side panels. I had been in two minds as to whether or not to use them, as it can make the side panels look a bit cluttered and busy, but in the end I decided to include them. The pinstripes and transfers had now been applied to the tank and side panels, and, after leaving overnight to check that all was well, they were ready for their final coat. See photo 36.24. Also note that the logos and pinstripes on the side panels were aligned with the top edges of the side panels, not exactly horizontal when on the bike, and I think this looked right as they'd look odd if not aligned with the panels themselves.

The final coat was the lacquer, which gives the paint its shine. Nick uses an expensive lacquer made by Max Mayer, as he finds that it gives a really high gloss finish. The parts were then baked at a low temperature (30°C for 30 minutes – it's normally about 70°) to help the lacquer set but without risking damaging the transfers etc. Note that two-pack dries through chemical reaction, which tends to give a far harder finish than cellulose, but you can aid the chemical drying process by gently heating it in the spray booth.

The tank and side panels were now finished – looking stunning and ready to be fitted to the bike! See photo 36.25.

So the tank etc were all done – but it's a big job: chemically cleaning the inside of the tank with three different chemicals, sealing the inside of the tank with proprietary sealant, stripping the paint off the tank and panels, blast cleaning, a coat of primer, removing the dents and bumps, applying several coats of filler and rubbing down each time, applying five coats of high build primer and then rubbing down, applying another three coats of high build primer and then rubbing down again, applying the copper-coloured undercoat, applying five coats of Candy Red, applying the transfers and pinstripes, applying the final coat of lacquer and baking. So don't forget, there's a lot of work in refurbishing a tank, and if you pay someone to do it for you, then now

197

HOW TO RESTORE NORTON COMMANDO

36.24 Transfers and pinstripes applied.

you know why it's not that cheap! The tank and side panels had a total of 16 coats of paint!

LESSONS LEARNT

• What colour to paint your bike? A big decision. And one you need to get right! I spent quite a while looking at different bikes with different colour schemes, before choosing mine. Do you try to go original (bearing in mind that details of the original colours used no longer exist) or try a totally different colour? Gold or silver transfers? On a MkIII do you include the words 'Electric Start' on the side panels? And do you colour in the 'Norton' imprint on the timing case the same colour as the tank (as some owners do) or leave it plain alloy (as I did)?
• I use chemicals to clean the gunge and rust off the inside of a fuel tank. Other methods are available.
• I seal my tanks after cleaning with POR 15, even if the tank isn't leaking. Some owners are against tank sealant. I think it works well if the tank is prepared well beforehand. Other products and a whole raft of different opinions are available.
• Stripping off paint is just as much of a pain these days as it used to be 'back in the day' – having proper strength paint stripper is a big help!
• Painting a tank isn't for the faint hearted.
• Candy paint is semi-transparent and gives a lovely depth to the finished paintwork (compare the original solid gloss black paint on my bike, with the new Candy finish).
• It's the lacquer that gives the paint its shine.
• It's such a childish thrill to get your paintwork back!

36.25 Tanks and panels lacquered – stunning!

Chapter 37
Fitting the tank & side panels

With the fuel tank and side panels painted, it was time to fit them – the last job! I began by fitting a new fuel cap to the tank. You can see the old and new caps in photo 37.1, which only just shows the corrosion and wear that was actually very evident on the old cap. I decided to just buy a new cap, as it's one of those parts that are actually cheaper to buy new rather than restore. I used the original split pin but found that the holes in the new cap were way too small for the pin, and I needed to use the Dremmel to open them out slightly. I then positioned the cap in place and tapped the split pin home (very, very gingerly!) using a small drift, as for the dismantling.

I then fitted my Roadster side panels; other models differ slightly. Both panels have strange-looking double-sided rubbers that fit to their bottom mountings, and these fit in-between the support plates and the frame and hold them fast at the bottom. The right-hand panel is then bolted to the top of the oil tank with two bolts, one slightly longer than the other. See photo 37.2.

The left-hand panel has two different mountings at the top: one mounting is a spigot on the frame, in about the 1 o'clock position, which slides into a rubber grommet on the side panel. The other mounting should be on the airbox (MkIII) with some weirdly shaped plastic clips – but I no longer had an airbox! As a result, I had bought a special bracket from Norvil that provided a new mounting point, this time with a small bolt. Needless to say, the new bracket didn't quite fit, but after some 'persuasion' it held the side panel perfectly in place. See photo 37.3. At least it's clearly not just me who has changed their MkIII airbox for an earlier air filter.

After this, I turned my attention back to the fuel tank. First of all I checked the fuel taps. These were clearly quite new and looked to be good, solid types (there's nothing worse than a leaking fuel tap), and so I had no hesitation in refitting them using new Doughty washers to provide a good seal. If you look at the fuel taps in photo 37.4, you can see that one tap has a tube inside the gauze, the other does not. The tap with the tube is the main tap, and that without, the reserve. You can fit them either way round. I tend to fit the main tap to the right, as that is the one I always turn on when getting on a bike – but it's up to you which side you fit them (just remember which is which, otherwise you could easily run out of fuel!).

Following this, I prepared to fit the tank by fitting the mountings to the tank. At the front, the tank sits on four large rubber washers each side (five for High Riders), held onto the

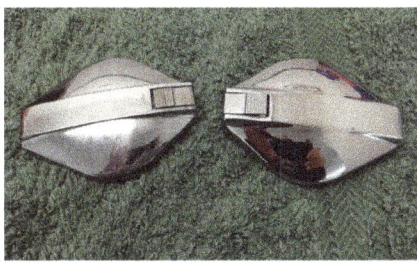
37.1 Old and new fuel cap.

37.2 Right-hand side panel bolted to the oil tank.

HOW TO RESTORE NORTON COMMANDO

37.3 Extra bracket to allow left-hand side panel to be mounted without the original air filter.

37.5 Ready to fit the tank with rubber washers at the front, foam padding near the back, fuel taps fitted, and rubber 'cotton reel' mountings to the rear with mounting strap.

37.6 Fitting the seat.

37.4 Nice, solid fuel taps. Main tap on the left with a tube in the filter, reserve tap on the right with no tube. Fit either way round as you prefer.

frame mounting bracket by two nuts with large penny washers underneath. At the rear there are two 'cotton reel' rubber mountings (Roadster tank) that attach to a strap under the main frame rail (there are different straps for different tanks). See photo 37.5. Note that there is also a rubber or hard foam pad that sits under the tank to the rear of the main tunnel. I didn't stick mine onto the tank, I just wedged it in before mounting the tank, as I wasn't exactly sure of the correct position. Having mounted the tank it seemed to be okay where it was, and I don't think it'll move; if it does I'll have to remove the tank and glue it in position.

Also note that I'd belatedly sprayed some of the underside of the tank with black paint where the metal was exposed, to prevent rusting. I didn't realise that the painters weren't going to paint the underside and so had left it as was. I therefore had to carefully mask the tank to protect the new paintwork and apply a couple of coats to the exposed metal, which I should clearly have done before I took it to the painters.

Before fitting the tank, I fitted the seatback. When I had bought the bike, the seat was loose and wouldn't shut properly. I realised that this was down to the plastic hinge (MkIII only, I think) not having been fitted properly. If you look at photo 37.6 you can see the mounting assembly. Basically, the plastic hinge is sandwiched on both sides with metal plates. The two plates you can see resting on the bottom of the seat will go either side of the plastic hinge and then bolt onto the frame. After this there's a small black rubber cover that clips over the top of the hinge and it's job done.

With the tank mounted, I attached the two (very expensive!) stainless fuel hoses to the taps.

The bike was now finished! Hurrah!

LESSONS LEARNT
- Some parts, like the fuel cap, are cheaper to buy new rather than restore.[1]
- Fitting the newly painted tank and side panels is a very stressful job. One slip and … ! Take your time and ensure that there is no possibility of damage at every stage.
- A bracket to hold the right-hand panel in place without the MkIII airbox is available from Norvil.
- Heaven is a good, solid fuel tap that doesn't leak. One tap should have a long tube on it, as the main tap, and the other without, for reserve. Make sure you remember which one you put on which side!
- Happiness is a completed bike! At this point, you know that it really was all worth it!

37.7 Bike finished! Hurrah!

---

[1] Note that Commando fuel caps are made from Mazak (or Zamak in America) which is a strong, light alloy, much used at the time for components such as fuel caps and car door handles. However, it does tend to suffer from corrosion, which causes pinholes, and can be difficult to re-chrome.

Chapter 38
Commissioning, teething & riding

COMMISSIONING

Having finished assembling the bike there were a few jobs still left to do to commission it. To begin with, I filled the engine with oil. I used Morris Lubricants' running-in oil to begin with, which will be changed to its 20/50 Golden Film engine oil after about 250 miles. I also used Hypoy 80-90w in the gearbox. See photo 38.1. I therefore filled the oil tank with oil, followed by the primary chaincase, via the clutch rod inspection cover. See photo 38.2. MkIIIs have an oil level plug in the chaincase; on earlier models the oil needs to be measured. I also filled the gearbox with oil through the clutch mechanism inspection hole. There is a level plug on the side of the outer casing, in about the 7 o'clock position.

With both sparkplugs removed, I then loosened the connection between the rocker oil pipe feed and the timing case and turned the engine over on the starter (it now goes at quite a speed!) until, to my great joy, oil started to pour out of the loose connection. See photo 38.3. This meant that there was no air lock in the oil pump and that oil was being pumped round the engine by the oil pump. Hurrah! It also meant that there

38.1 Engine and gearbox oil.

38.2 Filling the primary chaincase.

HOW TO RESTORE NORTON COMMANDO

38.3 Turning over the engine until oil dripped out of the rocker oil feed pipes.

38.4 Temporary fuel tank.

38.5 Tightening the front yokes.

was no need to undo the main oil pipe manifold to remove any air locks etc – good news. I then tightened the rocker oil feed pipe connections, along with those to the head, which I'd previously left loose, and turned the engine over again on the starter, for about 30 seconds or so, until oil came pouring out of the return pipe in the neck of the oil tank – oil was circulating properly!

I think that this is the best way of preparing the engine before starting – turn the engine over with the sparkplugs out until oil is seen returning to the oil tank. That way you know that you'll have instant oil pressure when the engine is first started for real. Having a starter motor, especially an upgraded one, helps, but it can be achieved just by kicking the engine over, too – especially if you primed everything as you went along.

After this, whilst waiting for my tank etc to come back from the painters, I hooked up a funnel to the fuel lines and used this as a small fuel tank to get the bike started – just to check that it did actually start and that there were no obvious issues (and anyway, I couldn't wait until the tank came back!). See photo 38.4. (Don't try this at home, kids!) This allowed me to check that the engine was running okay, and to address any issues, and to roughly set the carbs in the interim.

To my great relief, the engine started immediately (on the starter) and ran really nicely! I set the carbs roughly and sensed that the ignition timing was a bit retarded (the engine was very loud, with quite a hard exhaust note), but I knew that would soon be sorted and I was very happy.

After the tank and side panels arrived and were fitted, I removed the bike from the lift, with the aid of a neighbour (I didn't want any last minute disasters!) and the bike was almost ready to roll.

The next job was to spend five minutes bouncing the front suspension up and down to settle it, before beginning to finally tighten it up. I find that the forks and yokes benefit from this, as if you tighten everything up first, the front suspension can be slightly twisted and under uneven stress. To begin with, I tightened the mudguard mountings, followed by the bottom yokes (see photo 38.5), and then the front wheel spindle, which I torqued up to 60lb/ft. See photo 38.6.

I then set the ignition timing exactly, using a strobe. See photo 38.7. Usually I find that my initial static timing, completed when the electronic ignition is fitted, is pretty accurate. However, this time, the timing was a good five degrees retarded, and needed considerable adjustment to set correctly. I'm not sure why this was, but the engine immediately smoothed out and ran

COMMISSIONING, TEETHING & RIDING

38.6 Tightening the front wheel spindle.

much more sweetly – you can usually feel when the timing is right.

Following this, I was finally able to do what I've always wanted to do on a British bike, and that was to connect my vacuum gauges to the carbs in order to synchronise them exactly. However, I have to say that I found that by using the idle screws I wasn't able to alter the gauge readings to any noticeable degree, and I ended up with readings that were close, but not identical to each other, not far off where they had been when I first connected the gauges. See photo 38.8. I don't know if it's because of the Amal carbs, or the position of the tubes on the inlet manifold, or what, but the gauges gave much the same reading throughout.

However, I was able to balance the air screws on both carbs to give the cleanest running. I started with the pilot air screws about 1½ turns out and then turned them slightly in and out, until the engine ran the smoothest and fastest, which was very close to the starting position.

I then re-adjusted both idle screws on each carb by the same amount, to obtain the required idling speed. I set the idle at just over 1000 revs as you don't want it too slow on a new engine, as it's easy to starve the big ends of oil if the tickover is too slow. At this point, I discovered that I had the throttle cable a fraction too tight and I couldn't reduce the idle to where I wanted it, and so slackened the cable off, after which I could adjust the idle perfectly. The carburettor settings will be checked again at the first service, after a couple hundred miles or so.

I then checked and topped-up the oil in the oil tank, as it always drops slightly when the engine starts and oil is sent all around the engine. A couple of final jobs: check the tyre pressures and the rear chain tension. These are simple jobs, but ones that are easy to overlook in all the excitement – and it can be disastrous. A few years ago I took one of my Tridents out following winter storage, but forgot to check the tyre pressures first. The bike handled so badly, it was lethal, and I immediately turned back and spent half an hour checking the steering to try and discover the source of the problem, before the penny finally dropped. One tyre had 6lb pressure, and the other 8lb!

Having completed the above, I was ready to take the bike out onto the road for the very first time! It was early February but luckily the weather was unseasonably warm, and it was just dry enough to go for a short run. I went round the block a couple of times, and I have to say that this was the most sorted bike immediately after a rebuild that I've ever ridden! The engine was really smooth and pulled like a train – brilliant!

Anyway, there was a reason for that first, quick run (other than to put a smile on my face!) and that was to allow the head gasket and tappets/valves to settle in, as they can change quite dramatically in the first couple of miles, and so it proved to be in this case. When the bike had cooled down I checked and re-torqued the cylinder head nuts and bolts, and indeed, even after a short run, they were all slightly loose and required tightening back down. I then checked all the tappets, to discover that they had all opened up considerably from when I'd set them previously; they all had about a 20 thou gap. I therefore reset them all to six thou (inlet) and eight thou (exhaust). See photo 38.9. This sort of settling down isn't unusual and that's why it's important to check them soon after starting the engine for the first time.

38.7 Setting the timing with a strobe.

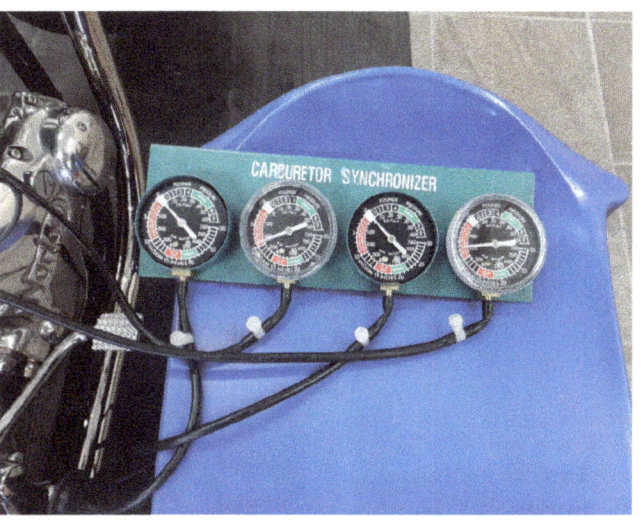

38.8 Checking the carbs with vacuum gauges.

HOW TO RESTORE NORTON COMMANDO

38.9 Checking and re-setting the tappets.

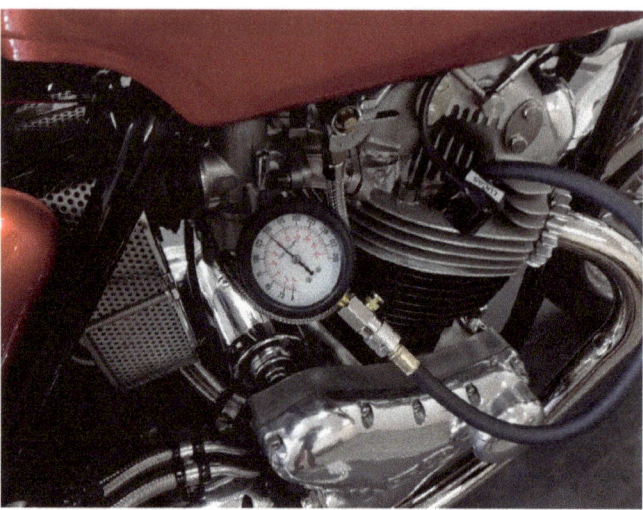

38.10 Compression test, timing side.

38.11 Compression test, drive side.

The only other thing that needed doing at this point was to sort the rear brake. I found that it worked okay, but only after pumping it a couple of times. I therefore re-adjusted the large nut on the operating rod on the master cylinder (the one that you're not supposed to touch in the first place), by screwing it further out, and that did the trick. The rear brake now worked fine – first press of the brake pedal. I also unclipped the clevis arm from the brake pedal and screwed it in a few turns to lower the height of the pedal, as it had been set too high.

I also took the opportunity to check the cylinder compressions. With the engine slightly warm, I removed the plugs in turn and replaced them with my tester. With the throttle fully open I turned the engine over on the starter. I was pleased to discover that both cylinders showed good compression, and that they were both almost exactly the same as each other. See photos 38.10 and 38.11.

TEETHING PROBLEMS

Suddenly, one day the starter motor simply stopped working – just like that. One moment it turned the engine over really quickly, the next moment, nothing: dead. Hmm. I guessed that there was no power getting to the solenoid (which sends current to the starter motor) as I couldn't hear a click from the solenoid, which you generally can if it's working – yet there was power to all the lights and indicators etc. I therefore used my multi-meter to test if power was going to the solenoid by putting one end to the terminal on the solenoid, and the other to earth and then pressing the starter button – nothing. So, as I had guessed, there was no power going to the solenoid.

I began to suspect that the starter button was the problem. I therefore opened the headlamp and found the multi-pin connection in there that carries the live feed to the solenoid. I connected my circuit tester to the relevant wire on the connector. I quickly discovered that power was going into the connector when the starter button was pressed, but not out again. It was the multi-pin connector that was faulty. I jiggled the connector, and, sure enough, the starter motor burst into life again. This was on a multi-pin connector that looked fine, and was locked with the metal clip that holds them tightly closed. I was surprised. I took the connector apart, cleaned it (again) and sprayed it with WD40 (again) and it's been fine ever since. So, those multi-pin connectors aren't to be completely trusted after all.

A few days after this I went to take the bike out for another run, the weather being incredible for mid-February, but I was instead greeted by a small pool of oil under the engine. Bugger! I soon realised that the oil was coming from the crankcase join at the bottom of the crankcase. A quick investigation revealed that I hadn't tightened the crankcase bolts up! The ones at the bottom were almost only finger tight. I immediately realised that after faffing about finding the correct bolt to go where in the crankcase when I first fitted the engine, I'd simply forgotten to tighten the bottom ones up – the three bottom crankcase bolts and the small screw were all only just over finger tight! And I'd ridden it like this!

COMMISSIONING, TEETHING & RIDING

Moron! I tightened everything and it's been oil tight ever since.

Again, one of my own rules after completing a restoration is to 'spanner up' before riding the bike. This means you begin with a small spanner, say 7/16in, and go round all the nuts and bolts on the bike of that size, checking that they're tight, then move on to a 1/2in spanner and so on (not forgetting Allen screws etc). I can virtually guarantee that you will find several nuts and bolts that haven't been properly tightened. Sometimes I really wish that I followed my own rules!

Another job I undertook was addressing the rather ugly/clumsy front calliper mounting plate. I realised that it was made of alloy, and so could be fairly easily machined. I removed the plate from the bike and after marking it out, I sent it to a local machine shop which duly milled the centre out of the plate, following my design. On return I fitted it to the bike, and I think it makes all the difference to the look of the front brake. It now looks far less clumsy, yet appears to still be strong enough to take the stresses demanded of it. Very pleased. See photos 38.12 and 38.13 of the bracket having been milled out and fitted to the bike.

Then I encountered a slightly unexpected problem – the engine was wet-sumping! In the text above, I mentioned that I checked the oil and found it required topping-up, and I discovered the reason for this was because the engine had wet-sumped. On my next ride out, when I stopped for a coffee, there was oil all over the rear of the bike and dripping from the air filter. By topping up the oil, when I started the engine, the excess oil in the engine was pumped back into the tank, causing it to overflow – mainly into the air filter box. Damn!

I immediately suspected the anti-drain valve in the timing case and drained the oil (see photo 38.14) before removing the timing casing for inspection. See photo 38.15. (If you used Wellseal on the joint, simply heat the casing slightly, which liquefies the Wellseal, and the casing will come off easily.) It was immediately clear that the anti-drain valve had jammed in the casing, fully open, as it had done before, and was doing nothing. I therefore took the radical, and always controversial decision, to fit an in-line anti-drain valve to replace the original.

As a result, I completely removed the valve from the casing and blocked off the small oil hole to the rear of it, in order to maintain oil pressure (see photo 38.16), as without the valve, oil could escape through the oil hole instead of going down the crankshaft. I then replaced the timing case.

38.12 The calliper mounting bracket having been milled out.

38.13 The modified bracket on the bike – looking better!

38.14 Draining the oil.

38.15 Timing casing removed.

38.16 Original valve removed and oilway blocked off.

I removed the valve because you most definitely don't want two anti-drain valves, as then you may well cause oil starvation.

At this point, I also removed the oil pipe union that feeds the rocker boxes, from the rear of the timing case. In order to check for oil flow later on. As part of this, I annealed the copper washers by heating them to cherry red and then quenching them. This serves to soften the copper and allow better sealing when the union is re-tightened. I then also left the washers standing in a jar of Coca-Cola for a couple of days. This removes any black scale from the washers, leaving them looking new. See photos 38.17 and 38.18.

I then bought an in-line anti-drain valve and fitted it in the oil pipe going from the oil tank into the engine (the outer pipe). In order to facilitate this, I drained the oil tank and removed the oil feed pipe, after which I cut a section out of it, just below the tank outlet, and inserted the anti-drain valve into the pipe.

I then primed the valve by re-filling the oil tank and then sucking oil through the valve – with a clear piece of pipe! (I really didn't want a mouthful of oil!) I also primed the remaining pipe with oil, using a small funnel. See photo 38.19. I reconnected the feed pipe to the inlet. I then chugged the engine over on the starter, to ensure I was getting oil flow out of the rocker oil feed union, before replacing the union with the newly softened ad cleaning copper washers, and then starting the engine and checking once again that I had good oil flow back into the tank. Since then the bike has run flawlessly and it has not wet-sumped at all; not one bit. Sorted. See photo 38.20 of the in-line valve in the oil feed pipe, under the oil tank.

However, the fitment of an anti-drain valve in the inlet pipe is highly controversial, and many mechanics will tell you never to do it. The problem is that there is a danger of oil starvation to the engine, mainly because the valve is now being sucked open rather than pushed open as it is before the oil pump, not after it. Firstly, the valve does need to be primed before use by sucking oil through it. If it's not properly primed, it can be full of air and so the valve won't open at all. This means no oil to the engine and it can lead to complete engine failure after only a few miles. Secondly, there is the possibility of the valve jamming closed during use, again leading to oil starvation and engine seizure.

However, all I can say is that I have fitted them to three of my bikes – one on each of my Triumph Tridents, and now one on the Commando – without any problems at all. None of my bikes wet-sump, and they all have good oil pressure – and the Tridents have been subjected to some 'spirited' riding over the years. I think that as long as the valves are properly primed, and you check your oil flow back into the oil tank when you first fit them, you won't have a problem.

But be aware that this is only my personal experience and some mechanics will have great joy telling you about all the engines they know that were wrecked by fitting such a valve, and telling you never to fit them, no matter what. However, I'm not sure how reliable such stories are, and if engines did seize, might they have seized anyway due to some other fault? You pay your money and you take your choice. (Several mechanics reading this will have now thrown the manual into the fire and danced on the ashes – it really is that contentious an issue!)

The last issue I had was a popping noise from the right-hand exhaust on deceleration – a classic sign of air in the exhaust. Sure

38.18 Copper washer softened and cleaned.

38.17 Softening and 'de-coking' copper washers!

COMMISSIONING, TEETHING & RIDING

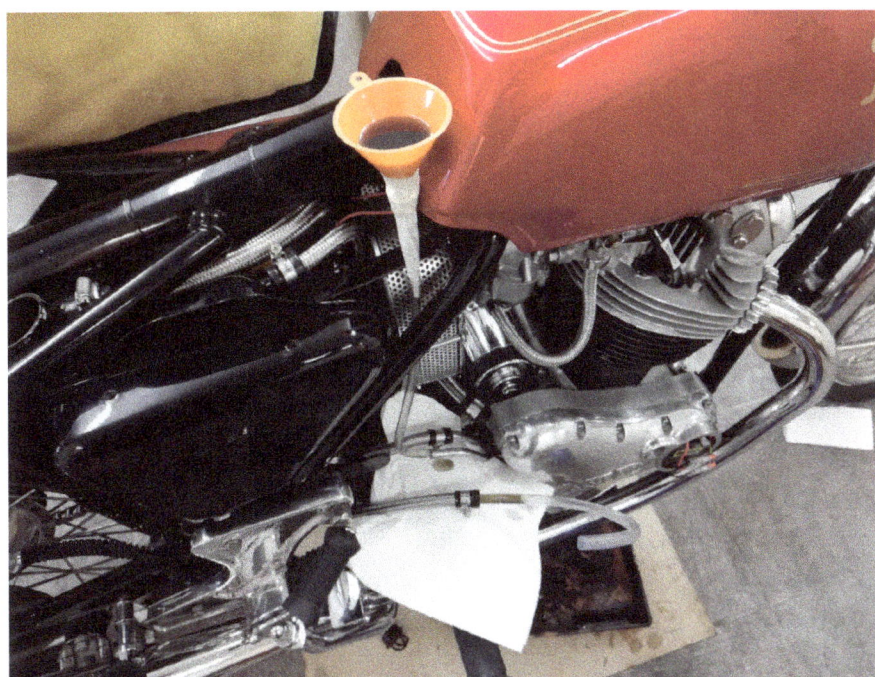

38.19 Priming the anti-drain valve and the oil feed pipe.

38.20 In-line anti-drain valve in situ in the oil feed pipe.

enough, the exhaust clamp had worked loose on the head (despite this being a MkIII with revised exhaust fittings). I followed the advice of many and tightened up both clamps when the engine was still very hot after each ride for the next few weeks. That seems to have done the trick. This same advice applies to owners of older machines, which tend to suffer more from loose exhaust clamps – tighten them after each ride, with the engine hot, for at least the first few rides. But, whatever the case, I think that it remains a perennial problem on earlier machines. I used my trusty rear suspension adjuster to hook round the fins on the clamps and tighten them that way.

RIDING

I can honestly say that I really like this bike already (did I just write that – about a Commando?!). The handling seems sharp, although I've been riding a bit gingerly so far, and the engine runs without any hesitation or flat spots etc and returns to a very steady 1000rpm idle every time – very impressed. Incredibly, the tension of the cylinder head spring seems to be correct. I have a little vibration at about 2000 revs, but after that it's really smooth – so I'll leave it as is for fear of upsetting it. I'm also amazed at how easily the Commando starts. It hardly needs any choke, and only requires tickling when starting from totally cold. My Tridents start okay, but only if you tickle all three carbs, hot or cold, and apply choke when cold.

The gear change is very clean and precise, and not at all stiff or notchy. It's probably not the best gear change in the world, but it's very good.

The front brake took a little time to bed in, but is now great, bringing the bike to a stop much more quickly and effortlessly than it would have done with a standard front brake. The rear brake is awesome, and will lock the back wheel without a problem.

The thing I'm probably most impressed with, though, is the legendary torque of the Commando engine. I know it's supposed to pull from low down – but having been used to Triples, I wasn't expecting it to be this good! It makes for some quite easy riding, without the need for constant cog swapping. Very, very impressed with the amount of grunt.

The clutch works! It disengages and it doesn't slip (now I've drained the excess oil out).

No oil leaks at all, so far. Fingers crossed.

So, very pleased; very pleased and very pleasantly surprised – so this is what a Commando is supposed to be like!

LESSONS LEARNT
• Don't forget to fill the engine, primary chaincase and gearbox with oil before starting the engine!
• Loosen the rocker feed pipe on the timing cover and turn the engine over until oil leaks out – you then know that oil's going through the oil pump and there's no air lock.
• Don't tighten the forks, yokes, wheel spindle and front mudguard until you've bounced them a few times.
• If you've got electric start, turn the engine over until oil starts coming out of the return pipe in the neck of the oil tank before starting the engine.
• Attaching vacuum gauges to the inlet manifolds wasn't quite as helpful as I'd hoped it would be.
• Always re-check tappets almost immediately after starting the engine – they can settle a lot.
• If you moved the adjusting nuts on rear brake master cylinder push rod, they need to be readjusted if the rear brake is to work correctly.
• Multi-pin connectors aren't infallible.
• Another golden rule of restoration is to 'spanner up' when it's all finished, just to check that everything's tight.
• Happiness is starting the engine for the first time!
• Nirvana is taking the bike out for a ride for the first time!

Chapter 39
Summing up

So, to sum up the whole restoration. When I began I was slightly worried about the whole process, mainly from my experience with Alan's Combat, back in the day. I knew that the Commando was rushed on to the market in just a few months, using an ageing engine, bolt-on support plates for the footpegs, and rubber mountings to try and reduce vibration. Not the most promising CV for a bike. However, for a start I think I was very lucky in finding a decent bike to restore from Frank Cuomo at Z1Classics and that helped a lot. The 850 MkIII isn't everyone's cup of tea as it's viewed as being a bit less of a pure racing machine, but I always wanted one, as it's got that magical ingredient: electric start. That's always been such a 'wow!' thing for me (I'm easily impressed!). Not only that but the MkIII is generally much better engineered than earlier models, and, as a mechanical type person, that was a big pull.

One of my biggest mistakes

SUMMING UP

was to then download the *Norton Workshop Manual* rather than buy a hard copy, as I found it really hard to read on my computer, for whatever reason. I therefore didn't really read it properly and so made a few silly errors, especially during the dismantling process. It was only later on in the restoration process that I bought a hard copy of the relevant workshop manual and that made a huge difference to my understanding of the various parts and processes. I would definitely recommend buying a hard copy at the outset of any major work on your bike.

Dismantling was fairly straightforward, if slightly error strewn due to the above. The main problem I encountered was with the MkIII airbox. I knew that it was going to be hard to remove; but not that hard! You basically have to wait until the cylinder head and cylinders are out of the way before you can remove the airbox easily. I managed to remove mine before this, but only after seriously 'adjusting' (bending) the top mounting to get it clear. That airbox is big!

As I dismantled the bike and began to buy parts I slowly discovered, to my surprise, that just about every single part for the Commando is still available, due to some wonderful parts suppliers. This is a really big bonus for any would-be restorer. Just about the only part not available is the giant airbox for the MkIII (!). I also discovered that there are many stainless steel parts available to replace the originals, so for someone like myself who is a stainless steel freak, that's a big bonus. Also, as with other models from the same era, there are many upgrades available too. There is in fact a wide choice of upgrades and in retrospect I should perhaps have spent longer choosing the correct ones for my requirements – although, in my case, time was a major influence on my restoration.

Beginning to rebuild the engine, I was struck by the basic and, indeed, slightly agricultural, nature of some of the castings. To begin with, the finish on the cylinder head was as rough as it comes, and then I found that the two crankcase halves didn't even match-up with each other. I have to say that even though I've worked on some slightly less than perfectly finished machines in the past, I was rather shocked by such woeful finishing – on one of the flagship models of NVT. Not great.

I found rebuilding to be relatively straightforward, especially as the Norton Workshop manual is a good, clear one, much better than many others I've worked with. I found that my usual method of partly dismantling and assembling the engine in the frame, rather than on the bench, worked well – apart from forgetting that the centre stand was attached to the engine, and not the frame! Having a bike lift also makes the job so much easier. I also found the dedicated technical helpline at Andover Norton to be very helpful (although I tried not to overuse it!) as well as the Norton Commando Facebook page and the technical forum on the Norton Owners' Club website.

I'm now very happy with my uprated front brake, but only after re-machining the calliper mounting bracket, which I think makes all the difference to the way it looks on the bike.

Having a good engineer to fit the new valve guides and mend the broken fin on the cylinder head was a real boon. Such work needs to be done properly.

In retrospect, I wish I'd sourced the stainless rims for the wheels myself, as I don't think the ones I've got on there are great quality.

Having a trusted local bike shop to help out is a real bonus. Support your local bike shop!

As I was expecting, some of the diagrams in the *Parts Catalog* in particular are misleading. Be aware. After all, they're parts catalogs, not manuals, so it didn't matter too much to them at the time if the diagrams weren't totally accurate.

I found all the parts suppliers were generally good, if not that fast. With other bikes I've done I've had next day delivery on parts. I don't think any of the parts suppliers I used managed that, but most delivered within two or three days of ordering.

Half way through the restoration I changed my mind and decided to fit an air filter from an earlier model rather than go for open bellmouths – purely for aesthetic reasons (I don't

HOW TO RESTORE NORTON COMMANDO

use my bikes enough to worry about bore wear from not using an air filter). I'm glad I did, as I think it's worked. The lesson being, always make a plan before starting the restoration, but be ready to change that plan. In my case, it was only after I started to reassemble the bike that I realised just how big the original airbox had been, and how big a hole it would leave if I just left the air filter out altogether (as I have done on my Tridents). It also meant that the carbs were correctly set and didn't need sorting to run with open bellmouths.

I decided to fit new Amal Premier carbs and I think it was a really good decision. Original Amals can wear quickly, and trying to refurbish them fully costs almost as much as buying new – and the new Premiers are far better than the originals anyway. Personally, I would only fit Amals to my British bikes, but that's a personal thing. Other owners fit single carb conversions, or Mikunis, or whatever and swear by them – fine. For my money, Amals are part of the DNA of the bike and I wouldn't change them. Each to their own.

I had the cases etc professionally polished this time, which meant that they were shinier than I could get them, and I didn't have the mess/dust/polish going everywhere, but of course it cost me money. If I'd have had more time I would have polished the alloy parts myself – but it was nice to get someone else to do it for me for a change, and the standard of finish is simply excellent.

I kept the engine pretty standard. I really don't need to go any faster than the bike already goes – if I ever hit the ton again, it's because the throttle's jammed! Also a lot of British bikes can become very brittle when tuned, so why court disaster? (Does anyone remember the story of the infamous Norton Commando Combat?!) I think it better to build the engine really carefully and properly and have a bike that goes well and doesn't leak oil etc rather than build a wild racer that breaks down all the time – but I'm a bit older now than I used to be and my values have changed.

I'm glad I've got a Boyer-Bransden power box fitted to the charging system on my bike, but I guess I don't really need it – no night riding or winter starting etc – so maybe, in my case, it was unnecessary – but it's a pretty invisible change and I am now confident with the charging system (I recently had problems with the original charging systems on both my Tridents).

I think entrusting the tank to my local bodyshop was a good idea, as I knew Nick and he knew what I wanted, and I was able to be fully involved at every step. He'd not painted a Norton tank before and so he used transfers for the pinstripes rather than painting them on, but I think the overall finish is excellent and you wouldn't really notice – that was fine for my requirements. I think in many ways it's better than if I'd have sent it away to a specialist, and definitely much, much better than (heaven forbid!) if I'd had a go at it myself!

So overall I'm pretty pleased. There's a couple of things I'm a bit unsure of: the slightly unwieldy original style front mudguard – one of those items that's eminently practical, but rather ungainly. I was considering a modern, cut down item, but the only ones I found required painting, so I decided against one. If there had been a smaller stainless or alloy item, I might well have gone for that instead.

I also have to say that, though I've only ridden the bike a little way to date, it's brilliant! It's just very smooth, and very light when on the move, and it pulls like a train – very surprised and very pleased.

The cost? A lot! The total restoration cost, including purchase of the original bike, was £15,600 (!). So, not the cheapest restoration in the world, but I did go for a 'no expense spared' restoration with all the trimmings and no corners cut, plus I started with a bike in better condition than I would have liked, and so it was relatively expensive to purchase in the first place. Whatever the case, I'm really happy with the restoration, and in my book it's been money well spent. Note that I could have completed the restoration for considerably less money if I'd wanted to (the uprated front brake and stainless nuts and bolts cost nearly £1500 on their own)

SUMMING UP

Some of the more major costs:
- Purchase of bike: £7000
- Tri Spark electronic ignition: £215
- Four-brush starter conversion: £130
- Chrome plating/polishing: £440
- Blast cleaning/powder-coating: £340
- Paint: £450
- Stainless fasteners: £700 (approx)
- Upgraded front master cylinder: £255
- Uprated front disc and calliper: £500
- Premier carburettors: £305
- New pistons: £99
- Boyer power box: £107
- Front mudguard: £115
- Rear mudguard: £80
- New cloth wiring harness: £150
- Wheel building: £400
- Cylinder head work: £160

So, I think that the Commando is one of those happy successes that shouldn't have been: it somehow just worked, against the odds. It should have been a dog, a mongrel, with an engine from an Atlas (and before) that was bored out beyond its natural limits and simply rubber mounted to try and reduce the inevitable vibration it produced, along with a frame that was new and untested, bolt-on mounting plates and a swinging arm that was also rubber mounted! The whole thing should have been a disaster, but somehow, it was a brilliant bike (I nearly said 'Triumph' but I thought that was inappropriate!). The rubber mountings became the wonderful 'isolastic' system – fit for a bike of the future. Just by tilting the engine forward the whole bike looked magnificent and immediately gained 20mph top speed in the eyes of everyone who saw it! The beauty of the machine was added to by the shiny alloy of the support plates, that, despite being a bit of an add-on, looked great! And then there was the name – the Commando! I'm no fan of much of what was going on in the British motorcycle industry at the time, but the marketing department hit the bullseye when it named its new bike the Commando. And the rest, as they say, is history!

Finally, I have created a Facebook page that contains updates, corrections, advice etc for those who have bought this manual. Please feel free to join:
Norton Commando Restoration Manual Updates
So, if there's any new or updated info, or if there are any corrections to the manual (heaven forbid!) then you'll find it on there.

All the very best with your own rebuilds. Keep the faith.

Chris Rooke

Chapter 40
Recommended publications & equipment

PUBLICATIONS

There are several essential and recommended publications if you are contemplating restoring or carrying out major work on your Commando. This book contains much of the guidance and information that you'll need when restoring a Commando, but there are some other publications that I would deem to be essential, which will go hand-in-hand with this manual. These are the *Norton Commando Workshop Manual* and the *Parts Catalog*[1]. If you look at photo 40.1 you can see two workshop manuals, one for the 850 MkIII and one for earlier 750 models and a parts catalog. I would consider these publications to be essential reading (along with this book, of course!) The Norton workshop manuals are quite clearly written and generally do go through how to carry out certain jobs in a clear and logical manner. Note that I bought two as I have tried to cover not just the 850 MkIII models in this manual, but obviously you just buy the one that's correct for your bike. They are readily available from the specialist suppliers listed in the next chapter.

The *Parts Catalog* is useful both in terms of ordering parts – if you have the part number when ordering then the parts' suppliers will love you, and you've more chance of actually receiving the correct part! – and also in terms of providing exploded drawings of different assemblies on the bike, which can be very useful; though they can also be misleading.

40.1 *Workshop Manuals* and *Parts Catalog*.

---

[1] For reasons best known to NVT, at some point in the early '70s, it started to issue its manuals etc in American English. Hence there is a *Parts Catalog* rather than a *Parts Catalogue*. I think this decision kind of sums up NVT: It was trying to somehow make its products more relevant and in-tune with the American market (by far its biggest market) and so chose to Americanise all its literature. However, in so doing I think it was losing the very thing that British bikes had going for them – Britishness. Just as owners of Harleys over here are somehow trying to buy into Americana and the American dream, I think that buying a Triumph or Norton in the states was getting your own piece of British culture (new and old) – NVT managed to completely lose this when marketing its bikes in an American way. Just my own little opinion of all that was wrong with the British motorcycle industry at the time. Rant over.

RECOMMENDED PUBLICATIONS & EQUIPMENT

You have to be aware that sometimes the exploded diagrams are far from correct and they can therefore be a hindrance, rather than a help. Take the exploded diagram of the rear wheel assembly on a MkIII as an example.

The other main thing to note is that I would *highly recommend* you buy *hard copies* of the manuals, rather than just download copies onto your computer. For reasons unknown, it's just much, much harder to read a manual on a computer screen. (No, I don't know why, but it just is!) One of my biggest mistakes I made on this rebuild was to only download the manuals and *Parts Catalog* at the beginning, rather than fork out on relatively expensive hard copies. Big mistake. It meant that I simply didn't read them, or if I did, I didn't read them properly, and this led to a few basic, easily avoidable errors (such as not removing the rear pistons from the brake callipers before disconnecting them). Later on, I bit the bullet and bought hard copies – so, so much easier to read, and packed full of vital information.

There are also some other publications that I would highly recommend you purchase. It may seem like a bit of an outlay to buy these books, but if you're planning major work or a complete restoration of your bike, they're worth it in the long run as they'll save you time and money. Also, the more you know and understand about Commandos, the better.

If you look at photo 40.2, you can see the following publications:
• *The Essential Buyer's Guide*; the clue's in the title. If you're thinking of buying a Commando to ride or restore, then this is a very good starting point.
• *The Haynes manual*; often derided, but easier to read than the Norton manual and a useful reference in the workshop.
• *The Norton Commando Bible*; all you ever wanted to know about the Commando, but were afraid to ask.
• *Norton Twin Restoration*; a very informative book, although slightly generic as it covers all Norton twins. Still very useful though.

The above are some books that I've bought and found useful, but

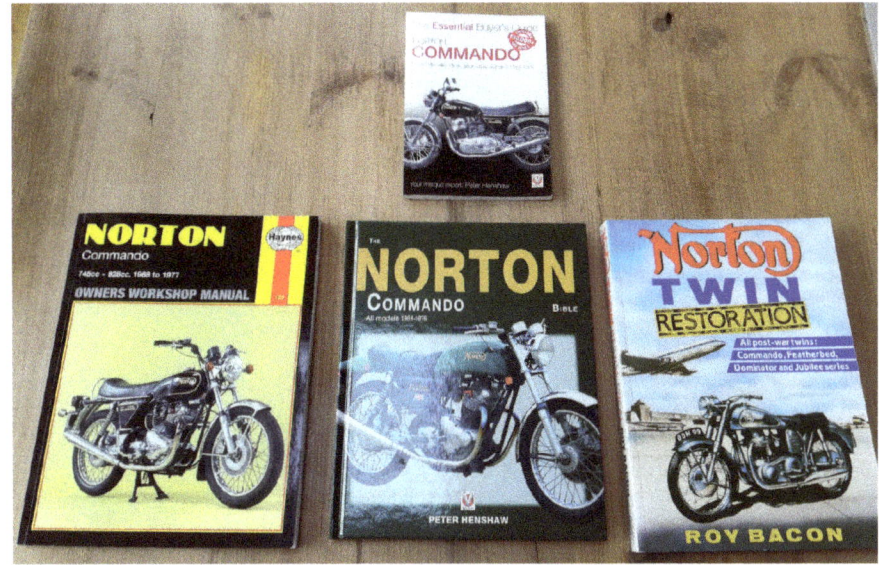
40.2 Other recommended publications.

I'm sure that there are also a number of other good publications about Commandos on the market not listed here.

GENERAL WORKSHOP TOOLS
Next up is an idea of the selection of tools required or recommended to carry out the restoration of a Commando; both ordinary workshop equipment and special tools for the Commando. If you look at photo 40.3 you can see some of my regular workshop tools:
• Three full sets of spanners in A/F, Whitworth and Metric sizes. On a MkIII there's a glorious mix of all three threads and sizes, so you need to be ready for anything and have as wide a range as possible. I think earlier models only have a mix of A/F and Whitworth – but be ready for anything!
• Adjustable wrenches, especially for larger nuts.
• Hammers, a selection of weights and styles is good.
• Wire brushes of different sizes and stiffness.
• A range of circlip pliers, to remove inner and outer fitting circlips.
• A magnifying glass helps with such things as wiring diagrams and examining bearings, etc.
• Mini wire brushes and old tooth brushes for cleaning, etc.
• Screwdrivers; you simply can't have enough, and ensure that you have a range of Phillips/cross-head screwdrivers – the heads are different and fit different screws – I also found that my screwdrivers made specifically for Japanese motorcycles: Japanese Industry Standard (JIS) fitted most cross-headed screws very well.

I would also recommend the following:
• Drifts of differing sizes to drive out bushes, etc.
• Wire cutters.
• Mini files for de-burring threads,

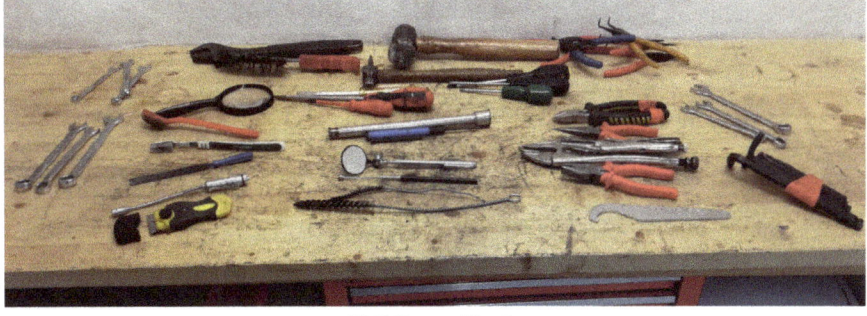
40.3 General tools.

HOW TO RESTORE NORTON COMMANDO

etc.
• A telescopic mirror for looking into such places as the front cylinder head stud opening.
• Mole grips of various sizes.
• A good set of Allen keys (plus some spares that can be cut down to fit the carb inlet manifolds).
• A small flexible torch – worth its weight in gold.
• A telescopic magnet – I couldn't work without it!
• Pliers of various sizes.
• A razor blade scraper, particularly useful for removing old gaskets, etc.
• Brushes to clean out oilways.
• A 'P' spanner, not only to adjust the rear suspension, but also to unscrew and replace inspection caps and exhaust pipe clamps.

As I say, this list is not exhaustive, but gives you an idea of some of the more common tools required.

MORE RECOMMENDED TOOLS

Looking at photo 40.4, there are more recommended tools:
• A set of funnels.
• A tap and die set – very good at cleaning old and damaged threads before reassembly.
• A digital vernier calliper – really useful for exact measurements.
• A strobe for setting the engine ignition timing exactly.
• A good quality set of imperial Allen keys – plus as many others as you can gather.
• A digital thermometer gun – very useful for testing the heat on exhausts etc when checking for even firing.

• A basic electrical tester – the main functions I use are circuit tester and voltage reading. Priceless.
• An impact driver – always good for removing those screws that are seized in.
• A 'Thor' lump hammer! An essential tool for gentle 'persuasion'! One side is copper, the other a very useful hide, which won't damage surfaces etc – always double check which way round it is before using!

SOCKETS

A very wide selection of sockets is essential – the more sockets the better. If you look at photo 40.5 you can see that there are a wide selection of AF, metric and Whitworth ½in drive sockets, including sets of deep sockets, which are very important. There's also a set of ¼in and ⅜in drive mini-sockets in the top of the photo – worth their weight in gold.

Probably the most important socket of all is the ¼in Whitworth socket in the bottom right corner of the photo. I bought this from Andover Norton and it's especially thin so it will slide into recesses other sockets can't reach, even the deep ones. Essential for several cylinder head nuts. Also note that there's a torque wrench there, which is an essential tool. I also bought a small torque wrench for some of the smaller nuts, which I used a couple of times – not in the photo.

SPECIAL TOOLS

In rebuilding the Commando, I used by far the most special tools that I've ever used to rebuild any engine before. I think that this is mainly due to the fact that they're all still available! How many times have I read a manual that recommends a special tool, only discover that it's no-longer available and that I'm supposed to make my own out of some spare angle iron and a castor from an orthopaedic bed (that I just happen to have lying around – not!) However, in the case of the Commando, every special tool I required was still available, and so I indulged! I mean, they're not that expensive and make the job so much easier – what's not to like? Looking at photo 40.6, you can see:
• A clutch compressor to enable removal and refitting of the clutch circlip – essential.
• A sprocket puller for the engine sprocket in the primary chaincase, and camshaft sprocket, if necessary.
• A tool to exactly centralise the rocker shafts when replacing them in the heads, ensuring free oil flow and proper fitting of the oval rocker caps, available from Norvil.
• A sliding hammer to remove rocker shafts from the head.
• A large pair of piston ring compressors, suitable for Commando pistons.
• A plate that is used to support the idler shaft in the timing case when removing the camshaft sprocket nut to prevent distortion (I never used this tool as I forgot I had it!).
• A special tool to allow the removal and replacement of the clutch actuating mechanism lock ring.
• A spring puller – another tool I didn't use as I forgot I'd bought it!
• A special peg tool for removing and

40.4 Recommended tools.

40.5 Full range of sockets.

RECOMMENDED PUBLICATIONS & EQUIPMENT

40.6 Special tools.

replacing the end plugs on Norton-Lockheed callipers, as well as the lock rings on the wheel spindles of some models.
• A front fork oil seal removal tool – very useful.
• A tool for locking the primary chain to enable the loosening and tightening of various nuts on the engine such as the front engine sprocket – worth every penny.

In the bottom left of the photo you can see the weird and wonderful special tool for removing the crankshaft pinion on the timing side. Not the cheapest special tool, but pretty essential, and it can be used on most engines of the era. After this there is a small tool that screws into the end of the camshaft and allows the timing case to be fitted without damaging the camshaft oil seal. Next to that is a timing plug that screws into the timing hole underneath the timing cover on MkIIIs and sets the timing at exactly 28 degrees BTDC (before top dead centre) and the adjustable timing plate in the primary chaincase cover can be set by it. Next to that is what looks to be a fairly standard ¼in Whitworth ring spanner, but is in fact a ring spanner with a very thin ring that goes over some of the cylinder nuts etc that normal ring spanners won't fit – also bought from Andover Norton. Finally, there are two flat spanners and I use these for removing and replacing the various inspection covers on the bike without damage.

POWER TOOLS
See photo 40.7. My second best-ever tool purchase, after my bike lift, was my DeWalt cordless impact driver. It cost a few bob (about £160) but it's worth every last penny: it just makes so many jobs so much easier! Highly recommended. There's also the general purpose cordless drill – used for polishing smaller or awkward parts with the requisite attachments and also for honing cylinders etc. Then there's the Dremmel. Such a useful tool. I use it all the time for cutting, grinding, polishing, cleaning, etc. It's important to have a wide variety of heads for it so it can be used in a wide variety of situations.

SPARE NUTS, BOLTS, WASHERS AND THINGUMMIES
See photo 40.8. I also keep a wide selection of spare bits and bobs – they always come in handy. I have a box of imperial stainless steel nuts and bolts and a box of metric. There are always nuts and bolts you need to replace on every job, and having a wide selection on hand just makes sense. I also keep boxes of: fibre washers, copper washers, neoprene rubber 'O' rings, stainless self-tapping screws of varied shapes and sizes, and a box of assorted split pins. I also have boxes of grommets, springs, circlips and spring washers. All of the above come in handy and are easily available on the internet. However, they do come with a warning: it doesn't matter how many spare copper washers or whatever you have, the size you want won't be there!

40.7 Power tools.

40.8 Boxes of odds and ends.

40.9 Oils and consumables.

HOW TO RESTORE NORTON COMMANDO

40.10 Cleaning equipment.

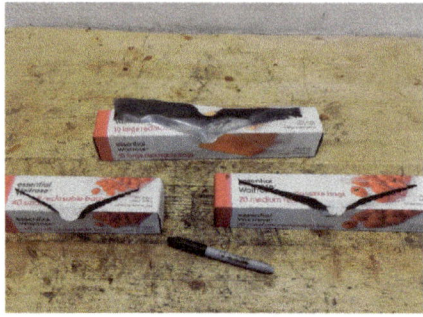

40.11 Freezer bags and a marker.

CONSUMABLES
See photo 40.9. It's always advisable to have as many consumables to hand as possible so you don't have to stop work whilst waiting for something to arrive that you've had to order:
• General grease and copper grease.
• Engine oil. I use Morris Lubricants running-in oil to begin with, followed by its 20/50 Golden Film. Morris oils are designed specifically for older motorcycles and I always use them – but the range of oils these days is massive and you pays your money and you takes your choice. (There are more opinions on what oil to use than anything else!)
• Satin black, gloss black and zinc galvanising aerosols always come in handy.
• Cellulose thinner (PVCu cleaner) is the only thing that will remove Wellseal – essential.
• WD40 – so much more than a lubricant. It also degreases, aids electrical connectivity and disperses water. Indispensable.
• ACF50 – this is what I use on my bikes over the winter to keep rust at bay. It can either be left on, or easily removed in the spring as required.
• White spirit – a very good degreaser.
• Brake cleaner and carb cleaner – both very good, and both very powerful/toxic. Only use outside.
• Hypoy 80-90 gear oil – to be honest, in my opinion, if the gearbox is built correctly then the choice of oil isn't too crucial. I use this standard hypoy oil.
• 140w oil for the swinging arm.
• Wellseal – the only sealant I ever use on my bikes. Some people say you don't need it, but I think that you might as well use it and create a really oil tight engine – there's no harm done.
• Brake fluid.

• A variety of Loctite products: thread seal, bearing seal – liquid and solid to lock parts and help keep threads oil tight.
• Tippex – always good for marking points on the engine: eg ignition timing and valve timing marks.
• Black trim wax – brings your rubber parts up like new.
• Engine assembly lubricant – essential to use this on wearing surfaces as you rebuild the engine.

KEEPING THINGS CLEAN
See photo 40.10. Okay, so I'm a bit obsessed with keeping my garage-cum-workshop-cum-showroom clean and tidy. These are some products I recommend:
• Heavy-duty wipes.
• Brush and dustpan and assorted brooms with different heads.
• A Dyson cordless vacuum cleaner – wonderful invention!
• Paper towel/garage tissue – I buy it by the absolute cart load. I used to use garage tissue but now I just use kitchen roll as I can buy it so easily at the supermarket. Essential.
• Old towels – every towel that is thrown out by my better half and replaced comes to me, and I have about 20 of them of all shapes and sizes. They protect work on the bench, stop little bits from rolling around, and protect the bench itself and any items being worked on. Can even be used as a towel!
• Rubber gloves – I use them a lot, especially during dismantling when dealing with an awful lot of oily/greasy parts. Saves your skin. I lost most of my fingerprints many years ago due to a high power green gel workshop cleaner – not a great idea: use gloves on the messy/oily bits.

FREEZER BAGS
See photo 40.11. One of the most important items in my workshop is freezer bags. Used to store parts during dismantling, keeping them safe and separate until required. Use a permanent marker to write what's inside. Available in small, medium and large. Absolutely essential.

OTHER ESSENTIAL TOOLS
See photo 40.12. A few other tools to mention are a blow torch, a good quality valve spring compressor, and a bench vice – generally speaking, the bigger the better. One other recommended tool, which I forgot to put in the photo, is a strobe for timing the ignition accurately. Not that expensive and a must if you want your engine to run as it should.

BIKE LIFT
See photo 40.13. By far the best tool/piece of equipment I ever bought for the workshop was the motorcycle

40.12 Blow torch, valve spring compressor and a bench vice.

RECOMMENDED PUBLICATIONS & EQUIPMENT

40.13 The best piece of equipment ever – the bike lift. (The Snowman likes it too!)

lift. Up until this point I'd always built bikes on the floor, and my knees and back are now suffering as a result. Having a bike lift where everything is at waist or chest height is just the best thing ever – they can be adjusted to different heights, as required. Not too expensive these days (around £300) and although they take up a bit of room in the workshop, I'd definitely invest in one if you're contemplating major bike surgery. They're brilliant, but I always ask a friend to help getting the bike on and off the main stand on the lift, as it's awkward/dangerous by yourself, and then strap the bike down carefully: you don't want your bike coming off the lift! (Remember that it nearly happened to me when I removed the engine head steady!)

LESSONS LEARNT

- This manual is designed to go alongside the *Norton Commando Workshop Manual* and not replace it. I strongly recommend you buy a hard copy for your model, rather than download one. Buy a *Parts Catalog* too, along with a *Haynes Manual*.
- You can never have too many tools.
- As with most things, buy the best quality you can afford. Handling and using good tools is a joy; poor tools make for a poor quality experience and finish.
- Just about every special tool required to dismantle and rebuild a Commando engine is still available – and new ones are being added!
- A bike lift and a cordless impact driver – two expensive items that are worth every penny!

Chapter 41

Recommended suppliers

RECOMMENDED PARTS AND SERVICE SUPPLIERS

(This is by no means an exhaustive list, but just some of the suppliers I used during my restoration.)

Andover Norton
Unit 6,
Wooler Park,
North Way,
Andover,
SP10 5AZ
Tel 01264 359565
www.andover-norton.co.uk
      A very good parts supplier that also has a dedicated technical helpline – which is great!

The Norvil Motorcycle Company Ltd
96-98 Cannock Road,
Chase Terrace,
Burntwood,
Staffs,
WS7 1JP
Tel 01543 278008
www.norvilmotorcycle.co.uk
      A very good supplier of Commando parts, and especially stainless steel ones. It has to be said, though, that its customer service leaves something to be desired.

RGM Norton Ltd
Haile Bank Farm,
Beckermet,
Cumbria,
CA21 2XB
Tel 01946 841517
www.rgmnorton.co.uk
      A very good parts supplier for Commandos. Good info on its website.

Old Britts
Washington,
USA
www.oldbritts.com
      Recommended as a parts supplier in the USA. Its website is also an excellent resource for technical info etc. USA shipping only.

Colorado Norton Works
Dolores, Colorado,
USA
www.coloradonortonworks.com
      Builder of custom Commandos and supplier of many different Commando upgrades etc – worldwide shipping.

Phoenix Marine Electrics
Newnham Grange,
Daventry,
Northamptonshire,
NN11 4NQ
Tel 07900 265426 (Ray Wild)
www.ebay.co.uk. Search for Phoenix-marine-electrics.
      Supplier of four-brush conversions for the MkIII Commando starter.

Venhill Engineering Ltd
21 Ranmore Rd,
Dorking,
Surrey,
RH4 1HE
Tel 01306 885111
www.venhill.co.uk
      Supplier of cables and brake lines etc. They will also make stainless hoses to your requirements.

Frost Auto Restoration Techniques Ltd
Albion Park,
Warrington Rd,
Glazebury,
Cheshire,
WA3 5PG
Tel 01706 658619
www.frost.co.uk
      Supplier of automotive tools and equipment, including POR 15 tank sealant.

RECOMMENDED SUPPLIERS

The Chain Man
18 Walton Close,
Stourport-on-Severn,
Worcestershire,
DY13 0LS
Tel 01299 212626
www.the-chain-man.co.uk
    Supplier of all types of chains for all bikes, including Commandos.

Vehicle Wiring Products
9 Buxton Court,
Manners Industrial Estate,
Ilkeston,
Derbyshire,
DE7 8EF
Tel 0115 930 5454
www.vehicle-wiring-products.eu
    Supplier of a wide range of electrical wiring and connectors etc.

Paul Goff
www.norbsa02.freeuk.com
    Supplier of LED bulbs and lighting.

Burlen Ltd
Spitfire House,
Castle Rd,
Salisbury,
Wiltshire,
SP1 3SA
Tel 01722 412500
www.burlen.co.uk
    Supplier of Amal carburettors and parts.

Morris Lubricants
Little Row,
Stoke-on-Trent,
Staffs,
ST4 2SQ
Tel 01782 410391
www.morrislubricantsonline.co.uk
    Supplier of engine oil for classic motorcycles, including the Commando.

Prestige Electro Plating
Unit 6,
Cliff St Industrial Estate,
Mexborough,
South Yorkshire,
S64 9HU
Tel 01709 577004
    A very good quality chrome plater and polisher. There is usually a long lead time, though – up to five months.

Smithcraft – classic motorcycle engine specialists
Dave Smith,
14 Ladybower Lane,
Poulton-le-Fylde,
Lancashire,
FY6 7FY
Tel 07757 880081
Email dave@rarr.org.uk
    Dave is a Triumph Trident engine specialist, but he also works on Commandos and other British bikes. He did a great job on my cylinder head.

Manhattan Motorcycles
641-643 London Rd,
Sheffield,
South Yorkshire,
S2 4HT
Tel 0114 258 2161
www.manhattanmotorcycles.co.uk
    A very good local motorcycle shop – support your local bike shop!

Two Brothers Coatings Ltd
Ball St,
Sheffield,
S3 8DB
Tel 07701 010607
    A very good local vapour-blast cleaner and powder-coating company.

D Middleton & Son
Unit 5,
Lady Ann Mills,
Batley,
West Yorkshire,
WF17 0PS
Tel 01924 470807
www.stainlessmiddleton.co.uk
    Supplier of dedicated stainless fasteners for Commandos.

Namrick Ltd
124 Portland Rd,
East Sussex,
BN3 5QL
Tel 01273 779864
www.namrick.co.uk
    Supplier of good quality stainless steel fasteners.

Z1Classics
(On Facebook)
    Stockist of many different imported bikes, mainly for restoration – and not just Kawasakis! A very good company to deal with.

Framptons
Framptons Classic Number Plates,
44 East Bank Rd,
Sheffield,
S2 3QN
Tel 0114 273 1151
www.framptonsplates.com
    A very good supplier of classic number plates. Probably best to ring them if you want pressed alloy plates like mine, as I can never find them on their website. They also know all the rules and regs etc regarding number plates, and what's legal, and what isn't. (All Commandos are now old enough to display black and silver number plates in the UK, if you so wish.)

There are also a few small specialist suppliers who make a limited amount of hight quality upgrades etc for Commandos, such as Donald Pender (www.tritonmotorcycleparts.com) and Mick Hemmings (www.mickhemmings.co.uk)

OWNERS' CLUBS
Norton Owners' Club
www.nortonownersclub.org
    The Norton Owners' club provides a great resource for all things Commando – and they run a technical forum for all those questions that aren't answered in this manual! Also on Facebook.

FACEBOOK GROUPS
• Norton Owners' Club
• Norton Commando
• Norton Commando Motorcycles
• Z1Classics
• Norton Commando Restoration Manual Updates (which supports this manual with updates and further guidance).

MORE FROM CHRIS ROOKE ...

Completed at home by an enthusiastic DIY mechanic who has great experience rebuilding bikes, this book covers the complete restoration of a Triumph Trident T150V and a Triumph T160. Every aspect of the dismantling, refurbishment and reassembly of these classic bikes is covered in great detail, accompanied by a host of clear colour photos.

ISBN 978-1-845848-82-8
Paperback • 27x20.7cm • 232 pages • 704 colour pictures

" ... informative and entertaining at the same time ... this is an excellent book for first-time and more experienced restorers; and could well save you far more than the purchase price by helping you to 'do it' the correct way. " (*Nacelle*)

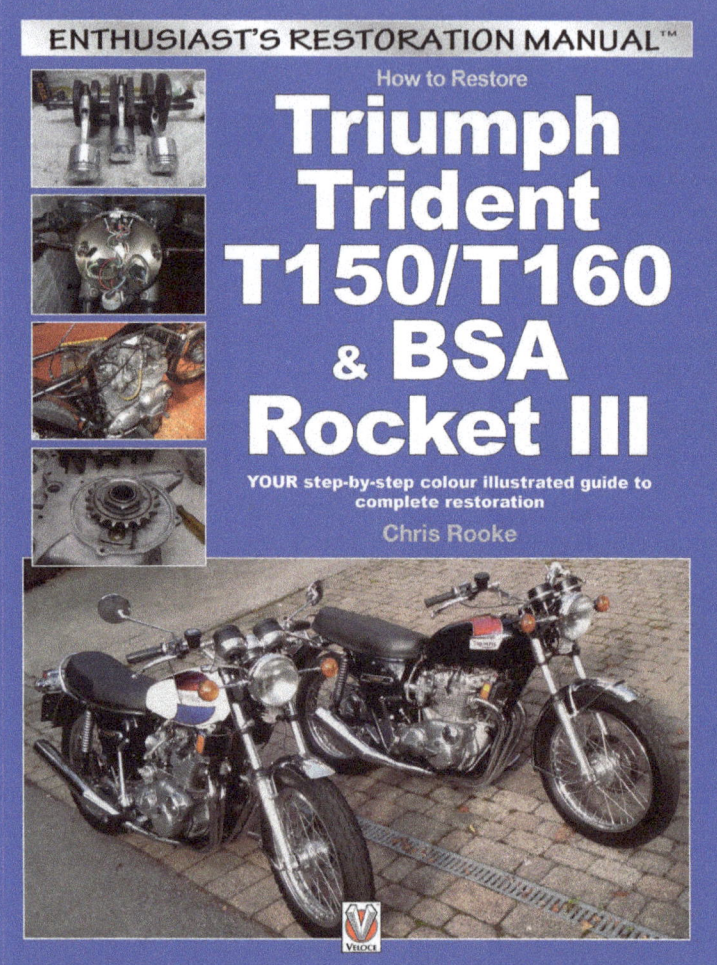

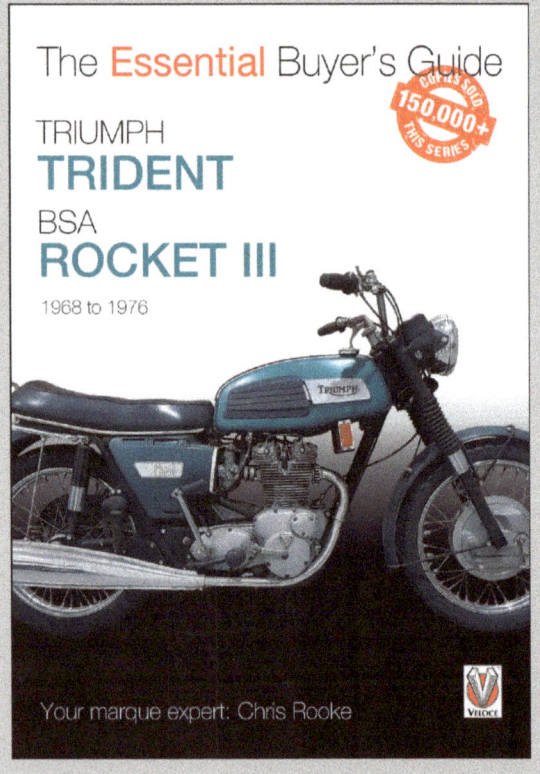

Benefit from Chris Rooke's years of experience with Triples, learn how to spot a bad bike quickly, and how to assess a promising one like a professional. This is THE COMPLETE GUIDE to choosing, assessing and buying the Trident or Rocket III of your dreams!

ISBN 978-1-787113-80-0
Paperback • 19.5x13.9cm • 64 pages • 90 pictures

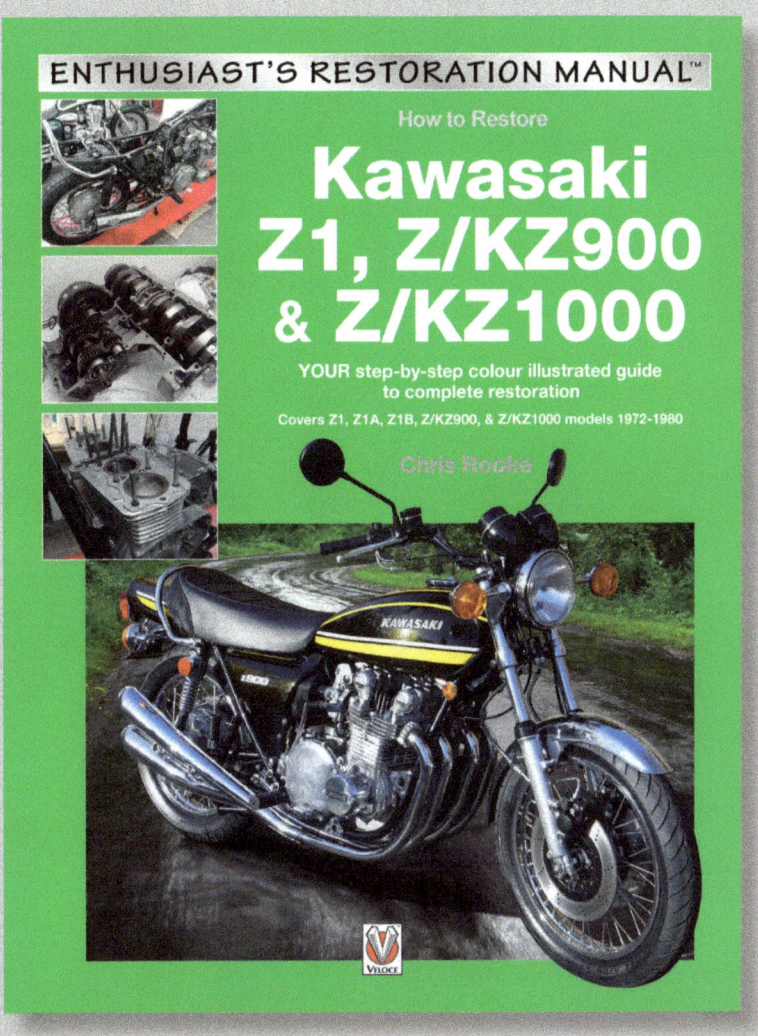

Written in a friendly and engaging manner by an experienced enthusiast, this manual provides a thorough and detailed restoration guide for the Kawasaki Z models, covering everything from dismantling, replacing, restoring and rebuilding, and is copiously illustrated with hundreds of original colour photos.

ISBN 978-1-787111-58-5
Paperback • 27x20.7cm • 224 pages
• 794 pictures

"The latest in possibly the best series of enthusiasts' restoration manuals ever published covers Kawasaki's [Z1] in intricate detail."
(*Old Bike Mart*)

For more information and price details, visit our website at www.veloce.co.uk • email info@veloce.co.uk • Tel +44(0)1305 260068

... AND MORE FROM VELOCE

Having this book in your pocket is just like having a real marque expert by your side. Benefit from Peter Henshaw's years of experience, learn how to spot a bad bike quickly, and how to assess a promising one like a true professional. Get the right bike at the right price!

ISBN 978-1-787116-52-8
Paperback • 19.5x13.9cm • 64 pages • 101 colour pictures

**Be the first to find out about new book releases, special offers and much more
Sign up to the Veloce email newsletter *On the Grid*, and get all the latest news delivered straight to your inbox:**

www.veloce.co.uk/On-the-Grid.html

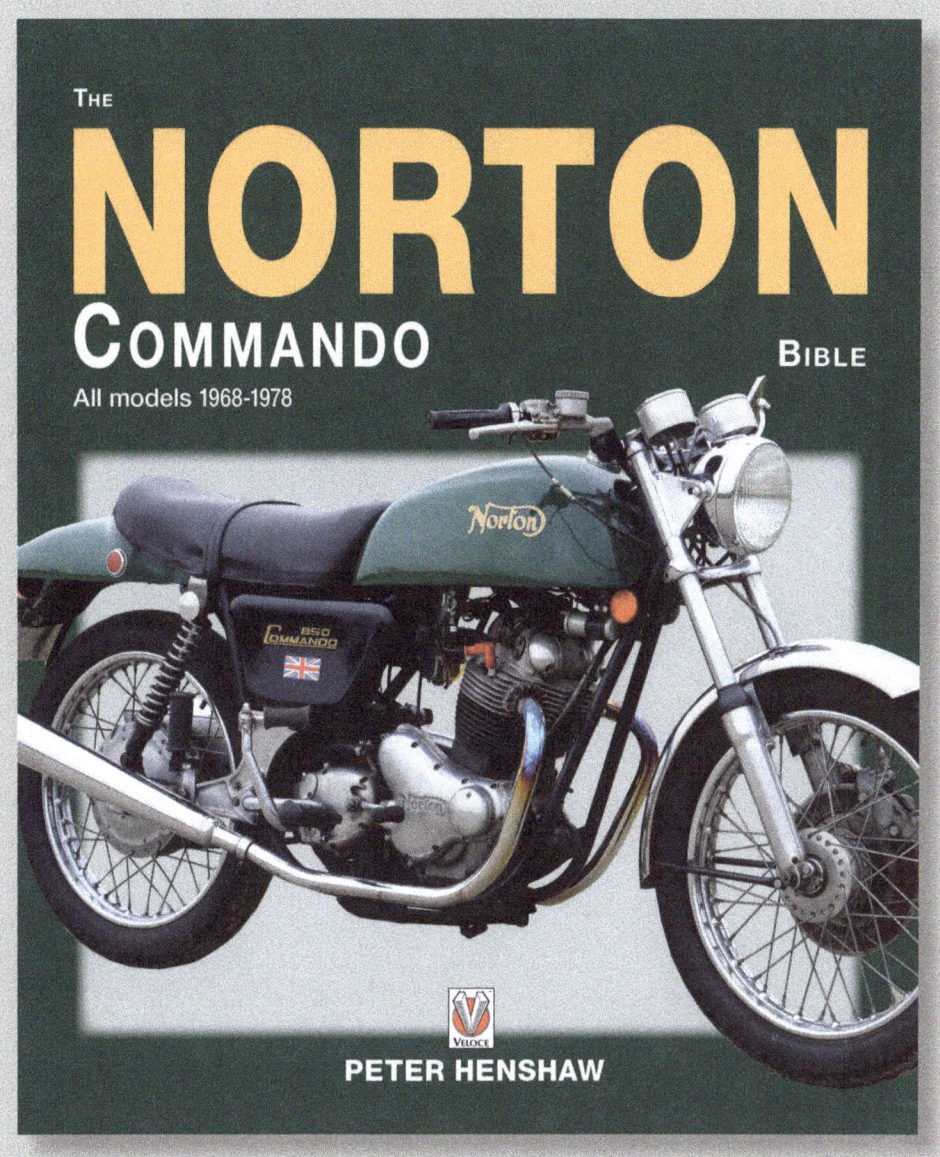

The story of the Norton Commando – its conception, design and production, and how it compared to the competition (British and Japanese). With insights into the company that built it, and guidance on buying a Commando secondhand, this is the fascinating history of a true British icon and essential reading for owners and restorers.

ISBN 978-1-78711-006-9
Hardback • 25x20.7cm • 144 pages • 163 colour and b&w pictures

For more information and price details, visit our website at www.veloce.co.uk • email info@veloce.co.uk • Tel +44(0)1305 260068

Index

Advance and retard unit 43, 44
Air filter 148-150
Airbox 33-35
Alternator 168, 169
Annealing 206
Anti-drain valve 110, 112, 205-207
Assimilator 34, 169, 170, 171

Backfire overload device 140, 141
Ballast resistor 26, 158, 172, 173
Battery 174
Battery tray 34, 160, 161
Big ends 70, 90-92
Bike lift 20, 216, 217
Boyer Powerbox 169-171
Brake pipes 191

Calliper removal 23, 24
Camshafts 68, 69, 93, 94, 113
Capacitor 26, 27, 33, 169, 170
Carburettors 33, 35, 144-152, 203
Centre stand 45, 97
Chainguard 183
Chroming/polishing 80, 81
Clutch 47, 49, 138, 141-143
Clutch (operating mechanism) 53, 54
Con-rods 70, 90-94
Condensers 26, 172, 173
Costs 210, 211
Crankcase oil filter 69
Crankcases 36, 37, 67, 68, 89, 92-94, 204
Crankshaft 70, 71, 90-94, 104, 112
Cush drive 77, 70, 181, 182
Cylinder barrels 62, 63, 114-118
Cylinder compression 204
Cylinder head 59-63, 119-125

Electronic ignition 172, 173
Engine breather 162, 163
Engine removal/replacement 66, 97, 98
Engine sprocket 50, 51

Gearbox 53-58, 126-132
Gearbox sprocket 56, 57, 127-131, 134
Grab rail 23

Exhaust 28, 29, 206, 207

Footrests 179

Fork yokes 73, 74
Frame 35, 80, 81, 95-97, 104
Front brake 72-76, 107-109, 190-192, 205
Front forks 72-75, 102, 103, 202
Front master cylinder 191
Front mudguard 104, 105, 107, 108
Front wheel 72-77, 82, 106-109
Front wheel bearings 76-79, 106
Fuel tank 21, 22, 193-200

Handlebar switches 23, 24, 164-167
Head races 74, 75, 103
Head steady 41, 42, 59, 60, 153
Headlamp 23, 25, 174
Horn 160-163, 174, 182, 183
Hydraulic primary chain tensioner 49, 50, 52, 139, 140

Ignition coils 26, 172, 173
Ignition switch 26, 174, 175, 177
Ignition timing 173, 202, 203
Indicators 26, 27, 174-176
Instrument binnacle 25, 174-177
Isolastics 95, 96

Kickstart 128, 129, 132, 179

LED bulbs 18, 169, 174-176
Locking the engine 54, 111

Main bearings 69, 89, 90
Manuals/publications 212, 213

Neutral indicator switch 128

Oil 36, 37, 201, 202, 216
Oil filter 37, 161, 162
Oil pipes 161, 162
Oil pressure relief valve 113
Oil pump 49, 50, 111, 112
Oil tank 160-162

Parts suppliers 218, 219
Petrol tank 82, 193-200
Pistons 62, 66, 67, 114-118
Primary chain 50, 51
Primary chaincase 37, 38, 46, 136-143
Primary chaincase oil seal 68-70
Push rods 62, 122, 123

Rear brake 179, 183, 184, 186-190, 204
Rear brake calliper 188-190, 192
Rear brake light switch 188
Rear chain 183
Rear chainguard 183
Rear light assembly 175, 176
Rear master cylinder 186-188, 192
Rear mudguard 29, 182, 183
Rear number plate 175, 176
Rear shocks 28, 101
Rear sprocket 29, 78, 79, 181-183
Rear wheel 29, 77, 79, 82, 180-185
Rear wheel bearings 77, 78
Rectifier 26, 33, 168-170
Rocker shafts 64, 121, 122
Rotor/stator 47, 48, 140, 141
Rules of the workshop 17

Seat 21, 22, 200
Side panels 193-199
Sidestand 44
Speedo 25, 29, 82, 174-176
Speedo drive 182
Sprag bearing 48, 49
Starter motor 47, 48, 52, 149, 150, 156-159
Starter solenoid 26, 27, 158
Stator/rotor 47, 48, 140, 141
Sump oil filter 36, 69, 93
Support plates 30, 31, 178, 179
Swinging arm 39, 40, 41, 98-100

Tacho 25, 82, 174-176
Tappet (adjusting) 203, 204
Tappet covers 124, 125
Tappets 63, 64, 116, 122-124
Timing case 42-44, 110-113
Timing chain 50, 111
Timing plug 37
Tools 213-217
Tyres 77, 79, 106, 107

Unsprung weight 82

Valve timing 110, 111
Valves 62, 64, 65, 119, 120
Vapour blasting 80, 81

Wiring 34, 168-171, 174-177, 204

Zener diodes 27, 168-170

www.ingramcontent.com/pod-product-compliance
Lightning Source LLC
Chambersburg PA
CBHW042226010526
44111CB00046B/2977